Strategic People Sourcing

Strategic People Sourcing

How to Build a Sustainable Talent Pipeline

Leigh Rodriguez

Publisher's note

Every possible effort has been made to ensure that the information contained in this book is accurate at the time of going to press, and the publishers and author cannot accept responsibility for any errors or omissions, however caused. No responsibility for loss or damage occasioned to any person acting, or refraining from action, as a result of the material in this publication can be accepted by the editor, the publisher or the author.

First published in Great Britain and the United States in 2026 by Kogan Page Limited

Kogan Page

Kogan Page Ltd, 2nd Floor, 45 Gee Street, London EC1V 3RS, United Kingdom
Kogan Page Inc, 8 W 38th Street, Suite 902, New York, NY 10018, USA
www.koganpage.com

EU Representative (GPSR)

eucomply OÜ, Pärnu mnt 139b -14 11317, Tallinn, Estonia
www.eucompliancepartner.com

Kogan Page books are printed on paper from sustainable forests.

ISBNs

Hardback 978 1 3986 2424 5
Paperback 978 1 3986 2421 4
Ebook 978 1 3986 2422 1

British Library Cataloguing-in-Publication Data

A CIP record for this book is available from the British Library.

Library of Congress Cataloging-in-Publication Data

A CIP record for this book is available from the Library of Congress

---

Typeset by Integra Software Services, Pondicherry
Printed and bound by CPI Group (UK) Ltd, Croydon CR0 4YY

To my mom: Thank you for the year of homeschooling when I didn't even believe in myself, for standing beside me through those teenage years when rejection felt bigger than me. You taught me to see myself clearly, to see that I was smart, capable, and even brilliant when the world made me feel less than.

And Mom, if it wasn't for those algebra lessons, I'm not sure where we'd be today (lol). Just kidding, but really, they taught me the most important lesson of all: never give up. Love you always.

To my beautiful wife, my greatest encourager and constant source of strength.

You believed in me when I doubted myself, and you pushed me to share what was inside me with the world. Because of you, I have found the courage to grow, to write, and to become the best version of myself.

This book is as much yours as it is mine.

I love you to the moon and back always.

CONTENTS

Introduction 1

1 **Rethinking Talent Acquisition** 3

The Catalyst for Change 3
Why Integration Matters 6
The Risks of Maintaining Silos 11
The Business Case for Integration 13
The Current Challenges 15
Why Alignment Matters in the Recruitment Process 16
Notes 29

2 **The Talent Pipeline as a Strategic Asset** 33

A Wake-Up Call in Recruitment 33
The Shift from Reactive to Proactive 34
Toward Recruitment Maturity and Organizational Readiness 46
Notes 48

3 **Defining Roles: Rethinking Sourcing and Recruiting** 51

Breaking Down Traditional Roles 52
Toward an Integrated, Collaborative Model 57
Technology as an Enabler 61
Culture of Shared Ownership 63
Notes 65

4 **Defining Key Skills and Responsibilities in the New Model** 67

Skills and Traits for an Integrated Sourcer (Talent Researcher) 67
Skills and Traits for an Integrated Recruiter (Talent Partner) 69
Realigning and Restructuring the Talent Acquisition Team: A Practical Guide 74
Notes 91

5 **Building Bridges: Cross-Functional Training and Skill Sharing** 93

The Strategic Imperative for Collaboration 95
From Handoffs to Handshakes: Forging a Cohesive and Empathetic Team 96
A Seamless Journey: Crafting a Superior Candidate Experience 98
From Theory to Evidence: Bridges in Action 100
The Architect's Blueprint: A Guide to Implementation 102
Fostering a Shared Mind: Workshops and Mentorship 103
Navigating the Headwinds of Change 105
Forging the Future with United Talent Teams 105
Notes 106

6 **Proactive Pipeline Building: Beyond the Requisition to the Talent Community** 107

The Paradigm Shift 107
The Strategic Imperative: Why Building Talent Communities is Non-Negotiable 109
A Powerful Engine for Diversity, Equity, and Inclusion 111
The "How-To": Core Strategies for Building Your Talent Community 112
Real-World Examples from the Field 116
Nurturing Your Talent Community 117
The Enablers: Technology, AI, and Analytics 119
Building a Sustainable Talent Advantage 121
Reflections 122
Notes 123

7 **Leveraging Technology and AI for Seamless Integration** 125

The Great Divide: Introduction 125
Anatomy of a Modern Recruiting Tech Stack 127
AI-Powered Sourcing and Intelligence Platforms 129
The Integration Blueprint: From Disconnected Tools to a Unified Workflow 131

The Importance of APIs and Native Integrations 133
Change Management is Non-Negotiable 135
Navigating the Human-AI Partnership 138
Training, Governance, and Data Hygiene 140
Notes 142

8 **Metrics That Matter: Measuring Success in a Collaborative Model** 143

The Myth of the Green Dashboard 143
From Activity to Impact: A New Measurement Philosophy 144
From Data to Action: The Continuous Improvement Framework 149
Telling a New Story 152

9 **Transforming Candidate Experience Through Collaboration** 155

The Ghost in the Machine 155
The Candidate's Journey Is the Team's Journey 156
Mapping the Moments That Matter 158
The Ripple Effect: The True Power of Candidate Experience 160
The AI-Powered Candidate Concierge 161
The Technology of Empathy 163
The Experience Is the Brand 164
Notes 167

10 **Navigating the Transition** 169

The Story of Innovate Inc. 169
The Anatomy of Resistance: Uncovering the "Why" 171
A Multi-Layered Analysis of Stakeholders 173
The Quiet Saboteurs: How Communication and Alignment Fail 176
The Collision of Misalignment: A War Fought with Spreadsheets 178
The Blueprint for a Successful Transition 180

The Strategic Communication Playbook 183
Sustaining the Momentum 186
Notes 188

11 **Future-Proofing Talent Acquisition: A Roadmap for Leaders** 189

The New Threat on the Horizon 189
The Obsolescence Trap: Diagnosing a Brittle TA Function 191
The Tides of Change: Forces Reshaping the Talent Landscape 193
The Roadmap to a Future-Proofed TA Function 195
Key Questions for Leaders 202
Notes 202

12 **The AI Revolution in Talent Acquisition** 203

Understanding the AI Toolkit for Talent Acquisition 204
Generative AI: The Creator 205
Conversational AI: The Concierge 206
AI and the Unified Front: A New Look at Chapter 1 207
From Proactive to Predictive: A New Look at Chapters 2 and 6 208
The AI Co-Pilot: A New Look at Chapters 3, 4, and 5 210
The Ethical Imperative: Navigating AI Bias and Ensuring Fairness 212
The Transparent Scorecard and the AI-Driven Narrative: A New Look at Chapters 8, 9, and 10 214
A Final Caution: The Soul of the Machine Is Human 215
What AI Cannot Replace 216
The Augmentation Framework: The Human + AI Partnership 217
A Final Reflection: The Human-AI Partnership 218
Notes 220

Index 221

The Importance of APIs and Native Integrations 133
Change Management is Non-Negotiable 135
Navigating the Human-AI Partnership 138
Training, Governance, and Data Hygiene 140
Notes 142

8 Metrics That Matter: Measuring Success in a Collaborative Model 143

The Myth of the Green Dashboard 143
From Activity to Impact: A New Measurement Philosophy 144
From Data to Action: The Continuous Improvement Framework 149
Telling a New Story 152

9 Transforming Candidate Experience Through Collaboration 155

The Ghost in the Machine 155
The Candidate's Journey Is the Team's Journey 156
Mapping the Moments That Matter 158
The Ripple Effect: The True Power of Candidate Experience 160
The AI-Powered Candidate Concierge 161
The Technology of Empathy 163
The Experience Is the Brand 164
Notes 167

10 Navigating the Transition 169

The Story of Innovate Inc. 169
The Anatomy of Resistance: Uncovering the "Why" 171
A Multi-Layered Analysis of Stakeholders 173
The Quiet Saboteurs: How Communication and Alignment Fail 176
The Collision of Misalignment: A War Fought with Spreadsheets 178
The Blueprint for a Successful Transition 180

The Strategic Communication Playbook 183
Sustaining the Momentum 186
Notes 188

11 **Future-Proofing Talent Acquisition: A Roadmap for Leaders** 189

The New Threat on the Horizon 189
The Obsolescence Trap: Diagnosing a Brittle TA Function 191
The Tides of Change: Forces Reshaping the Talent Landscape 193
The Roadmap to a Future-Proofed TA Function 195
Key Questions for Leaders 202
Notes 202

12 **The AI Revolution in Talent Acquisition** 203

Understanding the AI Toolkit for Talent Acquisition 204
Generative AI: The Creator 205
Conversational AI: The Concierge 206
AI and the Unified Front: A New Look at Chapter 1 207
From Proactive to Predictive: A New Look at Chapters 2 and 6 208
The AI Co-Pilot: A New Look at Chapters 3, 4, and 5 210
The Ethical Imperative: Navigating AI Bias and Ensuring Fairness 212
The Transparent Scorecard and the AI-Driven Narrative: A New Look at Chapters 8, 9, and 10 214
A Final Caution: The Soul of the Machine Is Human 215
What AI Cannot Replace 216
The Augmentation Framework: The Human + AI Partnership 217
A Final Reflection: The Human-AI Partnership 218
Notes 220

Index 221

Introduction

Why I Wrote This Book

I wrote this book because I believe the world of talent acquisition is at a crossroads. For years, I've seen organizations struggle with the same questions: How do we find the right people faster? How do we create sustainable pipelines? How do we bring humanity back into a process that has become so transactional?

This book is the culmination of my 27 years in the field years filled with wins, setbacks, lessons, and breakthroughs. It's for the recruiters who feel stretched thin, the sourcers who feel unseen, and the leaders who know there must be a better way.

I also want to thank the many talent acquisition leaders I've encountered along the way, those who showed me, sometimes painfully, how not to lead. Their examples of what leadership shouldn't look like pushed me to commit to leading differently: with authenticity, compassion, and courage.

And of course, this book is deeply personal. The lessons my mom instilled in me about persistence, problem-solving, and never giving up have carried me through every challenge in my career and inspired me to put these ideas into writing.

I want this book to be both a guide and a companion, something that sparks new ways of thinking, helps build stronger bridges between sourcing and recruiting, and, ultimately, empowers you to design talent strategies that last.

For leaders, it's a strategic roadmap to modernize talent acquisition by aligning your teams, technology, and partners around a shared vision of agility, authenticity, and data-driven excellence.

For recruiters and sourcers, it's a playbook filled with practical frameworks, communication strategies, and mindset shifts that help you move from order-takers to strategic talent advisors.

Whether you're leading a global team or filling one critical role, this book will help you rethink how talent is discovered, engaged, and nurtured. Each chapter offers insights that can be put into practice immediately, connecting strategy to execution, metrics to meaning, and people to purpose.

1

Rethinking Talent Acquisition

The Catalyst for Change

My career in talent acquisition (TA) has allowed me to both observe and reshape talent acquisition operations across various organizations, from small startups to multinational corporations. Each experience has highlighted a crucial reality: organizations often manage TA processes in ways that hinder both efficiency and effectiveness.

The most common issues I have identified within TA include recruitment processes that operate in a disjointed manner and teams that function independently rather than collaboratively. I have observed that the objectives of the TA team do not always align with the organization's goals, leading to a misalignment in hiring strategies.

In 2018, I had the opportunity to innovate and reshape the TA strategy for a major engineering client. Through this experience, I gained a thorough understanding of effective recruitment methods, which helped me build stronger connections among different teams. The organization underwent significant changes as their hiring processes improved noticeably, while this experience deepened my understanding of the extensive capabilities that an optimized TA function can offer. This experience serves as a foundation in my career, solidifying my commitment to developing more effective, cohesive talent management solutions that are strategically focused.

At the beginning of our engagement with the client, their TA department demonstrated strength through its diverse roles, which included recruiters, sourcers, recruitment coordinators, and administrative personnel. The organization appeared well-structured at first glance, but a thorough examination over the next 30 days revealed critical operational issues.

The flawed recruitment process led to numerous inefficiencies that severely hindered recruiters' ability to perform effectively. Sourcers struggled to find direction as unclear objectives resulted in wasted resources and failed to yield concrete outcomes. The situation worsened further because no team member understood the organization's Employee Value Proposition (EVP), which is a crucial factor in attracting the right talent and serves as a cornerstone for effective recruitment strategies.

The issues extended beyond mere disorganization; they revealed that the team was entirely chaotic. Team members experienced disengagement due to fragmentation and confusion, which hindered their ability to establish a shared mission or common goal. The team encountered recruitment challenges that surpassed their hiring needs, as they unintentionally worked against one another in a disjointed environment lacking both unity and clear objectives. The TA function was in crisis, illustrating an urgent need for strategic intervention and organizational realignment.

Despite the existing dysfunction, there was a remarkable opportunity to rebuild and redesign their approach while integrating their efforts. Instead of needing additional resources or staff, the team required proper alignment and collaboration, along with a shared vision, to function effectively. In the following months, we worked diligently to eliminate silos and clarify roles, while establishing processes that enabled team members to collaborate towards achieving shared objectives. The transformation was challenging yet profoundly rewarding. The project aimed to go beyond repairs by demonstrating how a unified TA strategy can drive transformation. My transformation experience led me to see TA as the strategic force propelling an organization toward success. Extraordinary results emerge when sourcing and recruiting teams collaborate, technology integrates with processes, and the entire organization adheres to a common vision. The content in this chapter and the upcoming ones builds upon past lessons to provide organizations with a strategic guide to redesigning their TA operations. This client's story taught me one critical truth: Integration is an essential requirement rather than merely a possible solution.

The Future Is Unified

Today's competitive job market has fundamentally transformed how companies recruit employees. Finding and retaining top talent presents serious challenges for organizations in this landscape. The TA environment has been reshaped by rapid technological advancements, evolving employee expectations and the global shortage of skilled workers. The traditional method of separating sourcing from recruiting has become outdated in modern hiring practices. To maintain a competitive edge, companies must adopt a cohesive strategy in their hiring processes.

Traditional TA methods create numerous gaps and misalignments, leading to significant miscommunication between teams. Sourcing teams often identify candidates who meet all technical requirements but may lack cultural fit due to limited collaboration with recruiters. Recruiters waste time reassessing candidates because sourcers fail to provide complete information. When there is misalignment in recruitment processes, companies risk losing highly skilled employees to their competitors.

This chapter underscores the necessity of integrating sourcing and recruiting into a unified TA process. By prioritizing collaboration and utilizing advanced technology, businesses can develop a flexible and effective TA system, ensuring all employees align with the company's objectives, which helps attract and retain top talent. This strategy offers significant benefits that enhance both the speed of filling positions and the long-term satisfaction of employees.

Moreover, this chapter emphasizes the significance of harmonizing sourcing and recruiting into a streamlined TA process. By fostering teamwork, employing cutting-edge technology and aligning with the company's objectives, businesses can establish a flexible, efficient, and innovative strategy for attracting and retaining talent. The advantages of this strategy are considerable and can positively influence everything from the speed of filling positions to the overall satisfaction of employees over time.

The Imperative for Integration

Talent acquisition has undergone a significant transformation over the past decade, evolving from a basic transactional role to a vital strategic force in business operations. Companies that do not adapt their recruitment strategies to today's competitive landscape will struggle to keep pace with rivals competing for top talent. To maintain industry leadership, organizations must address critical inefficiencies and misalignments resulting from disconnected sourcing and recruiting efforts. This strategic transformation is essential for enhancing the effectiveness of TA beyond mere process improvements. Organizations that integrate their recruitment practices will ensure their hiring strategies align with overall business objectives, leading to better talent outcomes and increased market competitiveness.

Why Integration Matters

To enhance collective capabilities and achieve shared goals, sourcing and recruiting teams must integrate their operations within the competitive talent marketplace. The current hiring landscape requires faster and more precise recruitment methods to attract high-quality candidates, making this alignment essential. The combined efforts of sourcing professionals and recruiters create an environment where each party leverages its unique strengths in the TA process, sourcers identify potential candidates through targeted outreach and market research, while recruiters assess these candidates to ensure they meet organizational needs.

Companies that establish this collaborative synergy not only streamline their hiring processes but also gain the advantage of attracting top talent before competitors can respond. An effective TA strategy emerges from these collaborative efforts, enabling organizations to thrive in a competitive job market.

Enhanced Candidate Experience

The candidate experience improves when sourcers and recruiters collaborate effectively to create personalized and efficient recruitment journeys. Imagine a scenario where a professional sourcer employs market research techniques alongside cutting-edge AI tools and dynamic talent networks to identify a promising candidate. The sourcer crafts a tailored outreach message that aligns with the candidate's professional experience and personal goals, establishing an immediate, genuine connection.

When a candidate shows interest but expresses concerns about career advancement opportunities, the sourcer notes key details, including the candidate's motivations, career development aspirations, salary expectations, and preferred work culture. The recruiter receives a comprehensive account of the candidate's perspective from the sourcer to fully understand their viewpoint. The recruiter utilizes these insights to conduct a call with the candidate, presenting the job opportunity in a way that perfectly aligns with their career aspirations. Recruiters actively address candidate concerns by outlining company career paths and clarifying hiring process expectations. This collaborative approach fosters an environment where candidates feel valued and understood, enhancing engagement levels often lacking in traditional hiring methods.

Throughout the recruitment process, the sourcer and recruiter maintain consistent and open communication. The candidate receives essential resources, including interview preparation tips and feedback after interviews, while staying informed about the hiring timeline through timely notifications. By streamlining conversations and reducing uncertainty, candidates enjoy a smoother and more pleasant recruitment experience. When the time comes to extend an offer, the candidate receives heartfelt congratulations from both the recruiter and the sourcer. This dual recognition deepens the candidate's sense of significance and belonging within the organization, highlighting the meaningful connections formed during the hiring process. The organization ensures the relationship remains active and nurturing, even if a candidate declines the job offer. The sourcer and recruiter keep open lines of communication to connect promising candidates with future job opportunities, strengthening the organization's talent pipeline. This strategic partnership transforms the hiring process from a purely transactional practice into an impactful consultative experience that builds trust and transparency while creating lasting connections in today's competitive talent landscape.

Improved operational efficiency

By creating a structured and repeatable process, recruiters and sources can enhance operational efficiency by minimizing wasted time and manual effort while also improving the candidate experience. The first step in boosting efficiency involves standardizing intake and requisition management through structured forms and kickoff meetings to align with hiring managers and set clear expectations from the start. AI and automation tools such as HireEZ or Entelo help streamline sourcing by identifying top candidates, ranking them, and automating initial contact, along with reminders for follow-ups to prevent candidate drop-off. A Candidate Relationship Management (CRM) system enables organizations to build talent pools, eliminating the need to start sourcing candidates from scratch for each new job opening. Recruiters access pre-qualified talent more quickly when they organize candidates by skills and engagement levels, which reduces submission time.

Automated scheduling tools like Calendly or Paradox, along with chatbots and SMS or WhatsApp follow-ups, allow recruiters to keep candidates engaged while minimizing response time. Shared tracking systems (like Trello, Asana, or ATS dashboards) and clearly defined handoff points between sourcers and recruiters prevent duplicated work. Weekly reviews of the recruitment pipeline enhance both alignment and operational efficiency. Teams maintain optimal sourcing strategies by regularly reviewing key performance metrics, such as time-to-submit and conversion rates, using data from Power BI or ATS dashboards.

When recruiters and sourcers combine structured intake with AI-driven sourcing, CRM talent pools, automated communication, seamless handoff processes, and performance tracking, they create a scalable hiring process that excels in efficiency and collaboration. This approach accelerates hiring processes while simultaneously improving consistency and candidate experience, resulting in better recruitment outcomes.

Alignment with Business Goals

A unified approach to TA helps ensure that hiring practices align with an organization's primary goals. When an organization plans to enter a specific geographical market, expansion requires the sourcing and recruiting teams to collaborate closely. This partnership enables TA teams to recruit candidates with essential skills, as well as expertise in local cultural norms and market regulations.

Targeted recruitment campaigns focusing on particular attributes allow teams to connect with potential candidates who have demonstrated their expertise in specific regions. The recruitment team can leverage local job boards and regional career fairs or tap into market networks to find talent that provides valuable insights and connections.

Through this strategic partnership, companies can ensure that every hiring decision contributes meaningfully to their strategic objectives. By aligning their TA strategy with the company's growth vision, organizations create skilled teams capable of effectively managing expansion into new markets.

Data-Driven Decision-Making

Organizations that merge their sourcing and recruiting activities with advanced analytics tools can monitor essential hiring metrics while uncovering trends and evolving their recruitment methods. When both teams share real-time data access, decision-making processes become more unified and aligned with business objectives. This integration enables recruiters and sourcers to assess vital hiring metrics, including time-to-fill, quality of hire, source effectiveness, candidate conversion rates, and engagement levels. Centralizing data within an Applicant Tracking System (ATS) or Business Intelligence (BI) dashboard allows teams to identify bottlenecks in the hiring funnel and enhance sourcing channels while adjusting outreach strategies based on historical success data.

The recruitment process must integrate market data to function effectively. Recruiters can make better decisions regarding candidate sourcing and engagement by leveraging market intelligence, which encompasses salary benchmarks, talent availability, competitor hiring patterns, and regional hiring demand. By understanding the current labor market, hiring teams can identify appropriate talent pools and offer competitive salaries and benefits. When market data indicates that a specific skill set has limited availability but high demand in a particular area, recruiters should consider searching in nearby markets or hiring remote workers. Utilizing compensation data helps organizations avoid losing potential hires due to non-competitive offers.

When sourcing data shows that a specific job board or referral system consistently delivers high-quality candidates who convert to hires quickly, organizations should shift their resources to optimize their impact. Once outreach methods become ineffective, organizations can implement immediate changes to enhance operational efficiency. Companies use advanced analytics to predict future hiring needs through historical trend analysis, allowing them to build talent pipelines proactively rather than merely responding to hiring needs as they arise. Recruitment predictive modeling tools analyze candidate behavior patterns to evaluate response times, discern engagement strategies that improve acceptance rates, and identify roles that may experience hiring delays based on historical data.

Integrating AI and machine learning (ML) into recruitment analytics enables teams to move beyond historical data and adopt predictive hiring approaches. AI provides insights to identify optimal candidate outreach times, recommend job description adjustments for competitive markets, and detect potential flight risks within the current workforce. The integration of sourcing and recruiting analytics provides unified data access to stakeholders, eliminating discrepancies and operational inefficiencies caused by siloed team activities. When teams share data access, they become accountable, as they can monitor their progress while measuring performance against benchmarks and adjusting strategies to meet hiring objectives.

Organizations become more adaptable to market changes through data-driven approaches. Recruiters who continuously monitor external labor market data can anticipate talent shortages and adjust their recruitment strategies according to industry trends, while building relationships with passive candidates in advance of demand spikes. Recruitment strategies can be modified swiftly when analytics reveal a decline in candidate responsiveness due to economic changes or increasing hiring competition. Continuous data analysis enables recruitment teams to uncover candidate behavior patterns while optimizing engagement methods and maintaining effective hiring strategies.

Organizations that combine internal recruitment analytics with external market data into their hiring strategies can safeguard their competitive advantage. Sourcing teams gain the ability to identify ideal candidates while developing data-driven talent strategies, resulting in more agile and strategic hiring decisions.

The Risks of Maintaining Silos

Companies face significant risks that can harm their hiring outcomes when sourcing and recruiting teams work in isolation from each other. Organizations suffer from inefficiencies that influence time-to-hire, candidate quality, and employer brand perception when they lack a cohesive collaborative approach. The following are critical challenges that emerge from disconnected hiring functions:

1. Delayed Hiring and Lost Talent

Hiring timelines become unnecessarily extended when sourcing and recruiting teams operate with misaligned priorities and inconsistent communication due to the absence of standardized processes. Slow hiring processes make companies vulnerable to losing exceptional candidates to faster-moving competitors. Despite high-quality lead generation by sourcers, the lack of defined handoff procedures and recruiter follow-up leads to candidates disengaging or accepting other offers before meaningful discussions occur. When team members cannot collectively track pipeline movement, they encounter duplicated work and missed follow-ups, prolonging the hiring process.

2. Inconsistent Messaging and Employer Brand Damage

Separate sourcing and recruiting processes generate conflicting information for candidates regarding job expectations, pay structure, company culture, and growth opportunities. When a sourcer emphasizes career advancement prospects in early communications but recruiters provide different information during interviews, candidates may feel confused, undermining their trust in the company. Such discrepancies can lead candidates to perceive the organization as disorganized, causing some to begin doubting the company's reliability. Inconsistencies between employer branding messages and candidate experiences can harm recruitment efforts by lowering offer acceptance rates and referral potential.

3. *Reduced Candidate Quality Due to Misalignment*

Without proper collaboration between sourcers and recruiters, organizations risk incomplete candidate evaluations. Sourcers assess candidates primarily on technical skills and immediate availability, while recruiters prioritize cultural fit and potential future contributions. The lack of a coordinated hiring strategy can lead teams to select candidates who meet certain requirements but fail to address other organizational needs. Sourcers focusing solely on specialized technical skills may overlook leadership qualities that hiring managers equally value. Hiring teams that are not aligned can create mismatches between employee capabilities and job requirements, resulting in high turnover rates and increased recruitment costs.

4. *Missed High-Potential Candidates*

Hiring teams forgo high-potential candidates when siloed hiring strategies obstruct knowledge-sharing, which could otherwise provide substantial value to the organization. Disconnected efforts between recruiters and sourcers hinder proper candidate matching for suitable roles, sometimes causing missed opportunities to fill various positions. Inefficient processes complicate the maintenance of a strong talent pipeline, forcing teams to restart sourcing with each new job opening. This lack of efficiency contributes to higher time-to-fill rates and escalating recruitment costs.

Organizations must establish a unified hiring process that unites sourcers and recruiters to work toward common goals to mitigate these risks. Implementing shared technology platforms alongside standardized handoff procedures and joint strategy sessions will enhance communication, maintain candidate engagement consistency, and lead to improved hiring outcomes. By removing departmental barriers, organizations can create a streamlined hiring system that focuses on strategic objectives and candidate satisfaction, resulting in faster position fills and better long-term workforce management and employee retention.

The Business Case for Integration

Talent acquisition leaders aiming for recruitment efficiency must prioritize the integration of their sourcing operations with recruiting functions as a strategic imperative. Organizations frequently discover that their sourcing and recruiting teams operate in isolation, leading to operational misalignment and missed opportunities. The business case for integration should present measurable improvements in key recruitment metrics and candidate experience, along with the positive impacts on business outcomes. By streamlining workflows and aligning sourcing and recruiting functions under one cohesive strategy, organizations can achieve faster hiring processes, strengthen their employer brands and enhance candidate conversion rates.

A shorter time-to-hire serves as a compelling justification for integration. The separation of sourcing and recruiting teams often results in miscommunication and redundant efforts, which can delay candidate handoffs and slow down the hiring process. An integrated team alleviates these bottlenecks by providing sourcers and recruiters with real-time candidate pipeline information and enabling collaborative priority tasks through standardized workflows. The alignment of sourcing and recruiting teams promotes quicker decision-making processes and reduces the risk of losing top talent to competitors, allowing hiring teams to fill key positions more efficiently. Companies that implement fully integrated recruitment systems have documented significant reductions in time-to-fill periods, enhancing productivity and revenue performance.

Integration also leads to higher candidate conversion rates, marking it as one of its key advantages beyond acceleration. Fragmented recruitment processes result in inconsistent candidate communication, creating confusion and diminishing engagement levels. An integrated recruitment model ensures that candidates transition smoothly from initial contact to job acceptance, featuring consistent communication and proactive involvement throughout each stage. This approach diminishes candidate drop-off, boosts response rates and culminates in improved hiring success. Organizations can achieve superior talent pipelining by merging sourcing with recruiting practices, enabling earlier engagement with passive candidates and fostering ongoing relationship building, which leads to proactive hiring practices.

Organizations gain significant strategic benefits when they align their goals through the integration of sourcing with recruiting functions. Through collaboration rather than working in silos, teams can connect hiring initiatives to business priorities and tailor recruitment methods to address the company's long-term workforce needs. The integrated approach empowers TA leaders to leverage data-driven insights to predict hiring trends, optimize sourcing channels, and improve resource allocation. This alignment shifts hiring efforts from reactive responses to establishing a proactive talent pipeline that supports sustainable business growth.

When sourcing and recruiting teams work together cohesively, they cultivate a stronger employer brand. Candidate perceptions of the organization can plummet and trust can erode when discrepancies arise in messaging across various recruiting and sourcing interactions. A unified team ensures consistent employer branding, which enhances the organization's value proposition and sets it apart from competitors. A well-integrated recruitment team fosters improved candidate interactions, leading to higher job offer acceptance rates and bolstering the company's reputation in the talent market. Organizations that prioritize the development of a unified recruitment strategy often enjoy better Glassdoor ratings, increased candidate Net Promoter Scores (NPS) and more effective referral pipelines contributing to their sustained success in TA.

Talent acquisition leaders can build a robust business case by showing the clear quantitative and qualitative benefits of integration through real-world examples or benchmarking data. Identifying key performance indicators, such as shorter hiring times, enhanced candidate interaction rates, better quality-of-hire metrics and cost efficiencies from recruitment optimization, is crucial. Organizations that have unified their sourcing and recruiting teams can highlight best practices and potential ROI through their success stories.

Talent acquisition leaders who address inefficiencies in siloed operations while showcasing the benefits of integration can transform this process into a vital business strategy. When sourcing and recruiting functions work together seamlessly, they enhance operational efficiency and elevate TA into a strategic asset that fosters sustained business success.

The Current Challenges

When a company's sourcing team finds multiple qualified candidates without proper communication of priorities to recruiters the hiring process becomes inefficient. The absence of proper communication between the sourcing team and recruiters results in wasted resources and lost chances to connect with excellent candidates. When companies bridge these operational gaps, they achieve streamlined and efficient hiring processes.

TABLE 1.1 Challenges of separate talent functions

Challenge	Impact
Fragmented processes	Duplication of efforts missed opportunities
Inconsistent candidate experience	Disjointed and unsatisfactory journey
Inefficiencies in time-to-hire	Loss of top talent
Misalignment with business needs	Uncoordinated talent strategy

So why should we prioritize collaboration? Uniting sourcing and recruiting creates a streamlined recruitment process that enhances every step of hiring. Talent acquisition in today's fast-paced hiring environment goes beyond merely filling open positions, it requires a strategic and agile approach that leverages data analysis. Integrating sourcing with recruiting signifies a comprehensive transformation that boosts each recruitment phase by improving efficiency and candidate quality while ensuring long-term workforce success.

Why Alignment Matters in the Recruitment Process

Sourcing and recruiting serve distinct functions, yet together they improve the recruitment process. Sourcers identify and cultivate relationships with top talent, while recruiters manage hiring logistics and assess candidate suitability for conversions. Working in isolation leads to inefficiencies, causing missed opportunities and inconsistent pipelines for hiring managers, while the time-to-fill increases. Organizations can enhance their recruitment process by integrating sourcing and recruiting functions to deliver quality hires more quickly.

1 **Precision in talent identification and outreach**
   Successful recruitment begins with talent market research and the proactive identification of qualified candidates. Collaborating between sourcing and recruiting teams from the outset allows them to establish clear standards for candidate profiles, essential skills, and cultural fit. The recruitment process is enhanced when sourcers utilize recruiter insights to refine search parameters, making outreach efforts precise and effective.

   Impact on recruitment process:

   - reduces time spent on unqualified candidates
   - improves engagement rates with customized messaging
   - ensures early alignment with hiring manager requirements throughout the recruitment process.

2 **Seamless candidate handoffs and pipeline optimization**
Recruiters take charge when candidates express interest but experience disjointed transitions due to insufficient context. Sourcers provide recruiters with complete candidate profiles, which include motivation details, skill evaluations, and any potential concerns in a unified format. This streamlines the screening process and speeds up decision-making.

Impact on recruitment process:

- faster movement from sourcing to interview stages
- higher interview-to-offer conversion rates
- the implementation of clear and informed transitions leads to lower candidate drop-off rates

3 **Enhanced candidate experience through consistency**
Candidates expect a recruitment journey that flows smoothly and keeps their interest. When recruitment processes become fragmented, they result in inconsistent communication and delays, which lead to decreased candidate engagement. The collaboration between sourcing and recruiting teams creates a cohesive candidate experience that offers consistent communication, clear expectations, and timely updates.

Impact on recruitment process:

- builds trust and improves employer brand perception
- reduces candidate ghosting through proactive engagement
- increases offer acceptance rates by maintaining momentum

4 **Data-driven recruitment strategy**
Integrated recruitment strategies utilize shared analytics to enhance hiring processes. By collectively tracking essential recruitment metrics, sourcers and recruiters can identify inefficiencies and make strategic data-driven decisions.

Impact on recruitment process:

- the approach determines hiring stages that slow down recruitment for process enhancements

- real-time market insights establish future talent strategies
- enhances diversity hiring efforts through targeted sourcing

5 Future-proofing talent pipelines

Recruitment serves a dual purpose: filling current positions while anticipating future workforce needs. Teams that collaborate effectively build talent pools and keep candidates engaged, ensuring they have qualified applicants ready for upcoming job openings. This approach reduces reliance on reactive hiring and strengthens workforce planning capabilities.

Impact on recruitment process:

- reduces time-to-fill by having pre-vetted candidates ready
- the plan enables strategic workforce development by creating extended talent pipelines
- improves hiring agility in competitive talent markets

A Recruitment Process Built for Success

Organizations that align sourcing with recruiting achieve more than operational efficiency, they transform their TA into a best-in-class, game-changing process. When companies merge their sourcing and recruiting functions into one streamlined approach, their hiring becomes more precise, candidate engagement increases, and data analysis improves decision-making capabilities, all of which helps secure their workforce for the future. Organizations adopting this model achieve competitive superiority through both attracting top talent and creating a sustainable hiring system that evolves with business requirements.

Lessons from Industry Leaders

REAL-WORLD EXAMPLE

Google's Recruitment Strategies and Team Integration

Google earns recognition for its innovative products while simultaneously achieving fame for developing groundbreaking TA methods. The analysis explores Google's integration of its sourcing and recruiting teams to improve hiring efficiency and reveals how it optimizes TA through best practices along with insights into industry comparisons and key lessons and challenges faced in merging sourcing with recruiting processes.

Google's Talent Acquisition Team Structure and Integration

Google maintains a recruiting organization that is centralized and highly specialized to achieve peak efficiency. Google has chosen to employ specialist recruitment professionals instead of distributing hiring duties across its general HR team. During its high-growth phase Google kept one recruiter for every 14 of its workforce which exceeded typical industry standards by a significant margin.[1] Google dedicates substantial resources to recruiting because they consider top talent as the essential input that leads to success.[2]

Specialized roles: The recruiting process at Google was divided into separate specialist roles to create an assembly-line method similar to a supply chain.

Key roles in Google's hiring team include:

- *Recruiting research analysts*: gather market and talent intelligence.
- *Sourcers*: concentrate their efforts on the proactive search and recruitment of potential hires.
- *Process coordinators and screeners*: process coordinators and screeners oversee interview scheduling and logistics management while conducting initial resume evaluations.
- *Recruiters for specific talent pools*: Google uses different recruiters to manage the hiring process for college students, technical positions, and executive searches.
- *Recruiting program/project managers*: oversee hiring programs and improve processes.

The organizational structure defines distinct yet complementary responsibilities for sourcers and recruiters. Sourcers focus on finding passive candidates through social media platforms, networking events, boolean search techniques and other methods. Recruiters begin building relationships with interested candidates after sourcing completes their process and proceed to guide them through interviews until they secure the hire.[3] Google achieves team specialization by keeping sourcers focused on creating top-notch candidate pipelines while recruiters deliver personalized candidate experiences and closing expertise.[4] Specialists have unified hiring objectives and work closely with distinct business units which allows them to collaborate with hiring managers while also sharing talent throughout the company when necessary.[5]

Google's central recruitment team maintained authority to internally staff executive and leadership positions instead of hiring externally.[6] The system provides comprehensive sourcing and recruiting solutions for all positions within the company under a single framework. Google treats TA as a fundamental strategic function because it recognizes its critical nature and therefore allocates extensive resources while promoting a recruitment culture that involves every employee from top executives to entry-level staff members.[7]

Key Methods Used by Google to Improve Their Hiring Procedures

The hiring model developed by Google established multiple best practices which have since been replicated throughout different industries.

- *Data-driven, structured hiring*: Structured interviews and evidence-based selection became widespread due to Google's adoption. Standardized interview questions with defined scoring criteria enhance hiring quality while saving time and minimizing bias.[8] Committees are usually responsible for making hiring decisions instead of single managers to maintain objectivity and uphold high standards during the hiring process.[9] The systematic approach shows strong predictive power for candidate success.[10]
- *Proactive sourcing and innovative talent pipelines*: Google avoids over-reliance on passive job boards. Instead, it sources talent actively and creatively. Google uses AdWords job advertisements connected to particular keyword searches for recruitment to target specific professional groups (for instance, engineering job ads appear when programming terms are searched).[11] Google hosted coding competitions such as the Google Code Jam which allowed top engineers to compete for prizes and fast-track their hiring process upon reaching the finals. These approaches generate a large pool of candidates outside traditional recruiting methods. Google heavily depends on employee referrals which access Googler networks to reveal top talent and consistently produce high-quality hires.[12]
- *Candidate experience focus*: Google designs every step of its hiring process to create a positive experience for candidates. Recruiters serve as friendly intermediaries who maintain candidate communication and engagement throughout the entire process from initial interaction to onboarding.[13] The recruiting team features coordinators whose responsibility involves managing interview scheduling and travel arrangements to prevent inconvenience to candidates. Google attracts applicants through its well-known employer brand

which features famous perks and an innovative culture along with programs such as 20% time yet the recruitment team continues to ensure every candidate experiences a responsive and respectful process.[14]

- *Continuous improvement and metrics*: Google historically trailed behind in formal HR metrics but progressively utilized its analytical approach to improve recruiting practices. The company monitors hiring sources and conversion rates along with other talent analytics to improve its methods through data analysis. Google conducted research to determine the most effective interview techniques for predicting performance and made process changes based on the findings which resulted in replacing brainteasers with structured interviews.[15]

Google has developed what Dr. John Sullivan has dubbed a true "recruiting machine" through their combination of rigorous selection methods, aggressive sourcing practices, exceptional candidate care, an inclusive company culture, and data-driven improvements which enables them to successfully attract superior talent.[16]

Google's recruitment approach shows how combining sourcing and recruiting teams through thoughtful and data-driven structures can generate exceptional results. Google's hiring success at scale results from combining a centralized model with specialized roles and a company-wide commitment to recruitment.[17] Google stands out as a talent magnet because they apply best practices like proactive candidate sourcing, rigorous and structured selection processes, and maintain an obsessive focus on candidate experience. Salesforce and IBM have implemented coordinated sourcer-recruiter teams following Google's approach according to.[18]

For companies aiming to improve their own hiring outcomes, the lessons are clear: Organizations must strengthen their recruitment capabilities together with clearly defined roles while taking advantage of technology and upholding an outstanding hiring culture. Organizations can create effective recruiting systems that transform hiring into an efficient scientific process through these actions.

REAL-WORLD EXAMPLE

Unilever's Purpose-Driven Talent Model and Talent Acquisition Strategy

The Purpose-Driven Talent Model together with Talent Acquisition Strategy at Unilever demonstrates their approach to integrating TA efforts with corporate purpose for improved organizational performance.

The Purpose-Driven Talent Model implemented by Unilever demonstrates organizational effectiveness improvements through the alignment of TA with corporate purpose. This case study examines Unilever's integration methods for sourcing and recruiting teams and their best practices in purpose-driven TA while comparing them to other industry leaders and providing lessons and challenges for organizations looking to merge sourcing with recruiting functions.

Unilever's Talent Acquisition Structure and Integration

Through its recruitment strategies Unilever ensures alignment with its foundational values and mission by maintaining a purpose-driven TA process. The "Future-Fit Plan" functions as a key initiative that helps employees develop skills that match their individual purpose and promote wellbeing and leadership behaviors. The framework enables employees to identify their purpose and build skills that serve their current roles and equip them for upcoming opportunities at Unilever or other organizations.[19] Unilever has approximately 30 percent of their office-based workforce actively participating in the Future-Fit Plan which creates an environment where recruitment processes integrate with sourcing strategies to match individual career goals with company objectives.[20]

The implementation of the "FLEX Experiences" platform enables Unilever employees to build professional profiles which allows them to be engaged in both short- and long-term organizational projects to improve internal mobility and agility. This system achieves efficient talent movement through aligned sourcing and recruiting efforts that match employee skills and career goals resulting in integrated talent management.[21]

Best Practices in Purpose-Driven Talent Acquisition

Unilever has implemented multiple best practices to enhance its TA process which is driven by purpose.

- Leveraging artificial intelligence (AI): Unilever collaborated with AI experts to improve its hiring operations. Potential hires complete digital tests that measure their capability in aptitude alongside logical thinking and risk assessment abilities. The suitability of candidates is determined by machine learning algorithms which compare their profiles to those of successful employees. The use of AI in Unilever's recruitment process enabled the company to save substantial time and resources while maintaining consistency with its purpose-driven organizational culture.[22]
- Equity, Diversity, and Inclusion (ED&I): ED&I principles form the foundation of Unilever's talent management strategy. The company created an Equity,

Diversity, and Inclusion Advancement Framework that identifies systemic inequities in its business operations and explores their fundamental origins. The company's framework helps Unilever build an inclusive culture that attracts and keeps diverse talent who support the company's purpose.[23]

Comparisons with Other Industry Leaders

The Purpose-Driven Talent Model of Unilever shares commonalities with strategies implemented by other top industry leaders.

- *Schneider Electric*: Schneider Electric has pursued the development of an internal talent marketplace which functions similarly to Unilever's approach to boost organizational agility and mobility of employees. Schneider Electric supports both individual career goals and company needs by offering employees the chance to participate in new roles and projects.[24]
- Cisco: Cisco supports internal movement by permitting employees to switch roles after specified periods to build an environment of ongoing growth that matches organizational goals. The approach integrates sourcing and recruitment processes with employee development plans while taking inspiration from Unilever's strategies.[25]

Lessons for Other Organizations

- Organizations working to merge sourcing and recruiting teams into a purpose-driven structure should study Unilever's approach for valuable insights.
- Align talent strategies with corporate purpose: Create systems that guide employees to connect their individual purpose with company objectives for increased workforce engagement and motivation.[26]
- Utilize technology to enhance recruitment: The implementation of AI systems and internal talent marketplaces can improve recruitment efficiency while supporting internal mobility and aligning TA with both employee goals and organizational objectives.[27]
- Commit to Equity, Diversity, and Inclusion: Build complete ED&I strategies that create an inclusive environment that draws and maintains diverse talent while supporting the company's mission.[28]

Challenges in Integrating Sourcing and Recruiting Teams

- A purpose-driven model creates specific challenges when merging sourcing and recruiting functions.
- Ensuring alignment: The continuous alignment of individual purposes with organizational goals demands sustained effort and strategic communication methods.[29]
- Managing technological integration: Careful planning is essential for implementing AI alongside internal talent platforms to guarantee they support current processes while obtaining employee acceptance.[30]
- Sustaining ED&I initiatives: The advancement of Equity, Diversity, and Inclusion depends on continual dedication and strategic adaptability in response to changing societal norms and workforce patterns.[31]
- Organizations that tackle these challenges and follow best practices will build a purpose-oriented talent model which merges sourcing and recruiting functions to produce a more dedicated and proficient workforce.

Tools and Exercises for Implementation

EXERCISE 1: MAPPING CURRENT PROCESSES

Objective: Analyze current recruitment and sourcing workflows to discover areas of inefficiency and missing elements.

Instructions:

- Develop process flow diagrams to represent existing workflows for sourcing and recruiting.
- Ensure your process mapping covers every stage starting with job requisition approval and continuing through candidate onboarding.
- Identify places where delays and miscommunications happen including situations where candidates receive repeated outreach or when screening standards are inconsistent.

- Use team member feedback to detect inefficient processes and problem areas.
- Consider possible integration opportunities that will enhance operational efficiency and coordination.

EXERCISE 2: TECHNOLOGY AUDIT

Objective: Perform an evaluation of existing tools to pinpoint compatibility issues and identify functional shortcomings.

Instructions:

- List all the technologies that sourcing and recruiting teams currently utilize including ATS systems along with CRM systems email platforms and scheduling tools.
- Assess each tool for how usable it is as well as how scalable and integrable it remains. Verify whether the ATS system operates smoothly with the CRM or if users need to enter data manually.
- Explore potential adoption of new systems that enable collaborative processes. One example of advanced technology includes an ATS with built-in analytics dashboards or a CRM platform that supports automated workflows for engaging candidates.
- Make sure selected tools fulfill both technical specifications and practical needs through consultations with IT and end users.
- Develop a cost-benefit analysis to guide decisions about advancing technology systems or merging current systems.

Laying the Groundwork for Change

Organizations need to use systematic planning and execution methods when transitioning to an integrated TA model. Organizations need to tackle cultural obstacles together with operational and technological challenges to establish effective cooperation between sourcing and recruiting teams. These steps illustrate the basic components essential for achieving effective integration.

FOSTER A CULTURE OF COLLABORATION

Trust and transparency combined with shared goals create an environment where collaboration can flourish. Establishing a collaborative culture requires the elimination of barriers between sourcing and recruiting teams.

- *Regular cross-functional workshops*: Conduct regular workshops to synchronize teams around organizational hiring priorities and recruitment goals while clarifying individual responsibilities. These sessions should encourage open dialogue, knowledge-sharing, and brainstorming.
- *Shared performance metrics*: Develop unified key performance indicators (KPIs) to evaluate the collective success of both sourcing and recruiting teams. For example, track metrics like the time-to-hire for critical roles, candidate satisfaction scores, or pipeline-to-placement ratios.
- *Employee recognition programs*: Provide recognition and rewards to team members who excel at working together with others. Showcasing successful stories inspires team members and strengthens the organization's culture of collaboration.
- *Leadership advocacy*: Acquiring leadership support is essential because their active promotion of integration initiatives establishes the organizational standard for everyone else. Leaders need to demonstrate teamwork through their actions and distribute resources that help implement changes.

INVEST IN TRAINING AND DEVELOPMENT

When team members gain the essential skills needed for an integrated model they adopt it more effectively which leads to superior results.

- *Sourcing and recruiting boot camps*: Create training programs that combine skills from both sourcing and recruiting domains. Sourcers receive training in behavioral interviewing methods while recruiters explore advanced sourcing techniques through boolean search utilization and data scraping.
- *Soft skills development*: Teach team members how to use communication, negotiation, and empathy skills to improve their

interactions with candidates. These abilities create a workplace that supports positivity and teamwork.

- *Microlearning modules*: Provide quick online courses together with video tutorials about topics including new recruiting technologies and diversity sourcing methods along with compliance rules. The method maintains consistent learning opportunities while avoiding excessive demands on team members.
- *Certification opportunities*: Team members should obtain industry certifications like SHRM Talent Acquisition Specialist or AIRS Certified Internet Recruiter to enhance their credibility and specialized knowledge.

ADOPT THE RIGHT TECHNOLOGY

Proper tools help organizations simplify their workflows while removing redundant tasks and generating data-driven insights that support informed decision-making.

- *Centralized data repositories*: Develop systems that combine sourcing data with recruiting information. When ATS systems are combined with CRM platforms candidate data becomes accessible to all stakeholders which minimizes communication errors.
- *AI-driven recommendations*: Use machine learning algorithms to pinpoint top potential candidates and develop customized engagement methods from historical data combined with role specifications.
- *Integration of communication tools*: Establish real-time connections between sourcing and recruiting teams through Slack or Microsoft Teams platforms. Set up automatic updates to notify stakeholders about key events like new candidates entering the pipeline and their movement through hiring stages.
- *Enhanced reporting dashboards*: Allocate resources to obtain sophisticated analytics tools which deliver comprehensive insights into TA metrics. The dashboard systems are capable of detecting trends which include the performance of different sourcing channels and identification of recruitment bottlenecks.

DEFINE CLEAR ROLES AND RESPONSIBILITIES

When team members experience unclear responsibilities, it results in both operational inefficiencies and interpersonal conflicts. A clear definition of responsibilities helps maintain accountability while ensuring seamless coordination between sourcing and recruiting teams.

- *Role playbooks*: Develop complete documentation to describe the detailed responsibilities of sourcers, recruiters, and all TA team members. Provide examples of required tasks, expected deliverables, and success metrics specific to each role.
- *Defined candidate handoffs*: Put in place specific procedures that guide the process of transferring candidates between sourcers and recruiters. Sourcers must supply comprehensive candidate profiles that incorporate initial contact details along with qualifications and availability to enable a smooth transition to recruiters.
- *Collaborative goal setting*: Ensure sourcing and recruiting targets support the company's overall mission and strategic plans. The recruiting and sourcing teams must both work together to meet the organization's diversity hiring goals and workforce forecasts.

STEPS FOR IMPLEMENTING INTEGRATED TALENT ACQUISITION

TABLE 1.2 Steps for implementing integrated talent acquisition

Step	Description
Foster Collaboration	Encourage collaborative work by establishing transparent communication through structured workshops, shared objectives, and recognition programs.
Invest in Training	Boot camps, certifications, and mentoring enable teams to learn integrated model operations through training programs.
Leverage Technology	Adopt technology solutions to improve integration capabilities through the use of centralized systems and AI-based analytical tools.
Define Clear Handoffs	Establish detailed handoff procedures while defining responsibilities to eliminate overlaps and prevent gaps.

Organizations aiming to succeed in the current competitive talent market must treat the combination of sourcing and recruiting as a strategic necessity. Organizations achieve their maximum potential and secure lasting success through collaborative efforts combined with advanced technology utilization and recruitment alignment with corporate goals.

Integration offers transformative benefits: The integration approach speeds up the recruitment process while improving candidate quality and delivers a smooth experience throughout the hiring journey. By empowering TA teams to proactively meet workforce requirements organizations improve their ability to adapt to the evolving business environment.

The successful implementation of integrated TA strategies by companies such as Google and Unilever illustrates both their practicality and benefits. The organizations in question improved their operational efficiency while simultaneously strengthening employer brands and developing strong talent pipelines. Through their examples we learn that integration represents more than just operational changes because it fundamentally alters the way organizations attract and maintain talent.

In summary, the insights shared in this chapter establish the foundation for a transformative approach to talent integration. As we move forward, the upcoming sections will explore the specific tools, methodologies, and innovative strategies that bring this vision to fruition. By grounding TA in the core principles outlined here, organizations can evolve into agile, future-ready entities. Those that embrace this transformation won't just fill roles they will create dynamic, scalable functions capable of driving sustainable growth and securing a lasting competitive edge in the global talent arena. The path forward is not only essential it is entirely within reach.

Notes

1 Sullivan, J. (2006) A Case Study of Google Recruiting, Dr John Sullivan, https://drjohnsullivan.com/articles/a-case-study-of-google-recruiting/ (archived at https://perma.cc/W5EN-D6HU)

2 Sullivan, J. (2006) A Case Study of Google Recruiting, Part 2, Dr John Sullivan, https://drjohnsullivan.com/articles/a-case-study-of-google-recruiting-part-2/ (archived at https://perma.cc/MMC7-N6DU)

3 Cracking Google's Code: Lessons From its Cutting-Edge Talent Management (2024) Talent Management Institute, www.tmi.org/blogs/cracking-googles-code-lessons-from-its-cutting-edge-talent-management (archived at https://perma.cc/M6L9-HA7R)

4 Sullivan, J. (2006) A Case Study of Google Recruiting, Part 2, Dr John Sullivan, https://drjohnsullivan.com/articles/a-case-study-of-google-recruiting-part-2/ (archived at https://perma.cc/3E7C-AFR7)

5 The 3 Big Secrets Behind Google's Famous Recruitment Process (2016) The Business Growth Agency, https://thebusinessgrowthagency.actioncoach.co.uk/3-big-secrets-behind-googles-recruitment/ (archived at https://perma.cc/2TZ5-YCDW)

6 Sullivan, J. (2006) A Case Study of Google Recruiting, Part 2, Dr John Sullivan. https://drjohnsullivan.com/articles/a-case-study-of-google-recruiting-part-2/ (archived at https://perma.cc/8LGF-Y53V)

7 Rushdi, Y. A. K. and Kamal, A. N. (2014) A Evaluation of Google's Organisational & Recruitment Culture, *Science and Education Publishing*, http://article.sapub.org/10.5923.j.mm.20140404.03.html (archived at https://perma.cc/GT8G-9GK5)

8 Badru, A., Chetty, T., Gigaba, S., and Khuluse, H. (2021) Case Analysis: Human Resource Management Strategy at Google, Research Gate, www.researchgate.net/publication/368987952_Case_Analysis_Human_Resource_Management_Strategy_at_Google (archived at https://perma.cc/P79G-BKYX)

9 Sullivan, J. (2006) A Case Study of Google Recruiting, Dr John Sullivan, https://drjohnsullivan.com/articles/a-case-study-of-google-recruiting/ (archived at https://perma.cc/8SBP-XRVD)

10 Badru, A., Chetty, T., Gigaba, S., and Khuluse, H. (2021) Case Analysis: Human Resource Management Strategy at Google, Research Gate, www.researchgate.net/publication/368987952_Case_Analysis_Human_Resource_Management_Strategy_at_Google (archived at https://perma.cc/88CB-2UDH)

11 Sullivan, J. (2006) A Case Study of Google Recruiting, Part 2, Dr John Sullivan, https://drjohnsullivan.com/articles/a-case-study-of-google-recruiting-part-2/ (archived at https://perma.cc/S3XM-NGVG)

12 Sullivan, J. (2006) A Case Study of Google Recruiting, Dr John Sullivan, https://drjohnsullivan.com/articles/a-case-study-of-google-recruiting/ (archived at https://perma.cc/482F-6GQ2)

13 Badru, A., Chetty, T., Gigaba, S., and Khuluse, H. (2021) Case Analysis: Human Resource Management Strategy at Google, Research Gate, www.researchgate.net/publication/368987952_Case_Analysis_Human_Resource_Management_Strategy_at_Google (archived at https://perma.cc/KE8D-UNVE)

14 Cracking Google's Code: Lessons From its Cutting-Edge Talent Management (2024) Talent Management Institute, www.tmi.org/blogs/cracking-googles-code-lessons-from-its-cutting-edge-talent-management (archived at https://perma.cc/F6R7-WLXS)
15 Badru, A., Chetty, T., Gigaba, S., and Khuluse, H. (2021) Case Analysis: Human Resource Management Strategy at Google, Research Gate www.researchgate.net/publication/368987952_Case_Analysis_Human_Resource_Management_Strategy_at_Google (archived at https://perma.cc/7ZCY-5US9)
16 Sullivan, J. (2006) A Case Study of Google Recruiting, Dr John Sullivan, https://drjohnsullivan.com/articles/a-case-study-of-google-recruiting/ (archived at https://perma.cc/VUT6-9SB6)
17 Ibid.
18 Cracking Google's Code: Lessons From its Cutting-Edge Talent Management (2024) Talent Management Institute, www.tmi.org/blogs/cracking-googles-code-lessons-from-its-cutting-edge-talent-management (archived at https://perma.cc/RHF7-WW96)
19 Unilever (n.d.) Providing Employability Skills for Life, www.unilever.com/sustainability/future-of-work/providing-skills-for-life/ (archived at https://perma.cc/AGL3-JL28)
20 Ibid.
21 Das, D. (2019) Unilever Launches New AI-Powered "Talent Marketplace," ESM Magazine, June 27, www.esmmagazine.com/technology/unilever-launches-new-ai-powered-talent-marketplace-77033 (archived at https://perma.cc/3MJV-8BZF)
22 Marr, B. (2018) The Amazing Ways How Unilever Uses Artificial Intelligence to Recruit & Train Thousands of Employees, Forbes, www.forbes.com/sites/bernardmarr/2018/12/14/the-amazing-ways-how-unilever-uses-artificial-intelligence-to-recruit-train-thousands-of-employees/ (archived at https://perma.cc/YVY9-RLJQ)
23 Unilever (2022) Equity for Impact, www.unilever.com/files/92ui5egz/production/7389005665eb8d074779b226bb4a8c4117786a2f.pdf (archived at https://perma.cc/XT2X-8SQQ)
24 Bersin, J. (2019) The Company As a Talent Marketplace: Unilever and Schneider Electric Show the Way, https://joshbersin.com/2019/07/the-company-as-a-talent-network-unilever-and-schneider-electric-show-the-way/ (archived at https://perma.cc/K4Q4-RD4U)
25 Ibid.
26 Unilever (n.d.) Providing employability skills for life, www.unilever.com/sustainability/future-of-work/providing-skills-for-life/ (archived at https://perma.cc/V7MR-WT5W)

27 Marr, B. (2018) The Amazing Ways How Unilever Uses Artificial Intelligence to Recruit & Train Thousands of Employees, Forbes, www.forbes.com/sites/bernardmarr/2018/12/14/the-amazing-ways-how-unilever-uses-artificial-intelligence-to-recruit-train-thousands-of-employees/ (archived at https://perma.cc/963F-8LLU)

28 Unilever (2022) Equity for Impact, www.unilever.com/files/92ui5egz/production/7389005665eb8d074779b226bb4a8c4117786a2f.pdf (archived at https://perma.cc/7S2L-Z73G)

29 Unilever (n.d.) Providing Employability Skills for Life, www.unilever.com/sustainability/future-of-work/providing-skills-for-life/ (archived at https://perma.cc/EA4D-DQTN)

30 Marr, B. (2018) The Amazing Ways How Unilever Uses Artificial Intelligence to Recruit & Train Thousands of Employees, Forbes, www.forbes.com/sites/bernardmarr/2018/12/14/the-amazing-ways-how-unilever-uses-artificial-intelligence-to-recruit-train-thousands-of-employees/ (archived at https://perma.cc/AL9G-ZAGL)

31 Unilever (2022) Equity for Impact, www.unilever.com/files/92ui5egz/production/7389005665eb8d074779b226bb4a8c4117786a2f.pdf (archived at https://perma.cc/Y7L8-8LYV)

2

The Talent Pipeline as a Strategic Asset

A Wake-Up Call in Recruitment

I still remember the morning I received an urgent call from one of my clients' CTOs: "We need a dozen data scientists yesterday." My stomach sank. At the time, I was leading the talent acquisition strategy for this fast-growing tech company as an external partner. Despite all our efforts, their internal recruiting model was perpetually reactive scrambling whenever a new project kicked off or a critical employee left. That morning, a high-stakes initiative had been greenlit unexpectedly, and there was no candidate pipeline in place.

I quickly pulled together my team for an emergency session. We scoured LinkedIn, engaged agencies, and leaned heavily on referrals—it was an all-hands-on-deck fire drill to source qualified people. We eventually filled the roles, but only after painful delays, premium salaries, and a lot of recruiter burnout. The experience was a personal tipping point.

Driving home late one evening after days of back-to-back candidate interviews, I reflected: How did we end up in this cycle of chaos? Why weren't we anticipating these talent needs? I realized the root issue wasn't the speed of hiring, it was the entire approach. The company was operating like firefighters, responding to talent "alarms" after they rang, rather than fireproofing their workforce with a proactive pipeline of skills. Their recruitment strategy was almost entirely requisition-driven, reacting to openings instead of planning ahead a model destined to struggle in a fast-moving environment.

In the months that followed, I worked closely with their leadership team to shift from reactive to proactive workforce planning. We built a process to forecast talent needs, nurtured relationships with high-potential candidates long before roles opened, and even identified internal employees for upskilling into future-critical positions. It wasn't easy—it demanded a mindset shift, new technologies, and a lot of patience, but it paid off.

A year later, when the company launched a major new product, they were ready. We already had a bench of pre-vetted engineers and scientists engaged and excited about the opportunity. Roles were filled within weeks instead of months with less stress, lower costs, and a stronger cultural fit.

This journey—helping a client move from last-minute scrambling to purposeful talent planning—reinforced for me just how transformative proactive sourcing strategies can be.

The Shift from Reactive to Proactive

My experience is far from unique. Many talent acquisition (TA) leaders have faced similar wake-up calls, realizing that yesterday's reactive recruiting tactics can't meet tomorrow's talent challenges. Traditionally, recruitment has been a transactional function: a hiring manager submits a requisition and the TA team rushes to fill it. This reactive recruitment often leads to frantic searches, suboptimal hires, and misalignment with business goals. In fact, 82 percent of Fortune 500 executives don't believe their companies recruit highly talented people—a telling statistic that reactive approaches aren't delivering the caliber of talent organizations need. Furthermore, skill shortages are becoming acute; for example, one study projected a 23 million talent deficit in the US by 2020 in critical fields.[1] The cost of waiting until a position is vacant is simply too high in today's competitive landscape.

Evolving to proactive and strategic workforce planning means anticipating needs, not just reacting to them. It's about looking around corners, identifying the skills your organization will require in 6, 12, or 24 months, and taking action now to ensure those capabilities are on hand. This shift is often described as moving up the "recruitment maturity" curve, from an administrative, backfill mindset to strategic talent stewardship. Proactive TA aligns closely with business strategy: Recruitment becomes a partner in future organizational planning, not an after-the-fact service.

The benefits of a proactive approach are significant. Companies that plan ahead can hire faster and better, because they've already cultivated candidates (or trained employees) for key roles. They reduce downtime from vacancies and avoid paying a premium for last-minute hires. Proactive TA also improves quality of hire—when you're not in panic mode, you can afford to be selective and attract the best. Moreover, it elevates TA's role to a strategic function that drives business outcomes, rather than a reactive cost center.

In this chapter, we explore how two global companies made this transformation. IBM, a century-old enterprise, reinvented its talent strategy by treating "Talent-as-a-Service," creating an agile internal talent marketplace to deploy skills on demand. And Johnson & Johnson (J&J), a company renowned for its innovation, built a proactive talent pipeline, using predictive analytics to foresee needs and engage future candidates well in advance. Through these case studies, we'll see how moving from reactive recruiting to proactive planning is not only possible, but game-changing. We'll delve into the tactics they used, the technologies enabling their success, and the lessons learned that you can apply to your own talent acquisition strategy.

REAL-WORLD EXAMPLE

IBM's Talent-as-a-Service (TaaS) Model—Agile Talent on Demand

Reimagining Talent Delivery at IBM

In the mid-2010s, IBM faced a pivotal challenge familiar to many large organizations: the tech landscape was shifting beneath its feet. The rise of cloud computing, AI, and other digital innovations meant that skills that IBM's workforce had relied on for decades were becoming obsolete, while entirely new skill sets were in sudden demand.[2] IBM's leadership recognized that to stay competitive, they needed to radically realign their talent with the evolving needs of the business. Diane Gherson, IBM's Chief HR Officer at the time, articulated the imperative clearly: IBM had to become a "skills-based organization," where employees were assessed and deployed based on skills rather than static job titles.[3] This vision laid the groundwork for IBM's "Talent-as-a-Service" model—an approach that treats talent supply as an on-demand service, dynamically matching skills to projects as needs arise.

Traditionally, IBM, like many companies, managed talent in a relatively linear way: employees were hired into specific roles, and when a new project started, managers either competed internally for available staff or opened a requisition to hire externally. This process was slow and siloed. IBM realized that in a world where business priorities can change overnight, a more fluid approach was needed. They asked a transformative question: *"What if we could access and deploy talent inside IBM as easily as renting capacity from a cloud service?"* In other words, could IBM create an internal talent cloud—a Talent-as-a-Service platform—to instantly match the right people to the right work?

How the TaaS Model Works

IBM's Talent-as-a-Service strategy centered on building an internal talent marketplace powered by data and AI. One flagship initiative was the development of the "Blue Matching" program. Blue Matching is an AI-driven platform that automatically catalogs employees' skills and experiences and matches them to project opportunities across IBM.[4] Instead of waiting for managers to fight over talent or for employees to apply for internal openings, Blue Matching proactively suggests matches: "Alice in the Finance unit has strong Python skills, which are needed on this AI project in the Research division." The system uses a proprietary algorithm to weigh an employee's current skill profile against the requirements of gigs and roles available elsewhere in the company.[5] Much of the skill data is collected automatically—IBM developed AI that can infer an employee's skills and proficiency by analyzing their work outputs, learning activities, and even the content of their communications (with appropriate privacy safeguards). This rich skill data fuels the matching engine.

From an employee's perspective, Blue Matching feels like an internal job board on steroids. At any time, an IBM employee can log into the system and see recommended opportunities—short-term projects, stretch assignments, or even full-time role openings—that align with their skills and interests. The platform doesn't just wait for employees to search, it nudges them to consider opportunities that they might not have been aware of, effectively "pulling" talent to areas of need in real time. For instance, a software developer in one business unit might receive a suggestion to contribute 10 hours a week to a cybersecurity project in another unit if there's a skills match. This dynamic allocation of talent is the essence of the TaaS model: Internal talent can be rented by teams that need it for as long as needed, then returned to the pool or onto the next project.

Managers, on the other side of the platform, gain agility in building teams. If a new client project kicks off that requires, say, expertise in blockchain, a manager can tap into the marketplace and quickly see a slate of internal candidates who have completed blockchain courses or have relevant project experience. Instead of initiating an external hiring process that might take months, the manager can assemble an "on-demand team" from within IBM in days or even hours. This fluid matching means project staffing is dramatically accelerated, and work doesn't stall waiting for the right talent. It also breaks down silos—an expert in one corner of IBM can be discovered and deployed by another corner, whereas previously that connection might never have been made.

Driving Internal Agility and Engagement

The impact of IBM's TaaS approach was significant and multifaceted. First and foremost, it injected tremendous internal agility into IBM's talent deployment. IBM effectively created a skills "market" inside the company where supply (employee skills) could meet demand (project requirements) continuously. This meant IBM could respond faster to changing business needs. As one IBM executive noted, internal talent marketplaces enable "swift resource reassignment, ensuring uninterrupted operations" even in times of rapid change.[6] In practical terms, when a new market opportunity arose or a project's scope changed, IBM could reallocate people with minimal bureaucracy—much like scaling cloud server capacity up or down on demand.

This agility proved especially valuable during unpredictable periods. For example, during economic headwinds in 2020–21, IBM, like many companies, instituted external hiring freezes in certain areas. Thanks to the internal talent marketplace, IBM could pivot by redeploying existing employees to priority roles, mitigating the impact of the hiring freeze. A LinkedIn analysis of 2023 trends highlighted IBM as a leader in this regard: faced with needing to tighten hiring, IBM leaned on its internal gig platform to unlock existing employees' potential and "ensure businesses harness their complete potential" without heavy external recruiting. In other words, IBM's TaaS model became a pressure release valve—rather than overburden remaining staff or leave gaps unfilled, the company tapped its internal talent cloud to keep projects moving and employees motivated with new opportunities.

Indeed, employee engagement at IBM rose as a result of these changes. Giving employees visibility of internal opportunities and the agency to apply their skills in new contexts made them feel more valued and empowered. IBM reported a significant increase in employee engagement levels after launching the Blue Matching internal marketplace.[7] People were energized by the chance to grow and take on stretch assignments. An engineer could pursue a passion project in AI, while a marketing specialist could spend a few hours a week with a product development team to broaden their experience. This dynamic not only kept employees interested, but it also clearly signaled that IBM was investing in their growth.

Another outcome was improved talent retention and reduced reliance on external hiring. When employees can find their next career move *within* the company, they are far less likely to look outside. IBM saw a measurable reduction in external hiring needs once the TaaS approach was implemented. Rather than immediately going to the market to hire for a new skill, IBM first looks internally. This has saved costs (external hires are typically more expensive) and preserved institutional knowledge. IBM essentially built an internal mobility escalator; as one role is vacated by an internal move, it might be backfilled by yet another internal move, and so on, with external recruiting being the last resort. This cascading internal movement is the opposite of talent hoarding—it's talent liquidity.

There's also a skills development advantage inherent in the model. As roles and projects are more fluid, IBM employees are continually encouraged to upskill and reskill. IBM paired the Blue Matching platform with a robust learning ecosystem called "Your Learning." If Blue Matching identifies a promising opportunity for an employee but they lack one minor skill required, the system integrates with Your Learning to suggest a course or module to gain that skill.[8] For instance, an employee matched to a project management gig might be prompted to take a short course in Agile methodology via the learning hub. This integration ensures that TaaS is not just about shuffling people around, but also about elevating their capabilities continuously. Every match becomes a development opportunity, and AI helps guide learning paths that align with IBM's strategic skills needs. IBM's approach thus fosters a culture of continuous learning, where employees see clear benefits to acquiring new skills (since it immediately opens new doors for them internally).

Crucially, IBM leveraged advanced technology and AI to make this all possible at scale. With over 350,000 employees globally, manually tracking skills and matching people to projects would be impossible. IBM's investment in AI for HR paid off in a big way. The company developed AI tools (such as the skills inference engine and the career matching algorithms) that could sift through vast amounts of data, from resumes, project records, and internal social networks, to paint a detailed picture of each employee's skills. One outcome of these AI-driven efforts was a sophisticated skills taxonomy and insight into skill adjacencies (e.g. knowing that someone proficient in one programming language could quickly learn another). Over time, as the AI "learned" from successful matches, the recommendations became more accurate and trusted by managers and employees alike. In fact, IBM's AI-based talent tools, including those underpinning TaaS, have achieved between 85 and 95 percent accuracy in matching people to opportunities according to IBM's internal assessments.[9]

The ROI of IBM's TaaS and AI talent initiatives has been impressive. IBM reported that its suite of AI-driven HR tools (which include the talent marketplace, AI skills inference, and others) saved the HR department $107 million and thousands of hours in one year. These savings came from faster hiring cycles, better internal fill rates, and automating labor-intensive tasks (like manually reviewing profiles or conducting lengthy skill surveys). $107 million in savings is not just a HR win it's a bottom-line business impact, demonstrating how a proactive talent strategy contributes tangible value. IBM's finance leaders greenlit further expansion of these tools once they saw the efficiency gains.[10]

Beyond the numbers, IBM's Talent-as-a-Service model also aligned talent with evolving project needs in a way that future-proofed the organization. Because IBM was continuously mapping its internal skills and identifying gaps, it could preemptively address areas where talent was lacking. For example, if data showed a shortage of cybersecurity experts for upcoming client contracts, IBM could quickly decide whether to retrain some internal developers in security or to hire consultants, well before the project start. This kind of workforce planning, informed by real-time skill data, turned IBM's talent acquisition into a strategic function. It wasn't only about filling today's jobs, it was about preparing for tomorrow's. In one instance, IBM's decision science team noticed an emerging need for quantum computing skills to support IBM's research division. Through the internal marketplace and learning programs, IBM identified engineers with strong mathematics backgrounds and offered them training in quantum computing, effectively creating a pipeline of quantum-ready talent internally before the demand fully hit.

Lessons Learned from IBM's TaaS Journey

Implementing a Talent-as-a-Service model at IBM was not without challenges. It required cultural change, new skills for managers, and trust in technology. IBM's experience offers rich lessons for any TA leader looking to build a more proactive, agile talent function:

- *Break down silos with data and transparency*: A key to IBM's success was making skills and opportunities visible across the organization. By using data and an open platform, IBM enabled talent to flow to where it was needed most. Lesson: Create a transparent skills database or talent marketplace so that no team operates in isolation when it comes to talent. Encourage a company-wide view of "talent supply" rather than each manager guarding their own bench.
- *Leverage AI to match talent to work*: IBM's use of AI for skill inference and matching was crucial. No human could have manually handled the scale of matching IBM needed. AI provided unbiased, objective matching based on skills, not on who managers personally knew, reducing favoritism and casting a wider net. Lesson: Adopt technology (AI, algorithms) to enable accurate matching and predictive talent analytics. These tools can identify non-obvious candidates and suggest career moves that benefit both employee and employer.
- *Cultivate internal mobility as a core culture*: Initially, some IBM managers resisted losing their star employees to other departments, and some employees were hesitant about trying gigs outside their comfort zone. IBM had to promote a culture where internal mobility is celebrated and supported (for example, by recognizing managers who develop talent that goes on to succeed elsewhere in the company). *Lesson*: Incentivize and normalize internal transfers and gig assignments. Make it clear from the top-down that the company values developing talent internally even if it means sharing people across teams. This might involve updating performance goals for managers to include talent development and mobility metrics.
- *Align talent strategy with business strategy*: IBM's shift was driven by a clear business need: the company's portfolio was changing and talent had to keep up.[11] HR and TA partnered tightly with business leaders to understand strategic direction (e.g. more cloud services, new AI products) and then proactively built the talent capabilities to support it. *Lesson*: Use workforce planning as a strategic exercise, not an annual HR ritual. Meet with business units regularly about future plans, identify what skills will be needed, and use a TaaS approach (internal re-skilling, talent pooling) to prepare in advance. By the time the business formally needs a role, you should have candidates or internal staff ready.

- *Invest in employee reskilling and learning*: One of IBM's mottos during this transformation was "Don't just find talent—build it." The TaaS model wasn't purely about shuffling existing skills around, it was also about elevating skills. IBM's integration of Blue Matching with the Your Learning platform meant that employees had a clear pathway to gain in-demand skills and see the career payoff of doing so. *Lesson*: Combine any talent marketplace or mobility program with robust learning and development. Provide resources (courses, certifications, mentorship) for employees to develop skills for the opportunities they aspire to. This ensures your proactive talent pool actually grows to meet future needs (and employees remain engaged learners).[12]
- *Measure and iterate*: IBM tracked metrics like internal fill rate, time-to-staff projects, employee engagement, and cost savings from its TaaS initiatives. The $107 million savings in one year was a powerful proof point. They also monitored the accuracy of AI matches and improved the algorithms over time. *Lesson*: Define success metrics for your proactive talent programs—it could be increased percentage of roles filled internally, reduced time-to-hire, higher retention of top performers, or cost avoidance. Use these metrics to refine the program and to demonstrate ROI to executives.

IBM's Talent-as-a-Service journey shows that even a very large, established company can dramatically increase its recruitment maturity. By moving to an on-demand internal talent model, IBM became faster, more flexible, and more strategic in how it deployed human capital. For TA leaders, the IBM case underscores the importance of breaking free from the old requisition-by-requisition mindset. When you treat talent as a continually flowing service, you ensure your organization has the right skills at the right time, not by luck, but by design.

REAL-WORLD EXAMPLE

Johnson & Johnson's Proactive Talent Pipelining—Planning for Tomorrow's Talent Today

Anticipating Talent, Not Chasing It

In today's fast-changing talent landscape, one truth stands out: if you wait until a requisition opens to begin recruiting, you're already behind. Johnson & Johnson (J&J), a global healthcare giant with over 140,000 employees and a presence in over 60 countries, embodies what it looks like to transform traditional recruitment into a proactive, predictive, and business-aligned function.

J&J's recruiting leaders recognized that reactive hiring practices posting a job and hoping the right person applies were no longer sufficient in high-growth, high-demand areas like digital health, biologics, and data science. These roles required a forward-looking talent strategy, one that anticipated hiring needs before they arose and built relationships with candidates long before an interview ever took place.

This transformation in mindset was intentional and driven by forward-thinking leaders like Sjoerd Gehring, then Vice President of Talent Acquisition and Employee Experience at Johnson & Johnson. Gehring championed a data-driven approach to recruitment, using advanced analytics and AI to enhance decision-making and create a more predictive hiring process. Rather than focusing solely on filling open roles, his team sought to understand future workforce needs, identifying emerging talent gaps and proactively shaping the company's ability to attract the right skills before the market demanded them.[13]

Workforce Planning and Predictive Analytics

At the center of J&J's approach was its Decision Science team, a workforce analytics function that helped forecast talent demand based on internal and external data. By analyzing business plans (e.g. a new product line or global expansion), industry trends, and demographic data (such as upcoming retirements in key departments), the team could identify skills that would be in short supply and begin building strategies to address them.

For example, when anticipating a surge in demand for viral vector scientists due to a growing focus on gene therapy, J&J didn't wait until hiring became urgent. The TA team built targeted outreach to academic researchers and biotech professionals in that niche. Simultaneously, internal R&D talent was upskilled through their AI-driven learning ecosystem, J&J Learn, a platform designed to build emerging skills before the business needed them.[14] This type of foresight turned hiring from a reactive scramble into a strategic, data-informed plan.

Candidate Relationship Management and Engagement

Forecasting talent gaps is only half the equation. The real power came from how J&J used that insight to build, nurture, and convert pipelines of passive candidates over time.

Their approach leveraged a recruitment Customer Relationship Management (CRM) system (Jibe, later acquired by iCIMS), which enabled recruiters to track passive candidate engagement, segment talent pools by skills and interests, and personalize communication at scale.[15] The CRM could, for instance, flag a data scientist repeatedly engaging with oncology-related content, prompting a recruiter to reach out personally about a relevant opportunity.

This marketing-like approach mirrored consumer engagement strategies treat each candidate as a potential customer, deliver value early, and maintain interest until the timing aligns. J&J's philosophy was clear: If you're building a talent pipeline, you're not managing requisitions you're managing relationships.

Diversity and Inclusion: Expanding Who Enters the Pipeline

A standout initiative was J&J's effort to increase representation in STEM roles by auditing and optimizing the language of job descriptions. Using augmented writing platforms like Textio, they identified that certain phrases were discouraging female applicants. After reworking job postings and outreach language to be more inclusive, the company saw a 22 percent increase in applications from underrepresented groups and a 26 percent rise in candidate response rates.[16]

This resulted in approximately 90,000 more women entering J&J's STEM pipeline in a single year. This effort exemplifies that pipelining isn't just about speed or cost it's about equity and access. By refining language and engagement tactics, J&J expanded its potential talent base and made critical roles more accessible to underrepresented communities.

Creative Sourcing Beyond the Career Page

J&J also understood that in high-demand roles, especially tech, the best candidates aren't browsing job boards. They built brand awareness through hackathons, innovation challenges, and data science competitions. By offering meaningful interaction with real healthcare datasets and access to J&J leaders, the company engaged passive tech talent who may not have previously considered healthcare as a viable or exciting industry. Even if participants weren't ready to move, these events planted a seed. When the right role opened, J&J was top-of-mind and the candidate was already warm to the brand.

Shine: Humanizing the Candidate Experience

J&J's "Shine" platform was originally built to improve communication with active candidates during the hiring process, but its philosophy extended into their pipeline management approach as well. Shine ensured candidates received regular updates, feedback, and transparency even if they weren't immediately moving forward.

For passive candidates in J&J's pipeline, this translated to periodic check-ins, newsletters, and relevant content updates. A recruiter might share an innovation story or send a "thinking of you" note. These small, authentic touches created connection and loyalty long before a job offer was extended.

Embedded Talent Planning in the Business

Crucially, J&J didn't view pipelining as a standalone TA initiative. Business leaders were active partners. When the company planned to open a new R&D hub in Asia, TA was involved from the start. They helped identify roles that could be filled by relocating internal employees, which would need local sourcing, and which required global recruitment. They then began community-building with local universities and biotech networks months before the facility launched.

Another example was the Procurement Leadership Development Program (PLDP), which prepared high-potential MBA graduates for senior procurement roles in anticipation of an aging workforce. Over 10 years, 119 leaders were trained and placed through PLDP, reducing reliance on external hiring and ensuring a strong cultural fit.

J&J's model is not exclusive to healthcare. Across sectors, leading organizations are implementing similar forward-focused strategies:

- *Tech*: Google and Microsoft invest in early-career development programs and university partnerships to create future-ready talent.
- *Manufacturing*: GE's "Edison Engineering" program creates internal pipelines of technical talent to address global shortages.
- *Finance*: Firms like JPMorgan Chase are using internal mobility platforms and predictive analytics to redeploy talent before gaps emerge.
- *Retail*: Walmart has implemented CRM tools and candidate personas to pre-engage high-potential frontline workers in local markets.

No matter the sector, the playbook is similar: use data to predict needs, engage talent early, maintain relevance through personalized content, and align with business strategy.

Why This Case Resonates

That morning with the CTO still lingers in my mind—the urgency, the scramble, the sheer weight of not being ready. It wasn't just another high-volume requisition, it was a wake-up call.

In the moment, we did what we always do in TA under pressure: pulled out every stop to deliver. We filled those data science roles, but the cost in time, in money, in team morale was steep. Driving home that week, exhausted from a blur of back-to-back interviews and agency negotiations, I couldn't stop thinking: this isn't just inefficient it's unsustainable.

What struck me most wasn't that we lacked effort or talent. It was that we lacked foresight. That company had so much ambition, so much growth ahead but their recruiting model was built entirely around reacting to open roles. It was like building the plane mid-flight, every single time.

That experience fundamentally shifted how I viewed my role as a talent advisor. I knew we had to help our clients move from reaction to anticipation from firefighting to fireproofing. And when we did, when we finally laid the groundwork for pipelining, workforce planning, and relationship-based sourcing, the difference was night and day. Launching that new product a year later with talent already lined up felt like stepping into a new era. Which is why the Johnson & Johnson case study has always resonated so deeply with me.

J&J didn't wait for a crisis to make the shift. They made a deliberate decision to reimagine their talent strategy before the gaps became painful. Their model stands in direct contrast to the experience I had and to what so many organizations still endure: reaction-driven recruiting that burns people out and misses the mark.

This case study isn't impressive because of J&J's size or resources. It's powerful because it proves that with the right leadership, data, and mindset, even the most complex talent challenges can be anticipated, planned for, and met with confidence. It's what I wish we'd had that morning when the CTO called and it's the blueprint I've used ever since.

Reflect on Your Talent Acquisition Strategy

1. Do you have a clear view of your organization's future talent needs and where gaps might emerge?
2. Are you treating pipelining as a strategic capability or a side project when time allows?
3. How are you using technology to deepen not just scale relationships with passive candidates?
4. Are you aligning pipelining with diversity goals and internal mobility strategies?
5. Do you have a measurable way to assess pipeline health, conversion, and quality?

Johnson & Johnson's proactive pipelining model is a blueprint for the future of talent acquisition. It blends data and empathy, analytics and inclusion, planning and personalization. By embedding recruiting into business strategy and building long-term relationships with both candidates and internal stakeholders, J&J created not just a pipeline but a competitive advantage.

Toward Recruitment Maturity and Organizational Readiness

The journeys of IBM and Johnson & Johnson beautifully illustrate a promising way forward for TA teams everywhere: moving from scrambling to strategic planning. Both companies understood that, in a fast-evolving world, whether it's the tech advancements at IBM or the intense competition for top talent at J&J, waiting until a hiring need arises just doesn't cut it. Instead, they took proactive steps to invest in innovative models and tools that help them anticipate and effectively meet their talent needs. What creative models could you explore? Which tools might give you an edge in the talent landscape?

A unifying theme is that recruitment maturity is about integration—integrating talent strategy with business strategy, integrating technology with human touch, and integrating talent acquisition with talent development. IBM integrated recruiting with internal mobility and learning, treating internal talent as the first resort. J&J integrated recruiting with analytics and relationship management, treating external talent communities as an extension of the organization. In doing so, both elevated their TA practices to deliver not just candidates to open requisitions, but agility and readiness to the entire organization.

For talent leaders reading this chapter, consider where your organization lies today on the reactive-to-proactive spectrum. Are you often surprised by urgent hiring demands? Do you struggle to find quality candidates under tight timelines? Those are symptoms of a reactive approach. The cure is to borrow tactics from cases like IBM and J&J:

- Proactive workforce planning with business leaders (know what's coming).
- Building internal talent marketplaces or talent pools (mobilize who you have).
- Nurturing external talent pipelines (engage who you will need).
- Embracing data and AI to guide decisions (work smarter, not just harder).
- Focusing on skills and potential, not just current titles (think horizontally and long term).
- Prioritizing candidate and employee experience in all these efforts (make it human-centric).

The payoff for making this shift is enormous. Instead of saying "We'll cross that bridge when we come to it," your team will already have built the bridge and have people ready to march across. The organization becomes resilient to talent vacancies and skill gaps—a true state of organizational readiness where talent is a source of agility, not a bottleneck. Moreover, TA professionals move into a more gratifying role. It's far more rewarding to act as talent strategists partnering with the business on future needs than to be perpetual firefighters tackling yesterday's emergencies.

The journey from reactive recruitment to proactive talent planning is a transformative one. It requires vision, change management, and sometimes new investment. But as IBM's and J&J's experiences show, it elevates TA from a support function to a strategic enabler. It enhances recruitment maturity, meaning your processes become more predictive, data-driven, and aligned with organizational goals. And ultimately, it ensures your company has the right people, in the right places, at the right times, which is the cornerstone of any successful business strategy.

TABLE 2.1 Reactive vs. proactive talent acquisition comparison

Aspect	Reactive Model	Proactive Model
Recruitment Trigger	Job Requisition Opened	Forecasted in Advance
Candidate Pipeline	Built After Need Arises	Built and Maintained Continuously
Business Alignment	Low; Hiring on Demand	High; Strategic Workforce Planning
Speed-to-Hire	Slow	Fast
Quality of Hire	Variable/Often Lower	Higher (Selective Hiring)
Talent Engagement	Minimal/Transactional	High (Relationship-Based)
Cost Impact	High (due to delays, premium offers)	Lower (Strategic Hiring)
TA Role Perception	Administrative/Transactional	Strategic Business Partner

As I learned from my own wake-up call years ago, making this leap can be the difference between scrambling to catch up and being confidently prepared. In the next chapters, we will continue to explore how organizations can implement these concepts in practice, delve into the role of technology like AI in proactive hiring, and examine other case studies of talent innovation. But the fundamental mindset should already be clear: don't wait for the future to arrive to start thinking about talent—anticipate the future, and let your talent strategy build the future you want.

Notes

1 Grewal, A. (2018) 9 Ways IBM is Reinventing Recruiting, LinkedIn, www.linkedin.com/pulse/9-ways-ibm-reinventing-recruiting-amber-grewal (archived at https://perma.cc/VJ22-AKA8)

2 Feloni, R. and De Luce, I. (2019) AI is Going to Change Your Career. IBM is Showing How That Can Be a Good Thing, *Business Insider*, July 29, www.businessinsider.com/ai-is-transforming-the-workplace-with-ibm-taking-the-lead-2019-7 (archived at https://perma.cc/H4QY-ENL3)

3 Ibid.

4 Stolz, R. (2018) How IBM Puts the Right Person in the Right Job, Employee Benefit News, January 7, www.benefitnews.com/news/using-cognitive-hr-systems-to-optimize-talent-deployment (archived at https://perma.cc/EV37-CW2S)

5 Ibid.

6 Gigged.AI (2024) Embracing the Internal Talent Marketplace: Transforming Internal Mobility in 2024, https://gigged.ai/embracing-the-internal-talent-marketplace-transforming-internal-mobility-in-2024/ (archived at https://perma.cc/C2CV-CHCP)

7 Stolz, R. (2018) How IBM Puts the Right Person in the Right Job, Employee Benefit News, January 7, www.benefitnews.com/news/using-cognitive-hr-systems-to-optimize-talent-deployment (archived at https://perma.cc/VBH9-Z97Q)

8 Feloni, R. and De Luce, I. (2019) AI is Going to Change Your Career. IBM is Showing How That Can Be a Good Thing, *Business Insider*, July 29, www.businessinsider.com/ai-is-transforming-the-workplace-with-ibm-taking-the-lead-2019-7 (archived at https://perma.cc/H4QY-ENL3)

9 Ibid.

10 Ibid.

11 Moore, T. and Bokelberg, E. (2024) How IBM Incorporates Artificial Intelligence into Strategic Workforce Planning, SHRM Executive Network

12 Feloni, R. and De Luce, I. (2019) AI is Going to Change Your Career. IBM is Showing How That Can Be a Good Thing, *Business Insider*, July 29, www.businessinsider.com/ai-is-transforming-the-workplace-with-ibm-taking-the-lead-2019-7 (archived at https://perma.cc/H4QY-ENL3)

13 McIlvaine, A. R. (2018) Data in the Driver's Seat, HR Executive, June 5, https://hrexecutive.com/talent-acquisitions-leaders-use-ai-to-improve-hiring (archived at https://perma.cc/59TA-84J4)

14 Ehret, M. (2024) Case Study: J&J's Skills-Based Approach, HRO Today, September 19, www.hrotoday.com/learning-development/case-study-johnson-and-johnson-skills-based-approach/ (archived at https://perma.cc/Q9ZU-NVF8)

15 iCIMS (2019) iCIMS Acquires Jibe to Provide Employers Best-in-Class Candidate Engagement and Recruitment Marketing Capabilities, www.icims.com/company/newsroom/icims-acquires-jibe-to-provide-employers-best-in-class-candidate-engagement-and-recruitment-marketing-capabilities/ (archived at https://perma.cc/J6WW-AC96)

16 Halloran, T. (2018) How Johnson & Johnson is adding 90,000 more women to their hiring pipeline, Textio Blog, January 3

3

Defining Roles: Rethinking Sourcing and Recruiting

I still remember the knot in my stomach as I sat in a late-night meeting with my talent acquisition (TA) team 14 years ago. We were in the throes of a critical hiring blitz for a new product launch, and things were falling apart. Our sourcers had built a list of promising candidates, and our recruiters were working overtime to shepherd those candidates through interviews. Yet, miscommunication and silos were undermining our efforts. One star candidate—the kind you dream of hiring—slipped away because the handoff between the sourcer and recruiter came too late. The sourcer thought the recruiter had reached out, the recruiter assumed the sourcer was still nurturing the candidate. In reality, no one had kept the candidate warm, and by the time we followed up, she'd accepted an offer elsewhere. I felt we had failed not just our hiring manager, but the candidate and ourselves. That night, as I replayed the scenario, a hard truth hit me: our traditional model, with sourcers and recruiters operating in separate lanes, was broken for the modern era. We needed a new approach.

Fast forward to six months later: the same team, but a very different outcome. We had reimagined our roles and processes. Sourcers and recruiters now worked as an integrated unit, supported by new collaboration tools and automation. For the next phase of hiring, every candidate had a seamless experience from first contact through offer. Our sourcer-recruiter pairs met jointly with hiring managers to plan strategy, and every touchpoint with candidates was coordinated in real-time through our tech platform. Not one candidate fell through the cracks. In fact, our time-to-fill improved by 30 percent, and hiring manager satisfaction was at an all-time high. The star candidate we lost became the cautionary tale that sparked a transformation in how we defined our roles and leveraged technology. This chapter is about that transformation—how rethinking the traditional definitions of "sourcer" and "recruiter" can revolutionize your talent acquisition strategy in a tech-enabled world. It's about moving from siloed functions to a collaborative, fluid model where every team member becomes a true talent partner.

Breaking Down Traditional Roles

The conventional separation of sourcers and recruiters emerged to create specialization and efficiency. Sourcers focus on discovery, engaging passive talent, and filling the top of the funnel, while recruiters drive relationship-building, process navigation, and closing. This relay model gained popularity due to its scalability, especially in high-volume environments. But as talent markets have evolved, cracks have appeared in the form of communication breakdowns, candidate drop-off, and blurred responsibility lines.

The sourcer-recruiter handoff long treated as a natural step is increasingly seen as a weak point in the process. It disrupts the candidate experience and can reduce accountability. While the model still functions in many organizations, particularly large-scale RPOs or tech companies, its limitations become obvious when candidate expectations, hiring manager needs, and speed-to-hire collide.

For decades, talent acquisition has typically been divided into two primary roles, each with distinct responsibilities: sourcers and recruiters. To understand why a rethink is needed, we must first understand the traditional definitions of these roles and how they operate in many organizations.

Sourcers (Talent Sourcers)

In the classic recruitment model, the sourcer acts as the organization's talent scout and market researcher. Their primary focus is identifying and attracting potential candidates, especially those not actively seeking new opportunities. This involves exploring professional networks, databases, social media platforms, and industry communities to uncover individuals with the right skills and experience. Sourcers are hunters by nature, skilled in advanced search strategies, talent mapping, and personalized outreach. Once potential candidates are identified, sourcers initiate contact through various channels such as email, InMail, or phone to spark interest in the organization or a specific role. Depending on the company's structure, the sourcer's responsibilities may end after generating qualified leads or they may extend into initial candidate screening to assess basic fit and motivation. Ultimately, sourcers are the drivers of the talent pipeline, measured by their ability to discover, engage, and convert passive prospects into active candidates.

Sourcers are often highly research-oriented. A sourcing expert, Ronnie Bratcher, described a true sourcer as someone who "will go down many paths… to identify and establish true content to give to the recruiter." In Bratcher's analogy, the sourcer is like a chef's prep cook: gathering all the raw ingredients so the recruiter (the chef) can craft the final dish (hire).[1] Traditionally, sourcers do not usually manage the full candidate relationship; they handoff interested candidates to recruiters after an initial vetting. As one industry article put it, unless they are working a full-cycle desk, sourcers spend less time with candidates and hiring managers than recruiters do, focusing instead on the research and first-contact phase.[2] In sum, the sourcer's responsibility in the traditional model is to *master the art of finding talent*: knowing where to look, how to attract interest, and delivering a slate of qualified prospects.

Recruiters (Talent Acquisition Recruiters)

If the sourcer is the hunter, the recruiter is the closer and coordinator. Once candidates enter the pipeline (whether through sourcing or direct applications), the recruiter takes over. A recruiter's duties traditionally include reviewing incoming applications, conducting in-depth phone or in-person interviews, and assessing candidates' qualifications against the job requirements. They serve as the primary *point of contact for candidates throughout the hiring process*, guiding them through interviews, gathering feedback from hiring managers, and ultimately negotiating offers and onboarding new hires. Recruiters also manage relationships with hiring managers, facilitating intake meetings to understand the role, updating on pipeline progress, and advising on selection decisions. In many ways, recruiters are the face of the company to the candidate and the bridge between candidates and the business.[3]

As Nikoletta Bika colorfully characterized, the recruiter role colorfully as the person who "takes all the ingredients from the sourcer and creates a compelling message to engage the candidate." The recruiter qualifies and sells the opportunity, shepherding the candidate until they (hopefully) say "yes" to an offer.[4] This requires strong interpersonal skills: the ability to build trust with candidates, to probe their motivations, and to address any concerns. Recruiters must also coordinate the logistics of hiring: scheduling interviews, gathering evaluations from interviewers, and ensuring a smooth process. Compared to sourcers, recruiters are more deeply involved in relationship-building and stakeholder management. They often handle multiple requisitions at once and are measured on outcomes like number of hires, time-to-fill, and quality of hire.

In the traditional split, the handoff between sourcer and recruiter is a critical junction. Typically, it works like this: Once a sourcer has identified and piqued the interest of a candidate, that candidate is handed off (sometimes literally via an applicant tracking system status change or an email introduction) to a recruiter for the formal screening and interviewing process. The recruiter then becomes the candidate's primary contact moving forward. This relay approach can be efficient—it lets each role focus on their "core competency."[5] The sourcer concentrates on generating leads and the recruiter concentrates on evaluating and closing candidates. Each role aligns with a different stage of the hiring funnel, which in theory maximizes specialization.

Advantages of the Traditional Split

There are reasons this model became popular, especially in large organizations with high hiring volume. First, it allows specialization of skills. Great sourcers often possess a research-oriented and creative mindset to find talent in hidden places, whereas great recruiters excel in persuasion, assessment, and negotiation. Separating the roles lets each group hone their craft. Second, it can increase capacity—a team of sourcers feeding into recruiters can fill pipelines faster than recruiters handling sourcing on their own. For example, a single recruiter only has so many hours in the day; by offloading the time-intensive search tasks to sourcers, recruiters can spend more time interviewing and interfacing with hiring managers. Many companies find this division of labor improves throughput when hiring needs are extensive. In fact, one model in use is the "relay" model, where "the sourcer identifies, contacts, and screens candidates, then hands them over to the recruiter who manages the process from interview to offer."[6] Each focuses on their part, ideally leading to efficiency.

Another benefit often cited is improved candidate sourcing quality. Sourcers, with their specialized focus, can devote more energy to proactive outreach and talent mapping than overburdened recruiters might. This can be critical for hard-to-fill positions. Dr. Magdalena notes that having dedicated sourcers can greatly help for niche or senior roles that require intensive headhunting, something a general recruiter may not have bandwidth to do deeply.[7] Meanwhile, recruiters ensure that once candidates are in process, they get the attention and guidance needed through to hiring.

Drawbacks and Challenges

However, split role model is not without problems. One fundamental challenge is the *potential for a fragmented candidate experience*. When a candidate is passed from one person to another mid-process, there is a risk of confusion or lost rapport. A candidate might form an initial connection with the sourcer who first reaches out, and then suddenly find themselves talking to a different recruiter who takes over. If this transition isn't handled seamlessly, candidates may feel like they are starting over with someone new who doesn't fully know their history. As one practitioner quipped about the relay handoff: the candidate "may not realise that their point of contact changed" and momentum can be lost if communication isn't smooth.[8] In worst cases, top candidates might disengage because the process feels impersonal or disjointed. From an internal standpoint, dividing roles can introduce coordination challenges. Sourcers and recruiters need tight communication loops to succeed. There must be consistent communication patterns between the roles.[9] When those break down, it leads to finger-pointing: "Where are my candidates, Mr. Sourcer?" versus "I need feedback on the people I've presented, Ms. Recruiter!"[10] Each role might optimize for their part of the process, sometimes at the expense of the overall outcome. For instance, a sourcer might be rewarded for the volume of candidates delivered, even if many are not truly hireable, thus flooding recruiters with suboptimal leads. Conversely, a recruiter might focus only on active applicants and not fully utilize the sourcer's pipeline, frustrating the sourcer.

Another challenge is when responsibilities blur or gaps emerge. Sourcers often do some initial candidate vetting, but how far should they go? If they pre-screen candidates too extensively, they might essentially perform recruiting tasks without the authority to move candidates forward, which can slow things down. But if they don't screen enough, recruiters might get candidates who aren't actually viable. Finding the right balance is tricky and often unclear, leading to duplicated efforts or missed steps. It's been observed that "decision-making around how much sourcing and when it is needed, alignment, prioritization, feedback loops and conflicts" can plague the sourcer-recruiter collaboration if not carefully managed.[11]

Despite these issues, the traditional model persists in many companies because it has proven workable at scale. Industry veterans note that there is no one-size-fits-all: "You can set this up any way you want – all have been proven to work, it's just a matter of what brings value to your business."[12] In practice, organizations have experimented with various configurations: Some use full-cycle recruiters who handle everything (often in smaller companies or for less critical roles), others use pods or squads where a sourcer-recruiter pair work together on a set of reqs, and some (especially tech giants and RPOs) maintain clear delineation between large sourcing teams and recruiting teams. Each approach has trade-offs. Before proposing a new integrated model, it's worth noting that even in the traditional thinking, leading voices acknowledged that individuals differ: "there are people who just want to research and hunt, people who want to engage and sell, and people who like to do both."[13] In many ways, the structure of roles should adapt to the people and the situation.

However, the modern talent landscape, with its fierce competition, emphasis on employer brand, and need for speed, has exposed the cracks in the old model more than ever. As companies strive to deliver a superb candidate experience and maximize hiring outcomes, rethinking the strict division between sourcers and recruiters has become a hot topic. In the next section, we examine why a new integrated, collaborative model is gaining traction and what it looks like in practice.

Toward an Integrated, Collaborative Model

There is a growing shift in TA toward recognizing that sourcing and recruiting are not separate or adversarial functions, but complementary components of a shared goal hiring the right people. In today's competitive talent market, both candidate experience and team efficiency are critical differentiators. As a result, organizations are moving away from siloed approaches and embracing integrated models where sourcers and recruiters collaborate closely or take on more fluid, cross-functional roles.

What exactly is an "integrated, collaborative" model for sourcing and recruiting? While it can take different forms, a unifying theme is *close partnership and shared ownership of outcomes*. Instead of a linear handoff (sourcer → recruiter), the process becomes more of a teamwork loop. Sourcers and recruiters plan together, execute together, and solve problems together throughout the hiring lifecycle. In some cases, this might mean merging the roles—training and expecting recruiters to do their own sourcing, and sourcers to engage candidates as deeply as recruiters would, effectively creating hybrid professionals. In other cases, it means keeping distinct roles but erasing the hierarchical or sequential nature of their interaction—for example, having sourcers and recruiters jointly attend intake meetings with hiring managers, regularly sync on pipeline progress, and even tag-team candidate communications so that the candidate feels they have a team working for them rather than being passed off.

One model of integration is often referred to as the "360° recruiter" or full-cycle talent partner approach. Here, each recruiter is responsible for the entire process from initial candidate identification to offer. This was actually how recruiting was done in earlier eras and in many smaller companies: one person builds the pipeline and also closes the hires. Many modern organizations moved away from it due to volume pressure, but some are moving back for certain roles to improve accountability and candidate experience. The benefit of a full-cycle approach is *consistency*: candidates have a single point of contact ("one throat to choke or one back to pat," as the saying goes) and the recruiter has end-to-end visibility and control. Masluk-Mueller notes this approach creates direct feedback loops that can "improve the sourcing itself through direct feedback" and make the process more lean for the candidate, though it may reduce capacity if one person has too many requisitions.[14] An integrated strategy doesn't necessarily require every recruiter to go 360°, but it does encourage cross-functional skill development so that no one is "just a sourcer" or "just a recruiter." Everyone on the team understands and can contribute to both finding and closing talent.

Another variant is the "pod" system: small squads consisting of, say, one recruiter, one to two sourcers, and perhaps a recruiting coordinator, who collectively own a set of requisitions or a business area. They operate as a micro-team, meeting frequently and dividing tasks dynamically. In this setup, rather than a formal handoff, the sourcer and recruiter might, for instance, co-manage a candidate through different stages. One practical implementation is having sourcers remain involved even after passing a candidate to interviews—they might continue to nurture the candidate with additional touchpoints or gather feedback, acting as a *secondary point of contact to ensure the candidate feels attended to*. The recruiter, meanwhile, might sometimes jump in earlier in the sourcing stage for high-priority roles or niche searches, effectively doing some sourcing work themselves (especially if they have lighter requisition loads). The key shift is cultural and procedural: no more "us vs. them" between sourcing and recruiting, but a united front where both roles feel jointly responsible for successful hires.

Some organizations have gone further by redefining titles to support this integrated ethos. For example, changing the title "Recruiter" to "Talent Partner" and "Sourcer" to "Talent Researcher" or similar, to emphasize that both are part of one TA team serving the business together. Spotify did exactly this in recent years: they embedded "Talent Partners" into each business unit and created "Talent Intelligence" and sourcing teams to support them, dissolving the old regional recruiter vs. sourcer structure.[15] The result was a more fluid team that worked globally and collaboratively, and Spotify saw tangible improvements from this change (more on that in the case study in Chapter 4). The semantic change from recruiter to *partner* is intentional: it signals that recruiters are expected to go beyond just filling requisitions to also proactively source and consult, and that sourcers are partners in strategic hiring, not just researchers in the back room.

In an integrated model, the boundaries between roles are intentionally fluid. Both sourcers and recruiters are viewed as talent acquisition professionals with complementary expertise—they may focus on different stages of the process, but they operate toward the same goal. The guiding principle is that no candidate or hiring manager should ever experience a drop in service when transitioning between team members. To ensure this, many organizations create overlap points, such as having sourcers join recruiter intake or screening calls to maintain context or having recruiters share feedback with sourcers to refine sourcing strategies. These practices break down silos and reinforce collaboration. Ultimately, the success of any integrated model depends on shared drive, mutual understanding, and strong communication. In high-performing teams, sourcers and recruiters are trained together, evaluated together, and occasionally rotate responsibilities to build empathy and strengthen partnership.

Shared Metrics and Goals

A practical element of the new model is aligning performance metrics for sourcers and recruiters. Traditionally, a sourcer might be measured on the number of candidates sourced or submits, and a recruiter on hires made. This can cause misalignment: e.g. a sourcer could hit their numbers by sending a flood of names that never convert to hires, or a recruiter could ignore sourced candidates and only hire inbound applicants, rendering the sourcer's work moot. Integrated teams instead set shared targets (sourcer-recruiter pair or team goals). For example, both could be jointly accountable for hires in their segment, time-to-fill, diversity of candidates, and candidate satisfaction scores. When both roles succeed or fail together, it incentivizes cooperation. As an anecdote, one global company found that by giving sourcers partial credit in the hiring metric (such as including sourced hires in both the sourcer's and recruiter's performance evaluation), the collaboration improved: sourcers focused on quality not just quantity, and recruiters became more responsive to sourced candidates, knowing those hires were a win for everyone.

Flexibility in Role Execution

Rethinking roles also means being flexible about who does what. In a collaborative model, it's less about *whose job* a task is and more about *getting it done efficiently*. For instance, if a sourcer has a particularly strong rapport with a candidate they found, the team might decide that the sourcer continues as that candidate's main contact even through later interview rounds, with the recruiter stepping in mainly for offer negotiation at the end. Conversely, a recruiter might directly source a few candidates for an urgent role while the sourcer is busy with another project. Essentially, the rigid boundaries become porous. This requires trust and clarity within the team to avoid stepping on toes. Many integrated TA teams hold daily or weekly stand-ups (a practice borrowed from Agile methodologies) to quickly sync on who is handling which candidates or tasks, ensuring nothing falls through the cracks and adjusting responsibilities on the fly.

Technology as an Enabler

Technology isn't just a helpful tool in modern recruiting it's the connective tissue that makes collaboration between sourcers and recruiters seamless, scalable, and strategic. At its best, technology transforms fragmented processes into unified workflows and bridges the gaps that traditionally led to dropped candidates, miscommunications, and inefficiencies.

Shared Systems, Shared Insights

The first and arguably most critical element is system integration. Shared Applicant Tracking Systems (ATS) and Candidate Relationship Management (CRM) platforms are foundational. When sourcers and recruiters both operate in the same system, data lives in one place. A note from a sourcing conversation, a response to outreach, or even a candidate's resume review history is instantly visible to the recruiter. This continuity ensures the candidate never has to repeat themselves and allows the recruiter to pick up the conversation exactly where the sourcer left off. For example, if a sourcer logs that a candidate is hesitant about compensation expectations, the recruiter can proactively address it in their first interaction. This type of knowledge-sharing, powered by real-time access, creates a smoother candidate journey and demonstrates to the candidate that the team is aligned and attentive.

Collaboration Platforms for Real-Time Syncing

Beyond the ATS/CRM, platforms like Slack, Microsoft Teams or integrated communication tools, have become crucial for live coordination. A quick message—"Candidate X is interviewing tomorrow, but her schedule is tight, let's skip the second screen"—can save hours or prevent missed opportunities. These tools support asynchronous updates across time zones and foster a sense of team unity, even in distributed environments.

Many high-performing TA teams create dedicated channels or threads for each requisition or hiring sprint, keeping sourcers, recruiters, and even hiring managers looped in. This creates a living log of insights, feedback, and decisions that are searchable and referenceable.

Visualizing the Pipeline Together

Modern talent teams are increasingly adopting Kanban-style boards (e.g. in Trello, Asana, or integrated recruiting platforms like Greenhouse or SmartRecruiters) to visualize candidate progress as a shared project. Rather than "owning" separate columns of the pipeline, sourcers and recruiters collaborate across the entire board. Each card or profile represents a live opportunity, with both roles contributing updates, tagging teammates, or attaching feedback. This approach reinforces that candidate progression is a team effort not a pass-off and helps identify blockers quickly. For example, if many candidates are stuck in the "awaiting feedback" column, both parties can intervene faster to push them forward.

Automation and AI-Powered Insights

Another layer of technological enablement comes from automation and AI. Candidate rediscovery tools, for instance, automatically resurface past applicants who match a new req. These can be invaluable for sourcers, reducing time spent on repetitive searches. Recruiters, in turn, benefit from pre-screening bots or scheduling assistants that remove administrative bottlenecks. Predictive analytics embedded in some modern platforms can suggest which candidates are most likely to respond to outreach or drop out mid-process giving sourcers and recruiters time to intervene. AI-generated outreach sequences, customized to a candidate's profile, further streamline the top of the funnel and ensure consistency in communication.

Creating a Shared Source of Truth

All of this technology converges to support one essential goal: creating a single, transparent source of truth for every candidate. In siloed systems, recruiters and sourcers operate with partial data each with their own spreadsheets, notes, or assumptions. In an integrated tech stack, the entire team sees the same picture. Every touchpoint is tracked. Every action is visible. Every delay or concern is flagged early. This level of transparency minimizes redundant outreach, ensures faster handoffs, and boosts accountability. It also empowers leadership with dashboards to view conversion rates, sourcing effectiveness, DEI metrics, and time-to-fill in real time allowing for quicker, data-driven course corrections.

Tech as Culture Catalyst

But technology alone is not enough. It must be paired with a culture of collaboration and user discipline. The best systems fail when teams don't consistently log interactions, share updates, or trust each other's inputs. Conversely, even modest tools can enable transformation when used with intention. When teams commit to documenting interactions, sharing learnings, and working out of the same platforms, technology becomes a cultural accelerant, not just a functional upgrade.

In short, technology is what makes the modern, integrated sourcing-recruiting model possible. It provides the infrastructure for real-time coordination, the intelligence for smarter decisions, and the transparency for truly shared ownership. As candidate expectations rise and competition intensifies, leveraging the right tools becomes not just a strategic advantage but a necessity.

Culture of Shared Ownership

Perhaps the most important aspect of the new integrated model is cultural. It requires fostering a sense that *"we're in this together."* Rather than sourcers feeling like their job is done when they hand off a candidate, or recruiters feeling sourcing is "not my problem," both start to think like talent advisors responsible for the full lifecycle. This doesn't mean every individual has to do everything, it means they care about everything. Sourcers celebrate when a hire is made (not just when a candidate is submitted), and recruiters value the groundwork done by sourcers (even for candidates who weren't ultimately hired, recognizing the market insights gained). In organizations with this culture, you'll hear language like *"our hire"* or *"our pipeline"* more than *"my candidate"* versus *"your candidate."*

Importantly, integrated does not imply chaos or lack of role clarity. In fact, it demands *more clarity upfront* in defining how collaboration works. Teams that succeed in this model often create guidelines or playbooks. For example: *At what stage does the sourcer introduce the recruiter to the candidate? How will they communicate updates to each other? If a candidate goes dark, who re-engages?* By defining these together, there is less confusion. The difference from before is that these guidelines are built together rather than carved along department lines.

The benefits of an integrated approach are compelling. Companies report faster hiring times when handoff delays are eliminated, improved candidate feedback because of seamless interactions, and even higher quality hires as the synergy between sourcing and recruiting yields better screening and engagement. Moreover, recruiters with diverse skill sets (sourcing + closing) are more adaptable to changing hiring needs. The tumultuous hiring environment of recent years, with rapid shifts from high-volume hiring to hiring freezes and back, favors teams that are agile and cross-trained rather than siloed.

The most powerful transformation isn't in org charts, it's in mindset. Integrated models require a culture of shared ownership. That means shared wins, shared metrics, and shared accountability. Both roles align on success outcomes like hires made, candidate satisfaction, and diversity impact not just activity metrics like reach-outs or screens.

Teams that succeed here build operating playbooks to define how collaboration works: Who updates the candidate when? Who follows up if a candidate goes quiet? How do we debrief a no-hire situation? These micro-processes create macro-impact.

This chapter challenges the long-standing division between sourcers and recruiters, arguing that the traditional model, though once efficient, is no longer fit for today's fast-moving, candidate-driven market. It traces the evolution from siloed roles to integrated partnerships, where collaboration, shared ownership, and technology redefine how talent is found and hired. The key takeaway is that the future of TA lies not in rigid roles, but in adaptable, aligned teams working toward a shared outcome: hiring great people faster and better.

Reflective Questions

1. In your current TA model, where do the biggest breakdowns occur between sourcing and recruiting?
2. How might redefining roles improve your candidate experience?
3. Are your team's performance metrics encouraging collaboration or reinforcing silos?
4. How can you use technology to increase visibility and reduce handoff friction?
5. What cultural shifts would be needed on your team to embrace shared ownership of hiring outcomes?

Notes

1. Bratcher, R. (2012) Sourcer or Recruiter – The Dividing Line, ERE.net, 6 September, www.ere.net/sourcer-or-recruiter-the-dividing-line/ (archived at https://perma.cc/C5R5-J2PT)
2. Weck, A. (2024) The Sourcer-Recruiter Relationship: Maximizing the Connection, ERE.net, 2 September, www.ere.net/the-sourcer-recruiter-relationship-maximizing-the-connection/ (archived at https://perma.cc/LLY8-YY6Q)
3. Bratcher, R. (2012) Sourcer or Recruiter – The Dividing Line, ERE.net, 6 September, www.ere.net/sourcer-or-recruiter-the-dividing-line/ (archived at https://perma.cc/C5R5-J2PT)
4. Vilas, N. (2017) What Are You? A Recruiter? A Sourcer? Or Both? SmartRecruiters Blog, January 30

5 Bratcher, R. (2012) Sourcer or Recruiter – The Dividing Line, ERE.net, 6 September, www.ere.net/sourcer-or-recruiter-the-dividing-line/ (archived at https://perma.cc/C5R5-J2PT)

6 Ibid.

7 Ibid.

8 Ibid.

9 Ibid.

10 Vilas, N. (2017) What Are You? A Recruiter? A Sourcer? Or Both? SmartRecruiters Blog, January 30

11 Ibid.

12 Ibid.

13 Ibid.

14 Masluk-Mueller, C. (2021) Sourcer vs. Recruiter: What's the Difference and Why It Matters, SmartRecruiters Blog

15 Singel, J. (2019) How to Build a Great Talent Acquisition Team, Part II, Spotify HR Blog, August 6, https://hrblog.spotify.com/2019/08/06/how-to-build-a-great-talent-acquisition-team-part-ii/ (archived at https://perma.cc/3YQC-TJ8Z)

4

Defining Key Skills and Responsibilities in the New Model

In a rethought model of sourcing and recruiting, the skill sets of sourcers and recruiters start to broaden and converge. Each role still has areas of focus, but the Venn diagram of their competencies overlaps much more than before. In this chapter we define the core skills and responsibilities for sourcers and recruiters working in an integrated, collaborative environment.

Skills and Traits for an Integrated Sourcer (Talent Researcher)

Advanced research and sourcing skills This remains foundational. An integrated sourcer still excels at finding talent through various channels, be it crafting boolean search strings on LinkedIn, data mining niche forums, or leveraging employee referrals. In fact, as recruiting processes integrate, sourcing specialists become even more valuable for their ability to unearth passive talent and build strategic talent pools. The difference now is that they might also use more of that knowledge internally, such as advising recruiters and hiring managers on market talent availability and sourcing strategy up front.

Candidate engagement and relationship building Unlike the old days where some sourcers stopped at initial contact, in the new model a sourcer must be adept at nurturing candidates. That means developing stronger people skills, listening to candidates' career aspirations, engaging in meaningful dialogue about the role and company, and maintaining rapport over time. An integrated sourcer often conducts initial phone screens or informal chats to qualify a candidate's basic fit and interest. They should handle these conversations nearly as well as a recruiter would, creating a positive first impression of the company. Emotional intelligence is key here: Sourcers need empathy and communication finesse, since they are no longer behind-the-scenes researchers only, but brand ambassadors initiating the company-candidate relationship.[1]

Collaboration and communication Working closely with recruiters and hiring managers means an effective sourcer in the new model is a great team player. They communicate frequently and clearly, updating recruiters about progress and candidate reactions, sharing sourcing difficulties or successes, and taking feedback to refine searches. In team meetings, the sourcer confidently presents data (like how many target candidates exist in a region or which competitor companies have talent we could tap) effectively becoming a talent advisor in their own right. Strong written and verbal communication skills are essential, as sourcers may now contribute directly to crafting outreach messages, employer branding content, or status reports for stakeholders.

Flexibility and adaptability Sourcers need to be more versatile than before. On any given day, they might pivot from deep research to jumping on a screening call at short notice, or from sourcing for one role to helping a teammate on another. Being adaptable, comfortable with shifting priorities, and wearing multiple hats is a prized skill. For instance, if a recruiter is out sick, an integrated sourcer might step in to keep candidates warm or even move them to the next step, rather than putting everything on pause. This agility ensures continuity in the hiring process.

Knowledge of the business and roles In the new model, sourcers are expected to have a stronger understanding of the roles they recruit for and the business context. Traditionally, some sourcers were very research-focused and relied on recruiters for the nuanced job understanding. Now, since sourcers engage with candidates more deeply, they must speak the language of the roles. That means knowing the must-have vs. nice-to-have skills, understanding the team's projects, and being conversant in the industry or technical terms relevant to the position. Some organizations address this by including sourcers in hiring manager intake meetings and debriefs, which helps build their role expertise. In effect, the sourcer's responsibility extends to being a subject matter talent scout, not just a name generator.

Data and analytics orientation Modern sourcers leverage data to track their sourcing efforts, so they should be comfortable with sourcing metrics and tools. In an integrated setting, this could mean analyzing which sources yield the best hire conversion or measuring diversity of the sourcing pipeline and adjusting strategy accordingly. They might use talent market insights (e.g. average salaries, competitor org charts, etc.) to advise the recruiter and hiring manager. Facility with talent acquisition software and analytics dashboards is thus a valuable skill. As Jan Tegze noted, recruiters (and by extension sourcers) must be part technologist; this is equally true for sourcers who often spearhead using new sourcing platforms or AI tools.[2]

Skills and Traits for an Integrated Recruiter (Talent Partner)

Consultative partnering In the integrated model, recruiters transform into true *talent partners*. They not only manage interviews and offers, but also collaborate from the beginning on how to fill the role. This means strong consultative skills with hiring managers, and the ability to influence and guide. For example, an integrated recruiter will use data from the sourcers and their own knowledge to set realistic hiring timelines, adjust job requirements if the talent pool is tight, and educate hiring teams on market conditions. They act as strategic advisors, not just order-takers. Consultative ability requires credibility (knowledge of the domain), communication (clearly setting expectations), and sometimes courageous leadership (pushing back on unrealistic demands in a tactful way).

Sourcing capability That's right, in this new world, recruiters also flex their sourcing muscles. A key skill for modern recruiters is proficiency in direct sourcing when needed. Recruiters should be able to conduct a boolean search, identify potential candidates on LinkedIn or in the ATS database, and reach out effectively. Even if a team has dedicated sourcers, integrated recruiters don't simply wait for candidates to appear, they proactively contribute to building the pipeline. This is especially important in critical or executive roles where a recruiter's personal network and outreach might make the difference. By having sourcing skills, recruiters also gain empathy for the top-of-funnel challenges and can better coordinate with sourcers. It closes the gap in understanding between the roles. As Glenn Cathey argued, there's no reason recruiters "can't source"; in fact, in many environments recruiters are expected to handle sourcing as part of their toolkit.[3] In integrated teams, even if not the primary responsibility, a recruiter is sourcing-savvy.

Candidate relationship management Recruiters continue to own the mid- to late stages of the candidate relationship. Skills in behavioral interviewing, candidate assessment, and selling the opportunity are crucial. One could say these have become even more important, because by the time a candidate reaches the recruiter, the recruiter must take a warm lead and turn them into a committed candidate. Storytelling about the company vision, addressing career development questions, and negotiating offers are part of this skill set. Additionally, because candidates might now interact with multiple team members, the recruiter ensures consistency they must be adept at keeping notes and context so candidates aren't asked the same questions repeatedly or given conflicting information. In essence, the recruiter orchestrates the candidate experience like a project manager with a personal touch.

Project management and coordination Integrated recruiters often act as project managers of hiring. They coordinate the efforts of sourcers, interviewers, recruiting coordinators, and sometimes external agencies in a cohesive plan. The ability to keep all these moving parts aligned is a key skill. This involves scheduling prowess, attention to detail, and follow-through. For instance, if a hiring manager is slow to give feedback, a recruiter in this model doesn't hesitate, they follow up persistently or escalate as needed, because they and the sourcer jointly own the outcome. Tools like Kanban boards or shared pipelines mean the recruiter frequently updates the status of candidates so everyone (including the sourcer) has visibility. In collaborative hiring, recruiters ensure nothing falls through the cracks from initial outreach to final offer.

Market intelligence and talent advising Much like sourcers, recruiters in the new model bolster their knowledge of talent market trends. They should be aware of salary benchmarks, competitor moves, and overall talent supply/demand in their industry. This intelligence, often gathered in partnership with sourcers or a centralized talent intelligence function, becomes part of the recruiter's arsenal when consulting the business. For example, an integrated recruiter might present to a hiring team: "We've engaged with 50 target candidates over the last month, many cite remote work flexibility as a concern. To attract them, we may need to offer hybrid options or adjust our pitch." This elevates the recruiter's role to that of a talent market expert, beyond just processing candidates.

Collaboration and team leadership Recruiters in a collaborative model often take on a bit of a leadership role within their pods or teams. They facilitate regular syncs with their sourcer counterparts, share credit and feedback generously, and mentor junior sourcers or coordinators. The skill here is leadership without formal authority, creating an environment of trust and motivation. For instance, a recruiter might notice a sourcer struggling with a particular role and volunteer to help source or to brainstorm new approaches, showing that it's *our* problem, not *yours vs. mine*. This kind of team spirit often radiates from recruiters who model it for the whole TA team.

Notably, *both roles now share some critical skills*: data-driven thinking, strong communication, and customer-service orientation toward candidates and hiring managers. The lines blur such that a job description for a modern recruiter and a modern sourcer will have more overlap than divergence. Both might list "stakeholder management" and "candidate engagement" as duties, though perhaps to different extents. Both will certainly list "collaboration" as essential.

Evolving Responsibilities

In practice, how do responsibilities shift? Here are a few examples of redefined responsibilities in an integrated team:

- *Joint intake of requirements*: Instead of only the recruiter meeting with the hiring manager at the start of a search, the sourcer is present too (or in some companies, the sourcer even leads the meeting, with the recruiter). The sourcer and recruiter together gather requirements, then internally decide who will tackle which aspects. The sourcer might take responsibility for mapping out target companies and talent pools from that meeting, while the recruiter outlines the interview plan and selection criteria. Both contribute to writing an appealing job posting, combining their knowledge of what will attract candidates.
- *Sourcing strategy development*: Previously often the sourcer's domain, now recruiters also contribute to strategy. In many teams the *recruiter and sourcer sit together to make a sourcing plan* for each role identifying key sources, employee referral possibilities, diversity sourcing tactics, etc. The recruiter's insight from previous similar hires and the sourcer's fresh research perspective create a stronger plan than either would alone. They decide on search priorities and allocate who approaches which segment of candidates. This spreads responsibility for building the pipeline.
- *Candidate screening and nurturing*: In an integrated model, the initial candidate contact might be handled by either role, depending on bandwidth and expertise. Sourcers may still do the outreach and a brief screen, but then *introduce the recruiter early*, e.g. inviting the recruiter to a second call or to send a follow-up note.

Conversely, if a recruiter sources a candidate directly, they might loop in the sourcer to help keep that candidate warm or provide additional information between interviews. The responsibility for ensuring the candidate stays engaged is shared. A sourcer might take on scheduling informational chats or sending "candidate care" emails (like a note sharing a company blog or press release) mid-way through the process tasks that traditionally fell to recruiters or coordinators. The guiding idea is that whoever is best positioned at a given moment will do the needed task.

- *Interview process involvement*: Sourcers in the new model don't disappear after handing off a candidate. Some companies have sourcers sit in on interview debrief meetings to hear the feedback on candidates they sourced this helps sourcers learn and refine future searches, and also allows them to clarify any context about the candidate that might help in decision-making. It also signals to the whole hiring team that the sourcer and recruiter are equal partners in filling the job. Meanwhile, recruiters might take on an earlier touchpoint with candidates, like conducting a brief introductory call even before a formal interview, especially if the sourcer wasn't available. The recruiter ensures the candidate is well-informed about next steps, regardless of who spoke to them first. Essentially, both roles overlap during the middle stages to reinforce the candidate's experience.
- *Closing and offer stage*: Traditionally the recruiter's territory, but even here the sourcer can play a supporting role. For instance, if a candidate trusts the sourcer they met first, that sourcer might join the recruiter in the offer call to congratulate the candidate and address any lingering questions. If a candidate declines an offer, sourcers and recruiters conduct a joint retrospective: Was it something in sourcing (e.g. wrong expectations set) or something in the interview process or offer details? By examining this together, they both learn. The recruiter still typically leads negotiation and closing, but in a collaborative culture they might brief the sourcer on how it went so the sourcer knows the outcome and can follow up with a friendly note to the candidate as well. These little touches reinforce teamwork.

To summarize, in the new model sourcers take on more of the front-end recruiter-like tasks and recruiters take on more back-end sourcer-like awareness. The result is a more resilient team. If one person is out or bandwidth is strained, the other can cover. Each understands the whole picture of hiring, enabling a seamless experience internally and externally.

This blending of skills does not mean the roles are identical. Think of it like a doubles tennis team: one partner might typically play at the net (closing the point) and the other at the baseline (setting up the shots), but a great team knows how to cover each other's area when needed and coordinate their moves. The net player (recruiter) still specializes in quick reflex volleys (offer negotiation, hiring manager counsel) and the baseline player (sourcer) in long-range shots (talent searches), but they operate as a unit covering the whole court.

With the roles and skills redefined in this integrated way, the next challenge is implementing this in a real organization. Change like this impacts people, processes, and sometimes even incentives. In the following section, we provide a practical guide to realigning and restructuring talent acquisition teams to foster this kind of collaboration and efficiency.

Realigning and Restructuring the Talent Acquisition Team: A Practical Guide

Transitioning to an integrated model of sourcers and recruiters working collaboratively requires thoughtful change management. It's not as simple as announcing "Okay, work together now!" it involves adjusting team structures, processes, and mindsets. Below is a practical guide for talent acquisition leaders (and teams) on how to realign roles for better collaboration and efficiency.

Assess Your Starting Point and Pain Points

Begin with a candid evaluation of your current talent acquisition setup. Where are the inefficiencies or breakdowns occurring?

Gather feedback from your recruiters, sourcers, hiring managers, and even recent candidates. Common pain points might include duplicate efforts, slow handoffs, inconsistent candidate communications, or frustration about workload imbalance. For example, you might find that sourcers feel disengaged once candidates are passed on, or recruiters feel overloaded with too many candidates to screen. Identifying these will help target what changes are needed most. Also assess team capabilities: Do your recruiters have sourcing skills? Are your sourcers interested in more candidate engagement? Understanding your team's strengths and development areas will guide how you redefine roles. Essentially, diagnose before you prescribe.

Secure Buy-In for Change

It's crucial to get leadership and team buy-in for the new model. Explain the why, perhaps using scenarios like Alex's story or internal metrics (e.g. "we lost X candidates due to slow follow-ups" or "time-to-fill for critical roles is above industry benchmark by Y%"). Present the collaborative model as a solution to these issues. It often helps to highlight success stories: case studies or examples of companies that improved results by integrating sourcing and recruiting (we'll soon discuss Spotify and Amazon, which you can reference). Getting buy-in also means addressing concerns. Team members might worry, "Will I be doing double work?" or "Is my role being eliminated?" Clearly communicate that the goal is to empower everyone, not to overload or cut jobs. Emphasize that *sourcers and recruiters will share success*. Leadership support is key if the head of TA and HR leadership endorse the change and align it with business goals (like faster hiring or better talent quality), it gains legitimacy.

Redefine Roles and Titles (if Necessary)

Decide on whether you will formally change job titles or descriptions to set the tone. Some organizations keep titles ("sourcer" and "recruiter") but rewrite the job descriptions to include collaborative duties. Others adopt new titles like "talent sourcer & coordinator" or "talent acquisition partner" to signal the shift. For instance, one company might redefine a sourcer's role to "Talent Sourcing Specialist responsible for talent research as well as initial candidate engagement and ongoing pipeline relationship management in partnership with Talent Advisors (Recruiters)". The recruiter's role might be "Talent Advisor responsible for managing the interview and offer process while proactively sourcing talent and collaborating with Sourcing Specialists on pipeline development." Publish these definitions internally (and to any external job postings) so everyone is clear. This formal step helps prevent slipping back into old habits because it's now in writing what each role encompasses, and that includes overlaps and teamwork.

Provide Joint Training and Cross-Training

To make the integrated model work, invest in training your team. Host workshops where sourcers and recruiters are trained together on topics like effective intake meetings, sourcing techniques, candidate interviewing, and employer branding. When done together, it not only upskills everyone but also builds mutual understanding. Encourage cross-training: a recruiter might shadow a sourcer for a day to learn advanced sourcing methods, and a sourcer might shadow a recruiter during candidate interviews or offer discussions. This shadowing can be eye-opening: a sourcer sees how candidate concerns later in the process link to what's promised in outreach, and a recruiter sees how challenging it can be to get responses from passive candidates. Cross-training breaks down the "mystique" of each other's work. It also prepares the team to fill in for each other when needed. Additionally, consider mentoring pairs assign an experienced recruiter to mentor a newer sourcer in communication skills, and a veteran sourcer to teach a recruiter some sourcing hacks. This knowledge exchange strengthens the team's overall capability.

Implement Collaborative Processes

Redesign your recruiting process to facilitate collaboration. Some concrete process changes include:

- *Joint kickoff meetings*: As mentioned, have sourcer-recruiter pairs meet the hiring manager together at the start of a search. Use a checklist so both their perspectives are covered (e.g. recruiter ensures role requirements are clear, sourcer asks about target companies or diversity needs).
- *Regular sync-ups*: Schedule brief twice-weekly sync meetings for each sourcer-recruiter pair or team. These meetings (even 15 minutes) are to update on candidate pipeline status, share new findings (like "found a new batch of candidates in X company"), and address roadblocks ("we need hiring manager feedback on Y candidate"). Keeping a frequent cadence prevents things from falling behind and fosters constant communication.
- *Shared tools*: Leverage tools that allow collaboration. Ensure both sourcers and recruiters have equal access to the ATS and can both update candidate records. Use tags or statuses that both can edit (for example, a status "Contacted by Sourcer" vs. "Screen Scheduled by Recruiter"). Consider a shared spreadsheet or dashboard for each active role that tracks candidates from source to offer, visible to all stakeholders. Transparency is vital. If your system allows, have a single "owner" field include both names or use a "secondary owner" field to denote the sourcer and recruiter assigned to each req so accountability is visibly shared.
- *Candidate handover protocol*: Define how and when candidates transition between team members to ensure smooth handover. For example, you may set that *once a sourcer has a phone call with a candidate and deems them suitable, the sourcer introduces the recruiter in an email to the candidate, expressing that they will continue with next steps*. The recruiter then immediately reaches out to schedule a deeper interview. This overlap (both contacting the candidate at handoff) reassures the candidate and keeps momentum. Document such protocols in a brief internal playbook and make sure everyone follows a consistent method.

- *Feedback loop*: Incorporate a formal feedback loop from recruiters to sourcers on candidate quality, and from sourcers to recruiters on outreach effectiveness. For instance, after a batch of first-round interviews, the recruiter can meet with the sourcer to discuss which candidates were on target and which weren't, giving specific feedback (e.g. "We realized we need more cloud experience, some of the candidates weren't strong there"). This helps the sourcer refine searches. Likewise, sourcers can inform recruiters about response rates ("Our emails mentioning flexible work got twice the response emphasize that in your calls"). Making this a routine part of process (say, a quick recap email or meeting after each hiring cycle) institutionalizes continuous improvement.

Align Goals and Metrics

Revise your performance metrics to support collaboration. If previously sourcers were measured on, say, "candidates sourced per quarter" and recruiters on "positions filled per quarter," think about combined metrics. One approach is to use "*req fill rate*" or "*time-to-fill*" for the sourcer-recruiter team as a whole. Another is to incorporate *quality of hire or retention of hire* metrics that both contributed to. If you still keep some separate metrics, balance them with shared ones. For example, a sourcer might have a goal for "% of sourced candidates that pass screening" (emphasizing quality), which the recruiter influences by giving feedback and by effectively screening, the recruiter might have a goal for "offer acceptance rate," which the sourcer influences by ensuring candidates are well-prepared and aligned early. Moreover, you can implement team-based incentives: perhaps a quarterly team bonus if the overall TA team meets certain hiring targets or satisfaction scores. Be cautious that metrics don't accidentally incentivize old silo behaviors. The mantra is to reward collective success.

On the qualitative side, include collaboration in performance evaluations. Managers should gather input from recruiters about the sourcers they work with and vice versa. Peers can rate how well each person communicates and supports the team. When people know that "teamwork" is literally part of how they're rated or bonused, they are more likely to embrace it in daily work.

Pilot the Changes with a Small Group

It can be wise to pilot the new integrated approach with one team or a subset of roles before rolling it out company-wide. Select a department or location where you have willing participants, perhaps the engineering hiring team volunteers to try pod structures with integrated roles. During the pilot, observe outcomes like speed of hiring, candidate feedback, and team morale compared to the old approach in other departments. Work out kinks in the process on a small scale. Piloting allows you to make adjustments (maybe you discover bi-weekly syncs weren't enough, and switch to daily quick check-ins, for instance). Also, pilot successes create internal case studies that you can use to persuade any skeptics when you expand the model. After a pilot (say three to six months), do a review, gather feedback from all involved, and then refine your playbook.

Communicate to Stakeholders (Including Hiring Managers and Candidates)

As you restructure internally, inform your hiring managers about what to expect. If their main point of contact was only the recruiter before, let them know they now have a *talent team* working with them. Encourage them to loop in both the recruiter and sourcer on relevant communications. Some managers may still direct all to the recruiter; it may take reinforcement to get them comfortable involving the sourcer. Show them the value (e.g. "Marcia (sourcer) is mapping the market for you and can provide insight on talent availability. Expect to hear from both of us.").

From the candidate side, while you don't need to announce internal changes, ensure the interactions are coordinated. For example, if two people will be communicating with the candidate, introduce both: "I'm

John, I lead hiring for this role, and you may also hear from Jane, my colleague who specializes in talent outreach we work together." This way candidates aren't confused by multiple contacts. Many companies already do this naturally (recruiter and coordinator, etc.), so it's about extending that clarity.

Foster a Culture of "One Team"

Beyond process, focus on culture. Encourage behaviors that exemplify teamwork. Celebrate wins as a team: when a tough position is filled, call out both the recruiter and sourcer contributions in team meetings. Use language that reinforces unity (leaders should talk about "our hiring goals" not "recruiters' goals"). Perhaps create joint team rituals, e.g., a weekly coffee chat for the whole TA team or a shared online channel where sourcers and recruiters post updates, candidate success stories, or even ask for help ("I need ideas to find data scientists anyone have suggestions?"). By creating an environment where asking for and offering help is normalized, you break down any remaining barriers. Senior recruiters and sourcers should model this by openly collaborating and showing that no task is beneath or beyond their role.

Also, mind the physical or organizational arrangement: if sourcers were in a separate "sourcing team" under a different manager, consider having them report into the same managers as recruiters for a unified org structure, or at least establish a strong dotted-line relationship. Some companies merge the teams entirely under one leader of talent acquisition, doing away with separate reporting lines for sourcing. The more the team members see themselves as part of one group, the better. To maintain some functional expertise, you can still have practice meetings (all sourcers meet to share tips, all recruiters meet for their topic), but those are secondary to the primary integrated team identity.

Monitor, Iterate, and Educate Continuously

After implementation, continuously monitor key metrics and team feedback to see if the changes are yielding results. Perhaps time-to-fill has improved or quality of hire is better. If some metrics haven't moved, analyze why does the process need further tweaks? Always be ready to iterate. Talent acquisition is dynamic; a model that works today might need adjustment tomorrow due to new tools (AI sourcing etc.) or changing hiring volume. Solicit feedback regularly, maybe quarterly surveys or retrospectives on big hiring projects, to learn what's working or not.

Keep investing in training and development. As new recruiters or sourcers join, onboard them not just to their individual role but to *how your team collaborates*. Include modules in onboarding like sitting with both a recruiter and a sourcer to see how they interact. Update your playbook as you learn new best practices.

Lastly, share successes with the broader organization. If the sales department is thrilled because the talent team filled all their roles 20 percent faster this quarter, make sure that story is told. It will solidify support for the integrated model and recognize the team's hard work.

By following these steps, organizations can move from a fragmented approach to a highly collaborative talent acquisition function. The practical effort is significant; it touches people's roles, daily habits, and comfort zones but the reward is a more agile and effective team, which ultimately means better hires and a stronger business impact.

To ground these concepts, let's examine two real-world case studies of companies that have approached the sourcing-recruiting role divide in innovative ways: Spotify and Amazon. Each offers insights into role integration and job scope redefinition in practice.

REAL-WORLD EXAMPLE

Spotify: Integrating Roles with "Talent Partners" and "Talent Councils"

Spotify, the global music streaming company, underwent a major transformation in its talent acquisition organization as it scaled in the late 2010s. Growing from a startup to a company hiring thousands worldwide, Spotify realized that traditional recruiting structures were not going to be effective. In 2019, under the leadership of TA head Jon Singel, Spotify "did a total makeover" of its recruiting team structure.[4] This makeover provides an excellent case study in rethinking sourcing and recruiting roles.

The Old Model at Spotify

Previously, Spotify's recruiting team was organized in a *very traditional way*: recruiters were grouped by business function and geography (e.g. one team of recruiters for R&D in Europe, another for sales in the US, etc.), and they generally did full-cycle recruiting for their respective areas. Sourcing was a part of recruiting, but there wasn't a specialized sourcing team or formal role differentiation; however, given the high demand, the recruiting team was having difficulty proactively sourcing while also managing the process. Essentially, they faced the classic strain of fast growth: too many roles, not enough capacity to map the market and engage passive talent thoroughly. Leadership recognized that they needed to "disrupt" their own model.[5]

The Integrated New Model (Talent Partners and Talent Councils)

Spotify restructured by embedding Talent Partners into each of the core global business units and creating centralized Talent Councils which are effectively domain-focused sourcing teams. Here's how it works.

TALENT PARTNERS

These are Spotify's recruiters rebranded. By name and design, Talent Partners are expected to be consultative hiring experts aligned closely with their business unit (e.g. Engineering Talent Partner, Marketing Talent Partner). They work globally meaning a talent partner for engineering might handle roles in Stockholm, New York, or London alike, focusing on the function rather than a local silo. Their job is full-cycle in the sense that they own the hiring process and relationship with their stakeholder (the department), but critically, they don't do it alone. They partner with the sourcing teams and other resources. The title "partner" emphasizes that they are integrated with the business and also partners with the sourcing function. Spotify explicitly stated that they wanted the TA team to "embed ourselves into the business and build global teams aligned to the business units."[6] By doing so, recruiters became true advisors sitting in on business unit resource planning, proactively understanding upcoming needs, and working with managers continuously, not just per vacancy.

TALENT COUNCILS (SOURCING TEAMS BY DOMAIN)

Spotify formed what they called Talent Councils essentially specialized sourcing teams organized by technical domain or job family across the company. For example, there might be a Talent Council for Technology (sourcing for all software engineering and data roles) and another for Commercial (sourcing for sales, advertising, etc.). These teams were "solely focused on pipe-lining" talent.[7]

In practice, that means the sourcers on these councils continuously map talent, engage passive candidates, and build networks in their domain, even if there isn't an immediate open job. They act as *internal headhunters* ready to supply candidates as needs arise. What's different here is the sourcing function was centralized and global they serve any role in their domain regardless of location or which hiring manager and they work in concert with the Talent Partners.

Integration in Practice

How do Talent Partners (recruiters) interact with the Talent Council (sourcers)? From accounts by Spotify's HR Blog, they developed a close-knit working relationship. At the kickoff of a hiring need, a Talent Partner would tap into the Talent Council for that domain to either start a new search or draw from an existing pipeline. Sourcers from the council might already have a roster of potential candidates (since they pipeline in advance), or they'd quickly spin up targeted sourcing efforts. They would then feed candidates to the Talent Partner, but not in a blind handoff. Because both sourcers and recruiters were part of the TA department and considered equals in delivering hiring results, there was shared planning and feedback. The Talent Partner might say: "We need more candidates with cloud infrastructure experience for this role," guiding the sourcers; while sourcers might advise: "We're seeing a lot of interest in remote work among design candidates, can the hiring team be flexible?" thus influencing recruiting strategy.

By aligning on domains, sourcers became true experts in their talent markets, and by aligning recruiters to business units, recruiters deeply understood their stakeholder needs. The matrix structure (partners by business, councils by skill area) meant every hire involved both a Talent Partner and a Talent Council member working collaboratively. This is a sophisticated integrated model: not simply pairing one sourcer to one recruiter, but a networked team where any given recruiter might work with different sourcers depending on the role, and vice versa, under unified leadership and goals.

Results and Benefits

The restructured model quickly showed positive results. Spotify reported that within one quarter of implementing it, they saw a 26 percent increase in hires (Q2 vs. Q1 of 2019) after having stagnated before.[8] This jump can be partly attributed to having a dedicated pipelining engine via Talent Councils—roles were being filled faster because candidates were already in play. Also, aligning globally allowed them to surpass hiring goals; they noted by mid-year they had already hit more than 50 percent of the annual hiring target.[9]

Qualitatively, the relationship with the business improved. Being embedded made Talent Partners privy to strategic discussions and workforce plans, so they could anticipate needs rather than just react. Jon Singel commented that the team became "more strongly aligned to the business... than ever before."[10] The *all-hands-on-deck* approach meant that when hyper-growth spikes occurred, the sourcing team could swarm on hard roles while recruiters managed the influx, or recruiters could pitch in sourcing where they had connections flexibility increased.

One particularly forward-thinking aspect of Spotify's approach was how they evolved the sourcer role beyond just finding external talent. In 2024, Spotify shared that they shifted to heavily focus on internal talent mobility sourcing treating current employees as a source pool and "sourcing" them into new internal opportunities.[11] This again saw the collaboration of talent partners and a kind of sourcing function (now looking internally). The same principles applied: breaking silo between internal recruiters and those who might search for internal candidates. It underscores a culture of sharing talent and fluid roles.

Spotify's case demonstrates that role integration can be achieved by restructuring team design—they didn't merge sourcer and recruiter into one role, but rather created a structure where each could specialize *and* collaborate without barriers. The Talent Councils ensure sourcing is not neglected; the Talent Partners ensure business alignment and closing. Both parts are connected through joint goals and open communication. It's like having a dedicated engine for sourcing continuously running, fueling the recruiters who are steering the hiring with the business a two-engine system working in tandem.

For other organizations, Spotify's approach highlights: (a) the value of renaming roles to change mindset (recruiters to Talent Partners); (b) the effectiveness of dedicated sourcing teams if well-integrated with recruiters; and (c) the importance of aligning with business needs rather than rigidly by geography or silo. Spotify's model might be particularly useful for companies that have to hire in multiple locales and want to avoid duplicated sourcing efforts in each region a centralized sourcing team can serve all, while local/business-aligned recruiters personalize the delivery.

REAL-WORLD EXAMPLE

Amazon: Specialized Scale and the "Sourcing Recruiter" Hybrid

Amazon, one of the world's largest companies, provides a contrasting case study in how sourcing and recruiting roles can be defined and integrated at massive scale. Amazon's talent acquisition challenge is unique in its sheer volume and variety from hourly fulfillment center workers to senior machine learning scientists. Over time, Amazon has developed a recruiting machine known for its relentless drive and innovative approaches. Rather than blending roles completely, Amazon often uses highly specialized roles, but it has introduced hybrid notions like the "Sourcing Recruiter" and emphasizes tight collaboration between every part of the hiring process. Let's explore Amazon's approach.

Scale of Amazon's Recruiting Operation

To set context, Amazon's recruiting volume is staggering. In 2021, amid a labor shortage, Amazon *hired 500,000 employees worldwide in one year*, doubling its headcount an achievement described as "breathtaking" by industry observers.[12] They also reportedly received over 30 million job applications in a year.[13] These numbers are unheard of outside of perhaps government hiring. Handling this kind of volume requires a highly systematized approach with clear role delineation, yet also efficiency and coordination to avoid collapse under its own weight.

Role Specialization at Amazon

Amazon's recruiting model typically involves several roles: Recruiters (sometimes called "Client Lead Recruiters"), Sourcing Recruiters or Sourcers, and Recruiting Coordinators, among others. The interesting twist is Amazon often labels certain sourcers as "Sourcing Recruiters," effectively acknowledging them as a hybrid. A job posting for a Technical Sourcing Recruiter at Amazon describes the person will "cultivate talent sourcing channels, develop relationships with hiring managers, and close searches against tight deadlines."[14] This suggests that Amazon expects even those focused on sourcing to carry requisitions and be accountable for closing some roles. The description further notes the Sourcing Recruiter "will work with a team of peers including Client Leads and Recruiting Coordinators focusing on candidate search and placement, process improvement and strategy development."[15] The language is telling: rather than sourcers handing off candidates to recruiters and stepping away, they are focusing on "placement" and working alongside client lead recruiters.

In effect, Amazon created a two-pronged recruiting role: the *Client Lead Recruiter* who is the primary liaison with the business and often the final decision-maker in hiring processes, and the *Sourcing Recruiter* who is tasked with finding candidates and often screening them. But both are considered recruiters, just with different emphases. They foster a "collaborative team environment and a strong service-oriented culture," a phrase directly from their job ad indicating that working together is a core expectation.[16]

Integration Points

How do these roles interact at Amazon? Typically, a Client Lead (let's say for a software engineering team in AWS) will partner with one or more Sourcing Recruiters who focus on that domain. The sourcing recruiters identify passive candidates, reach out, and do initial phone screens. They might then present qualified candidates to the Client Lead Recruiter (and the hiring manager). The Client Lead then coordinates interviews and offers, but the Sourcing Recruiter remains involved, often managing the candidate relationship up to a certain interview stage. It's akin to the "relay model" we discussed, but Amazon mitigates the pitfalls by keeping the sourcing recruiter as a consistent figure to the candidate. In many cases, the candidate might not discern a big difference the sourcing recruiter is simply "one of the recruiters from Amazon" who contacted them initially and guided them through early interviews, and then another recruiter steps in for final rounds and offer logistics.

Moreover, Amazon's culture of metrics and process discipline forces alignment. Sourcing Recruiters and Client Leads share the same ultimate targets making hires that meet Amazon's high bar ("bar raisers" in Amazon parlance ensure quality). If a hire fails or a req is unfilled, it reflects on the whole team. Data is used intensively: every week the team reviews pipeline metrics, where any bottlenecks are everyone's concern to solve. For instance, Amazon's recruiting is extremely data-driven—they know exactly how many candidates at each stage, conversion rates, etc. A sourcer whose candidates consistently fail at hiring manager review gets feedback and training; a recruiter whose offers are declined examines if initial outreach (by sourcers) was attracting the right motivations. This culture pushes continuous collaboration and improvement.

The "Recruiter-on-Demand" Example

During my time at Amazon, particularly within the AWS division, I witnessed firsthand how the organization built scalable recruiting engines designed for both speed and precision. When hiring demands surged, the team adopted what could be described as a recruiter-on-demand model—mobilizing dedicated recruiters and sourcers who worked in tandem but with distinct focuses. Some were embedded with hiring teams, managing candidate relationships and interview logistics, while others concentrated exclusively on sourcing and market mapping to keep talent pipelines full. This deliberate division of responsibilities created a rhythm of efficiency: sourcers generated momentum at the top of the funnel while client-facing recruiters ensured consistent communication and alignment through to offer acceptance. The model also proved effective in broadening representation across candidate slates, as sourcers were intentionally tasked with diversifying outreach strategies and talent pools. The experience underscored a principle central to Amazon's playbook—scalability comes not from blending every role, but from clearly defining and tightly integrating them around shared goals.

Amazon's Efficiency and Integration Culture

Amazon is renowned for its relentless focus on performance and operational precision, and this ethos extends deep into its recruiting function. Within TA, coordination is almost surgical—teams operate with shared urgency and accountability. During high-volume hiring periods or "hiring blitz" events, it's common to see sourcers and recruiters working side by side, often on-site, to meet aggressive goals. Sourcers might be generating fresh candidate leads in real time while recruiters are conducting interviews or extending offers the same day. The lines blur intentionally; everyone does what's needed to deliver results. In practice, sourcers and recruiters are viewed as peers: each contributing distinct but equally critical expertise. This parity fosters respect across the function: sourcing updates carry as much weight in business meetings as recruiting updates because both directly impact hiring outcomes. Amazon's leaders care less about who fills which role and more about how the team collectively achieves results. The structure and mindset reinforce a simple truth efficiency at scale is achieved through integration, not hierarchy.

Another aspect is career path fluidity: Amazon often promotes or transitions sourcers into recruiter roles over time, and vice versa, recruiters might choose to specialize and become sourcing experts. This creates personal integration many Amazon recruiters have done sourcing and know what it entails. Institutional knowledge is shared.

Results

It's hard to argue with Amazon's results: they hire at a volume and speed that's industry-leading, while maintaining a reputation (mostly) for quality through their Bar Raiser program. They manage "huge recruiting volumes across a wide range" by industrializing each part of the process.[17] The integrated yet specialized model is one reason they can onboard hundreds of thousands of people in a year. By having sourcing recruiters laser-focused on filling the top of funnel, Amazon ensures no req goes unnoticed; by having client lead recruiters focusing on closing and stakeholder management, they ensure the business is served. Both roles operate within one of the most standardized recruiting processes around (from uniform interview loops to centralized hiring decision meetings). Everyone knows their part and the handoff moments are clearly defined by standard operating procedures which reduces the kind of confusion or gaps that smaller firms with less process might encounter.

One measurable outcome is diversity hiring: Amazon has reported improvements in diversifying hires partly by using sourcing to ensure slates of candidates include wide representation.[18] Specialized sourcers can dedicate time to find underrepresented talent that a busy full-cycle recruiter might not. The integrated model then funnels those candidates through the same rigorous process, with recruiters and sourcers jointly accountable for diversity metrics.

Key Takeaways from Amazon's Approach

- For other companies, Amazon's model shows that *you can maintain specialization but still integrate roles tightly.* The introduction of a "Sourcing Recruiter" hybrid role is one way to do that essentially making your sourcers into a type of recruiter with a foot in both worlds. It's a recognition that sourcing doesn't exist for its own sake; it exists to produce hires. So Amazon builds that expectation into the sourcing role itself. A company implementing this could, for example, have "Recruiter I" positions that are sourcing-heavy and "Recruiter II" that are closing-heavy, but both under the recruiter career ladder working as a team.
- Amazon also demonstrates the importance of process clarity. Integration doesn't mean lack of structure; on the contrary, it may require even more structure to manage handoffs smoothly. Amazon's meticulous documentation and metrics create a backbone against which human collaboration happens.
- Finally, Amazon's scale highlights technology's role. They employ advanced ATS and CRM systems and even AI tools (with caution, after a failed AI recruiting tool taught them lessons about bias). These systems facilitate information flow so that a candidate sourced in one part of the company can be considered by another if applicable this cross-pollination is another form of integration at an enterprise level.

Comparison to Spotify

While Spotify integrated by creating global partners and councils but still somewhat distinct in function, Amazon integrates by ensuring functional roles overlap and support each other at each step, with a culture that glues them together. Spotify's model might be more flexible and creative (alignment by values, internal mobility focus, etc.), whereas Amazon's is highly efficient and regimented. Yet both aim to avoid the pitfalls of a pure silo model.

Amazon's case study teaches us that even in the largest organizations, the synergy of sourcing and recruiting can be optimized by clearly defining roles that collaborate, using hybrid role definitions and enforcing a one-team mentality. The result is a recruiting function that is not only extremely productive but also robust to handle shifting demands something Amazon demonstrates year after year.

The evolving world of talent acquisition demands that we rethink long-standing role definitions. The stories and analyses in this chapter underscore a pivotal realization: whether an organization is a high-growth tech darling like Spotify or a behemoth like Amazon, success in hiring increasingly hinges on *integration, collaboration, and flexibility* in our approach to sourcing and recruiting. The traditional siloed model with sourcers hunting in one corner and recruiters closing in another is giving way to a more fluid partnership model. This shift is driven by the need for speed, the importance of candidate experience, and the recognition that identifying and hiring talent are two sides of the same coin.

In practice, rethinking roles means breaking down barriers: encouraging sourcers to be more like recruiters and recruiters to be more like sourcers, until the lines are blurred in the best way possible. It means establishing new team structures or communication rhythms so that no candidate ever falls through the cracks due to "whose job" it was. It means cultivating key skills in our teams data-savvy, marketing-minded, relationship-oriented professionals who can adapt to whatever the talent market throws at them. The future of talent acquisition belongs to those teams that can operate as *harmonious units*, not isolated functions.

By implementing an integrated model, organizations can expect to see tangible improvements. Better collaboration leads to faster hiring cycles; shared responsibility yields richer candidate pipelines and higher quality screening; unified goals drive a culture of collective accomplishment. Candidates, for their part, benefit from a smoother journey, they interact with well-informed recruiters (or sourcers) at every step, and sense the cohesion of the team behind the process. This positive experience can become a competitive advantage in wooing top talent.

However, making this shift is as much about mindset as it is about process. Leaders must champion a one-team ethos, and team members must embrace learning aspects of each other's roles. There may be challenges along the way change often brings temporary growing pains. But as we saw through Alex's fictional experience (one likely mirrored in many real companies), the cost of maintaining the status quo can be far greater: losing great people, fracturing team morale, and impeding the company's growth.

Modern talent acquisition is no longer about "sourcers vs. recruiters" it's about talent acquisition as a collaborative craft. By redefining roles and fostering collaboration, companies can build talent functions that are not only more efficient and innovative, but also more resilient in the face of change. In a space defined by connecting people to opportunities, it's only fitting that we first connect and empower our own people our sourcers, our recruiters to work as one. The result is a win-win-win: for employers, for talent acquisition professionals, and for the candidates whose lives we ultimately change through our work.

TABLE 4.1 Traditional vs. modern sourcing and recruiting roles

Aspect	Traditional Model	Modern Integrated Model
Role Definition	Separated sourcers and recruiters	Integrated talent partners
Workflow Model	Sequential handoffs	Continuous collaboration
Collaboration Level	Low; silos between roles	High; shared ownership
Technology Use	Minimal (basic ATS)	Advanced (AI, CRM, automation)
Candidate Experience	Fragmented	Seamless and personalized
Accountability	Fragmented	Shared and transparent
Skill Focus	Narrow (sourcing or recruiting only)	Broad (full talent spectrum)
Business Alignment	Low; reactive hiring	High; strategic workforce planning

Notes

1 Weck, A. (2024) The Sourcer-Recruiter Relationship: Maximizing the Connection, ERE.net, September 2, www.ere.net/the-sourcer-recruiter-relationship-maximizing-the-connection/ (archived at https://perma.cc/3456-GRDB)
2 Tegze, J. (2023) 10 Skills Recruiters Will Need in 2024 and Beyond, Full Stack Recruiter Newsletter, November 6, https://newsletter.fullstackrecruiter.net/p/ten-skills-recruiters-will-need-2024 (archived at https://perma.cc/7LSK-EHKH)
3 Cathey, G. (2014) Sourcing vs. Recruiting – What's the Difference? Boolean Black Belt blog, April 7, https://booleanblackbelt.com/2014/04/sourcing-vs-recruiting-whats-the-difference/ (archived at https://perma.cc/DH4T-UP5V)
4 Singel, J. (2019) How to Build a Great Talent Acquisition Team, Part II, Spotify HR Blog, August 6, https://hrblog.spotify.com/2019/08/06/how-to-build-a-great-talent-acquisition-team-part-ii/ (archived at https://perma.cc/AE5E-Y7VW)
5 Tegze, J. (2023) 10 Skills Recruiters Will Need in 2024 and Beyond, Full Stack Recruiter Newsletter, November 6, https://newsletter.fullstackrecruiter.net/p/ten-skills-recruiters-will-need-2024 (archived at https://perma.cc/7LSK-EHKH)
6 Singel, J. (2019) How to Build a Great Talent Acquisition Team, Part II, Spotify HR Blog, August 6, https://hrblog.spotify.com/2019/08/06/how-to-build-a-great-talent-acquisition-team-part-ii/ (archived at https://perma.cc/AE5E-Y7VW)
7 Tegze, J. (2023) 10 Skills Recruiters Will Need in 2024 and Beyond, Full Stack Recruiter Newsletter, November 6, https://newsletter.fullstackrecruiter.net/p/ten-skills-recruiters-will-need-2024 (archived at https://perma.cc/7LSK-EHKH)
8 Ibid.
9 Ibid.
10 Ibid.
11 Singel, J. (2019) How to Build a Great Talent Acquisition Team, Part II, Spotify HR Blog, August 6, https://hrblog.spotify.com/2019/08/06/how-to-build-a-great-talent-acquisition-team-part-ii/ (archived at https://perma.cc/AE5E-Y7VW)
12 Sullivan, J. (2022) Amazon Recruiting – A Case Study of a Giant Among Children. DrJohnSullivan.com, January 17, https://drjohnsullivan.com/articles/amazon-recruiting-case-study-part-1/ (archived at https://perma.cc/3A33-JHTE)
13 Ibid.
14 Ibid.
15 Ibid.
16 Cathey, G. (2014) Sourcing vs. Recruiting – What's the Difference? Boolean Black Belt blog, April 7, https://booleanblackbelt.com/2014/04/sourcing-vs-recruiting-whats-the-difference/ (archived at https://perma.cc/DH4T-UP5V)
17 Ibid.
18 Singel, J. (2019) How to Build a Great Talent Acquisition Team, Part II, Spotify HR Blog, August 6, https://hrblog.spotify.com/2019/08/06/how-to-build-a-great-talent-acquisition-team-part-ii/ (archived at https://perma.cc/AE5E-Y7VW)

5

Building Bridges: Cross-Functional Training and Skill Sharing

It was early in my career, and I was a fresh-faced recruiter, eager to make my mark. We had a critical role open—a senior software engineer with a niche skill set in real-time data processing. The sourcing team, a separate entity in our fairly siloed organization, had been hard at work. Or so I thought. One Monday morning, a list of 10 candidates landed in my inbox from Mark, a senior sourcer. On paper, their resumes ticked many of the keyword boxes we'd discussed. I diligently started my screening calls, full of optimism.

By Wednesday, that optimism had curdled into a uniquely demoralizing frustration. My first call was with a candidate who, while technically proficient, clearly had no interest in our industry; he was just looking for any remote job that met his salary floor. The second call revealed a brilliant engineer who was completely misaligned with our collaborative, fast-paced culture; he described his ideal environment as one where he could work on a single problem alone for months. Call after call followed a similar pattern. These individuals weren't bad candidates, but they were bad candidates *for us*.

When I finally sat down with Mark, a palpable tension hung in the air. "They all have the skills you asked for," he stated, a hint of defensiveness in his tone. "But they aren't a fit for *this* role, for *this* team," I countered, probably with more exasperation than was helpful. "How am I supposed to know about the 'vibe' of the team?" he shot back. "I find people with the skills on the req." We were speaking different languages. He was focused on the *what*—the technical qualifications, while I was focused on the *who* and the *why*—the person who would thrive in the role and the reasons they'd want to. That particular search dragged on for months, a monument to our mutual misunderstanding, costing the company untold productivity and leaving everyone involved, including the candidates, with a sour taste.

Fast forward a few years, to a different company with a more integrated approach. We had a similar challenge: a highly specialized principal data scientist role. This time, however, before the sourcing team even began their search, we held what we called a "search calibration summit." Sarah, the lead sourcer, and I sat with the hiring manager, the VP of Engineering. Sarah didn't just ask about programming languages and years of experience. She asked probing, second-level questions: "Can you describe the personality of the most successful person who's ever been on this team? What was it about them, beyond their technical skill, that made them great?" "What is the business problem that this person's work will solve in the next 18 months?" "If a candidate asks me what the biggest frustration of this role will be, what should I honestly tell them?"

I, in turn, shared market intelligence, explaining that candidates with this profile were often motivated more by the complexity of the data sets than by title or even compensation. I brought up the candidate personas we typically saw for these roles—the ex-academic, the startup veteran, the corporate researcher—and we discussed which persona would be the best fit.

Following this, Sarah shadowed two of my initial screening calls for a different but related role. Afterward, she said something that stuck with me: "I see now. You're not just screening for skills, you're testing for curiosity." It was a breakthrough. I, in turn, spent an afternoon with her as she demonstrated her advanced sourcing techniques, mapping out entire teams at competitor companies and using custom search strings that felt like a secret code. The result? The first slate of five candidates Sarah presented for that principal data scientist role was breathtaking. Every single one was not only technically qualified but also context-aware and culturally aligned. We hired our top choice from that first slate. The time-to-fill was 28 days. The bridge, it turned out, wasn't that hard to build, but it required a deliberate blueprint.

This chapter is about drawing that blueprint. It's about the transformative power of cross-functional training and skill sharing between sourcing and recruiting teams. In an increasingly complex and competitive talent market, the traditional assembly-line approach—where sourcing finds and recruiting qualifies and closes—is no longer sufficient. We need a more holistic, collaborative, and intelligent system. Building these internal bridges isn't just a "nice-to-have," it's a strategic imperative for optimizing candidate quality, enhancing communication, and, ultimately, achieving superior hiring outcomes.

The Strategic Imperative for Collaboration

The decision to intentionally weave together the sourcing and recruiting functions is not merely an operational tweak, it is a profound strategic choice. A unified talent acquisition front creates a value chain that delivers superior talent, and its benefits ripple through every facet of the hiring process, from the quality of the candidate pool to the morale of the hiring team itself.

Beyond Keywords: Elevating Candidate Quality to True Alignment

The most immediate and impactful outcome of this partnership is a dramatic uplift in candidate quality. This happens when the search moves beyond simple keyword matching into the realm of genuine candidate alignment. In a siloed environment, a job requisition is often treated as a simple checklist. The result is a job description that reads like a sterile shopping list of skills, attracting a wide but shallow pool of applicants who are merely qualified on paper.

A collaborative approach produces something far more powerful: a holistic "candidate persona." This persona, co-created by the sourcer, recruiter, and hiring manager, includes not only the required skills but also the desired competencies, motivations, working styles, and cultural attributes. For example, instead of just "five years of Java," the persona might specify "a developer who values clean code, enjoys pair programming, and is motivated by solving complex logistical challenges."

This detailed persona becomes the sourcer's true north. When they understand the type of person who will succeed, not just the skills they possess, their search becomes incredibly targeted. They can look for evidence of these traits in a candidate's online presence, past projects, or university affiliations. This deeper insight comes from immersion. When a sourcer has shadowed a recruiter's screening calls, they internalize the intangibles. They hear the candidate's passion, or lack thereof, for certain projects, their communication style, and their unspoken cultural assumptions. They begin to recognize the subtle difference between a candidate who lists a skill and one who can passionately articulate how they used that skill to solve a real-world problem. This richer understanding helps them to present candidates who are not only technically proficient but also far more likely to align with the team's dynamics and the company's values.[1]

Conversely, when a recruiter understands the art and science of talent mapping from their sourcing colleagues, their feedback becomes exponentially more valuable. Instead of a vague "these candidates aren't quite right," the feedback becomes a strategic adjustment: "The last slate was strong on backend skills, but we need to pivot toward front-end experience. Can we target companies known for their strong React developers?" This expertise extends beyond just finding people; when recruiters understand the art of market mapping, they become invaluable partners to the business. They can confidently walk into a meeting with a hiring manager and set realistic expectations about the true availability of a niche skillset, transforming a potentially frustrating search for a "purple squirrel" into a strategic conversation about talent realities, potential compromises, or alternative approaches.

From Handoffs to Handshakes: Forging a Cohesive and Empathetic Team

Silos breed inefficiency and misunderstanding. In a disconnected model, the relationship between sourcing and recruiting can become transactional and, at worst, adversarial. Sourcers feel like resume factories, judged on volume, while recruiters feel like they are panning for gold in a river of irrelevant profiles. Feedback sessions can become tense, blame-oriented meetings.

Cross-functional training dismantles these walls by fostering a shared language and, more importantly, mutual empathy. It creates a foundation of psychological safety, where team members feel safe to ask questions, admit mistakes, and challenge ideas without fear of retribution. When a recruiter spends an afternoon watching a sourcer meticulously build a complex boolean search string, testing and refining it for an hour to uncover just three promising profiles, they gain a newfound respect for the craft. They see it's not a simple database query but a form of digital detective work. When a sourcer sits in on a difficult offer negotiation, they understand the delicate balance of persuasion, psychology, and business acumen the recruiter must manage to bring a prized candidate across the finish line.

This shared experience erodes the "us versus them" mentality and replaces it with a shared sense of purpose. Intake meetings become more productive because jargon is replaced with shared understanding. Communication becomes clearer because it's rooted in a mutual appreciation of each other's challenges and contributions. The entire talent function begins to operate with the trust and cohesion of a single, high-performing team, which is the very foundation of an exceptional organization.[2]

The Velocity of Trust: Accelerating the Hiring Pipeline

In talent acquisition, speed matters, but speed without quality is just a faster way to make mistakes. A truly collaborative model increases the velocity of the entire hiring pipeline precisely because it builds in quality from the start. When trust and mutual understanding flourish, the process accelerates naturally.

Better initial candidate submissions from context-aware sourcers mean recruiters spend less time screening out misaligned profiles. Think of the cumulative hours saved across an entire talent team when the initial "pass-through" rate from sourcing to recruiting review jumps from 30 percent to 60 percent. If a team of 10 recruiters each saves just four hours a week on screening, that's 40 hours of reclaimed time every week—the equivalent of hiring an entire new team member. That time can be reinvested in higher-value activities like proactive candidate relationship building and strategic partnership with hiring managers.

This efficiency impacts more than just time-to-fill. It dramatically improves leading indicators like "time-to-quality-slate"—the time it takes to present the first set of viable candidates to a hiring manager. A shorter cycle here builds immense credibility and confidence with the business. With higher-quality candidates entering the process, recruiters can move more quickly to engage, interview, and close. The handoffs become seamless because the groundwork has been laid with shared intelligence, leading directly to a faster time-to-fill and a more agile response to the needs of the business.

A Seamless Journey: Crafting a Superior Candidate Experience

Candidates can sense organizational friction from a mile away. In today's transparent world, a poor candidate experience can quickly tarnish an employer brand. Consider the journey of a talented marketing professional, Maria, being pursued by two different companies for a similar role.

At Company A (the siloed company), Maria receives an initial LinkedIn message from a sourcer that is generic and slightly misrepresents the role. A week later, a recruiter calls, asks her to repeat much of the information from her LinkedIn profile, and seems unaware of the specifics of the sourcer's initial message. The recruiter schedules an interview with the hiring manager but provides little preparation material. Before the interview, Maria gets an automated email from a third person, a coordinator, with a different job description attached. She goes into the interview feeling confused and undervalued.

At Company B (the collaborative company), the sourcer's outreach is personalized, referencing a recent campaign Maria led and connecting it to a specific challenge the team is facing. The handoff to the recruiter is seamless. The recruiter's first words are, "Hi Maria, my colleague David was so impressed with your portfolio, and we're all excited to chat with you." The recruiter provides a detailed prep guide, including bios of the interviewers and a clear overview of the key priorities for the role. Every communication is consistent, professional, and makes Maria feel like the company is working in concert to recruit her. She goes into the interview feeling prepared, respected, and excited.

Which company do you think she will choose? When sourcing and recruiting teams are truly aligned, they present this unified and compelling front. This consistency not only enhances the candidate experience but also powerfully reinforces the employer brand as a place that is organized, respectful, and genuinely interested in the individual.

Investing in Your People: A Culture of Continuous Growth

Finally, cross-training is a direct investment in your most valuable asset: your people. It is a powerful tool for professional development and retention. In many organizations, sourcing is seen as a junior or entry-level role, with a vague career path. By creating a culture of skill sharing, you build formal bridges for career progression. When sourcers are exposed to the full recruitment lifecycle, they gain invaluable insights into influencing, negotiating, and closing candidates, opening new career pathways into recruiting or leadership roles. When recruiters learn advanced sourcing and market intelligence techniques, they become more strategic advisors to their hiring managers and more resourceful problem-solvers.

This commitment to skill enrichment makes team members more versatile and valuable. It fosters a culture of learning where knowledge is shared freely, not hoarded. This transforms the talent function from a group of individual contributors into a true "center of excellence." This boost in capability and collaboration can significantly improve job satisfaction and engagement, as team members feel more connected to the broader mission and see the tangible impact of their strengthened partnership on the business's success.[3]

From Theory to Evidence: Bridges in Action

The principles of collaboration are best understood through the stories of organizations that have successfully put them into practice.

Engineering a Unified Front at a Global Tech Company

Consider the immense challenge faced by a global technology giant, which must constantly attract highly specialized technical talent in a fiercely competitive market. To manage this complex, high-volume recruitment, the most effective talent acquisition functions are designed for deep integration and specialization. It's a common best practice in such high-stakes environments for teams of sourcers, recruiters, and coordinators to work in close, pod-like concert. These teams often focus on a specific business division, such as cloud computing or gaming, which allows them to build deep market knowledge and execute a cohesive strategy.

A day in the life of a recruiter in this model looks vastly different from their siloed counterpart. Their morning might start with a 15-minute stand-up meeting with their dedicated sourcer and coordinator to review the pipeline for their top three roles. The sourcer might report, "I'm seeing low response rates from our outreach in the fintech space, but high engagement from candidates in the healthcare tech industry. I suggest we pivot our focus." The recruiter can immediately use this information to update the hiring manager. Later that day, the recruiter and sourcer meet jointly to prep for a new intake meeting, co-authoring questions for the hiring manager to ensure they get the clarity they both need.

The process begins with a unified strategy. A cornerstone of this integrated approach is the joint intake meeting. Having sourcers and recruiters sit together with hiring managers from the very beginning ensures a unified understanding of a role's true requirements, preventing the "game of telephone" that plagues siloed teams. This initial unity is sustained by a strong emphasis on data-driven feedback loops. By analyzing data from their Applicant Tracking System (ATS), these teams can pinpoint which sourcing channels yield the best candidates and refine their strategies accordingly. This reflects the broader industry shift toward data-informed recruitment, turning raw data into actionable intelligence. The key takeaway from observing these large-scale operations is that a structure promoting both deep specialization and intense collaboration is not just beneficial it is essential for success, allowing the entire talent function to operate with agility and precision.

Scaling Rapidly Through Collaborative Partnerships at Atlassian

Atlassian, a software company renowned for its collaboration tools like Jira and Confluence, naturally extends its cultural philosophy to its own talent acquisition practices. This became particularly critical around 2021, when the company faced the need to significantly scale its hiring efforts to meet ambitious targets. Such rapid expansion can easily strain internal processes and lead to inconsistencies if sourcing, recruiting, and any external partners are not working in tight coordination. To meet this challenge, Atlassian leaned into its collaborative culture to manage the demand.

Their approach involved a powerful blend of internal alignment and strategic external partnerships. To achieve significant hiring goals, Atlassian strategically engaged external talent partners, embedding them within their teams to help build top-of-funnel pipelines.[4] This model can only succeed with exceptionally tight collaboration. It requires a shared understanding of candidate profiles, constant communication, and unified goals between the external partners and the company's internal sourcing and recruiting managers to ensure alignment and success.

Internally, Atlassian has long fostered this collaborative spirit through hands-on "sourcing blitzes" for particularly hard-to-fill roles. Imagine a conference room (or a dedicated virtual space) for a day, where a team of sourcers and recruiters focus on a single, critical role. There's a shared project board, a live feed of potential candidates, and a palpable energy as the teams work together, sharing search strings and outreach templates in real-time. This isn't just about finding candidates, it's about shared problem-solving and rapid learning. New hires in sourcing and recruiting go through onboarding modules that explicitly cover the roles and challenges of their counterparts, setting the stage for better collaboration from day one. Furthermore, by emphasizing shared team goals around time-to-hire and quality of hire, they foster a "we're in it together" mentality.

Atlassian's approach during its significant scaling phase highlights the importance of robust collaborative frameworks that can extend beyond internal teams to include strategic partners. It demonstrates that effective collaboration is a cornerstone of achieving ambitious hiring targets efficiently and sustainably.

The Architect's Blueprint: A Guide to Implementation

Knowing the benefits of collaboration is one thing, making it a reality is another. Building these bridges requires a deliberate and thoughtful blueprint, one that moves from planning and design to execution and sustained improvement. This is not about a single memo or a one-off meeting, it's about fundamentally re-engineering how your teams interact.

Laying the Cornerstone: Securing Buy-in and Defining Success

No significant organizational change can succeed without a strong foundation. The first step is to secure vocal and visible support from leadership. This requires presenting a clear business case that articulates the return on investment. Don't just talk about happier recruiters, talk about the business impact. Your presentation should include a current state analysis (e.g. "Our average time-to-fill for senior engineers is 95 days, putting Project X at risk"), a proposed solution (e.g. "A three-month cross-training pilot program"), the required investment (e.g. "10 hours per team member per month"), and the projected ROI (e.g. "A projected 20 percent reduction in time-to-fill, saving X dollars in lost productivity").

Once leadership is on board, the next step is to work with the teams to define what success will look like. Move beyond vague goals like "improve collaboration" and establish clear, measurable objectives. This could be reducing the candidate rejection rate at the initial screen by 15 percent, improving hiring manager satisfaction scores by 10 percent, or decreasing the average time a candidate spends in the pre-interview stages. Knowing your destination is the first rule of any successful journey.

The Immersion Experience: Shadowing and Joint Projects

The most effective way to build empathy is through shared experience. The core of any cross-training program should be structured immersion. Arrange for sourcers to shadow recruiters during intake meetings and live screening calls. Provide them with a simple observation guide: "What were the top three motivators for this candidate? What aspects of our culture resonated most? What question from the candidate revealed a potential concern?" This turns passive listening into active learning. Conversely, have recruiters sit alongside sourcers as they navigate complex market mapping exercises. Let them see the methodical process of identifying target companies, mapping out talent, and crafting personalized outreach.

Take this a step further by creating joint project teams. Assign a sourcer and a recruiter to co-own a challenging requisition from start to finish. This shared accountability transforms the process from a sequence of handoffs into a continuous, collaborative partnership. They will strategize together, debrief together, and celebrate the win together.

Fostering a Shared Mind: Workshops and Mentorship

Alongside direct immersion, create regular forums for structured knowledge sharing. These workshops should be practical and led by the team members themselves, which reinforces their own expertise. A "Sourcing for Recruiters" workshop could include these modules:

- **Module 1: The Sourcing Mindset** Moving from reactive to proactive talent engagement.

- **Module 2: Boolean and Beyond** Mastering search logic on different platforms.
- **Module 3: Market Intelligence Tools** Learning to use tools to provide data-backed insights to hiring managers.
- **Module 4: Crafting Compelling Outreach** A/B testing messages and measuring response rates.

A "Recruiting for Sourcers" workshop could cover:

- **Module 1: Candidate Motivation and Psychology** Understanding what drives candidates beyond compensation.
- **Module 2: Storytelling the EVP** How to articulate the company's value proposition in a compelling way.
- **Module 3: Navigating the Screening** Call Techniques for probing for skills, motivation, and culture fit.
- **Module 4: Introduction to Closing** Understanding the key elements that lead to a successful offer acceptance.

Complement these group sessions with a mentorship or buddy program, pairing individuals from each function to foster an ongoing, informal learning relationship. This creates a safe space for asking questions and sharing challenges, such as "How would you have handled this objection?" or "Can you show me how you found that profile?" that solidify the professional bonds that underpin a truly collaborative culture.

Launching, Learning, and Sustaining Momentum

It's wise to begin with a pilot program, testing and refining your approach with a single, receptive team before a full-scale rollout. When you launch, communicate the "why" with enthusiasm, ensuring everyone understands the benefits to their own work and career growth. Once underway, the work is not over. It is crucial to measure your progress against the objectives you initially set. Track the relevant KPIs, gather regular feedback from participants through surveys and focus groups, and be willing to iterate on the program. If a particular workshop isn't resonating, change it. If teams need more time for joint projects, find a way to provide it.

Finally, sustain the momentum by celebrating successes, sharing learnings widely in team meetings and newsletters, and embedding these collaborative practices into your standard operating procedures and new-hire onboarding. True transformation occurs when these new behaviors become simply "the way we work."

Navigating the Headwinds of Change

The path to integration is not without its challenges. Proactively addressing potential resistance and logistical hurdles is key to a smooth implementation. Team members may be resistant to change, comfortable in their current routines, or concerned about taking time away from their pressing targets. It is leadership's role to frame this initiative not as an addition to their workload, but as an investment that will make their work more effective and rewarding in the long run. Applying principles of change management is critical here. For instance, using Kotter's model, a leader would first create a sense of urgency by highlighting data on hiring inefficiencies, then build a guiding coalition of enthusiastic sourcers and recruiters to champion the effort.[5]

Furthermore, you must be prepared to prove the value of your efforts and maintain momentum after the initial excitement fades. The "flavor of the month" syndrome is a real danger. This requires a commitment to tracking metrics that demonstrate a clear return on investment, both in efficiency and quality. Sustain the program by making it a core part of your talent acquisition culture, not just a one-time project. By anticipating these challenges, you can navigate them effectively, ensuring that the bridges you build are strong enough to last.

Forging the Future with United Talent Teams

The journey from a siloed set of functions to a unified talent acquisition ecosystem is one of the most powerful transformations an organization can undertake. The principles and practices laid out in this chapter are more than just a guide to operational efficiency, they are a blueprint for building a lasting competitive advantage. The future of talent acquisition belongs to those who cultivate these interconnected teams, for the bridges you construct today will carry the talent that defines your organization's tomorrow.

As the leader of this critical function, the true work begins now, with reflection and intentional action. Ask yourself: What is the unvarnished truth about collaboration on my team today, and what is the real cost of our current disconnects? If I could architect the ideal workflow from scratch, what would it achieve for my candidates and hiring managers? And most importantly, what is the single most courageous change I can champion to dismantle the biggest barrier and begin forging this united front?

The path is paved by such intentional reflection. Your leadership in building these alliances will not only redefine your team's capabilities but will also fundamentally shape the future talent landscape of your entire organization.

Notes

1. Allen, D. G. (2019) *The Oxford Handbook of Talent Management*, Oxford, Oxford University Press
2. Lencioni, P. M. (2002) *The Five Dysfunctions of a Team: A leadership fable*, San Francisco, CA: Jossey-Bass
3. Hackman, J. R. and Oldham, G. R. (1976) Motivation through the design of work: Test of a theory, *Organizational Behavior and Human Performance*, 16 (2), 250–79
4. Talentful (n.d.) How Atlassian Made 939 hires Across 10 Countries, www.talentful.com/case-studies/atlassian/ (archived at https://perma.cc/P369-HDGC)
5. Kotter, J. P. (1996) *Leading Change*, Boston, MA, Harvard Business School Press

6

Proactive Pipeline Building: Beyond the Requisition to the Talent Community

The Paradigm Shift

I remember the exact moment the paradigm shifted for me. I was a few years into my talent acquisition (TA) career, and my CEO walked into my office with a look of controlled panic. The air in the room suddenly felt thin. "Our top competitor just launched a new feature," he said, his voice quiet but tense. "The one our head of product innovation was supposed to build." The role had been open for four agonizing months, a gaping hole in our strategic roadmap. In that moment, the low hum of the servers in the building felt like a ticking clock, counting down our lost revenue and evaporating market share. I realized the vacancy wasn't just an HR problem on my weekly report, it was a public failure, and I was the accountable owner. I could already feel the weight of the stares in the next leadership meeting.

This scenario, this feeling of being hopelessly behind the business need, is the predictable outcome of a system I've spent my career trying to dismantle: the traditional, requisition-based recruiting model. I call it the "firefighting" model, because that's precisely what it feels like. We all know the drill because we've all lived it. A need becomes urgent, a requisition is approved with a sigh of relief from a beleaguered hiring manager, a job description is hastily posted, and the frantic scramble begins. It's a process that treats the acquisition of a company's most vital asset—its people—as a low-level, transactional emergency response rather than a core business strategy. It's a framework that forces talented, capable recruiters into a perpetual cycle of catching up, leading to longer hiring times, painful compromises on candidate quality, and immense pressure to just fill the role—any role—to stop the immediate pain.

But what if, at that moment, I could have calmly looked my CEO in the eye and responded, "It's a concern, but we're already moving. We have three highly qualified members of our product innovation talent community who we've been nurturing for months. They've seen our tech blog, they attended our last virtual workshop, and they understand our mission. I have two of them tentatively scheduled for exploratory conversations this week." That response changes everything. It's the reality of a strategic alternative that goes beyond simple pipelining. It's the shift from building a list to cultivating a talent community.

I want to be very clear about this distinction, as it's the central thesis of this chapter. A pipeline is a one-way street, it's a list of names that we, the company, have sourced for our benefit. A community is a two-way relationship, it's a living network of talented individuals centered around a shared professional interest, where the company acts as a valuable facilitator and a hub of knowledge. The goal is no longer just to source talent when we need it, but to become a center of gravity for that talent in our industry, independent of any open role. When you build a true community, you are never starting from zero.

This chapter is my playbook for making that fundamental shift. Together, we will dismantle the reactive model and walk through the blueprint for building a true talent community from the ground up. I will argue that by shifting from a transactional mindset to a community-building strategy, TA teams can dramatically shorten hiring times, elevate the quality of every single hire, and finally earn their rightful place as indispensable strategic partners to the business. We will explore the core strategies I've used to build, nurture, and grow these communities, and examine the technology and analytics needed to drive and prove your success. It's time to stop fighting fires and start building a gathering place.

The Strategic Imperative: Why Building Talent Communities is Non-Negotiable

The allure of the old requisition model is its deceptive simplicity. A need arises, an action is taken. It feels orderly and logical on a spreadsheet. But I've learned that this linear approach is a dangerous illusion in today's complex, candidate-driven talent market. To truly make the case for change in your own organization, you must move beyond anecdotal frustration and dissect the deep, compounding costs of the old way, building an irrefutable business case for the new, community-focused model.

The Compounding Cost of a Vacancy

The most visceral pain point of reactive recruiting is the empty chair, but the term "cost of vacancy" is too sterile. It's a slow-burning crisis with cascading consequences across the organization. I break these down into four categories when I speak with my leadership teams.

1. **Financial costs:** This is the easiest to calculate and the hardest to ignore. For a revenue-generating role like a sales executive, you can multiply their quota by the length of the vacancy. For an engineering role, you can calculate the cost of a delayed product launch in terms of lost sales or market share. Beyond this, there are the hard costs of reactive recruiting itself: inflated fees for last-minute agency help, premium costs for job board postings, and the advertising spend required to make noise in a crowded market.
2. **Productivity costs:** This is where the damage starts to spread. The vacant role's responsibilities don't just disappear, they are absorbed by the existing team. I've seen teams of five trying to do the work of six, leading to a 20 percent increase in workload per person. This isn't sustainable. Quality drops, deadlines are missed, and innovation grinds to a halt because everyone is too busy covering the basics to think about the future. It's a recipe for burnout.
3. **Cultural costs:** This is the most insidious cost. When a key role sits empty for months, it sends a message: either leadership doesn't see

the role as critical or our company isn't attractive enough to fill it. Morale erodes. Your best employees, the ones picking up the slack, start to feel undervalued and overwhelmed. Their engagement drops, and soon enough, they begin to take calls from recruiters at companies that seem to have their act together. An open req can become a catalyst for wider attrition, turning one problem into many.

4 **Opportunity costs:** This brings us back to my opening story. What is the cost of the product you didn't launch, the market you didn't enter, the competitor you couldn't counter? In a fast-moving economy, the inability to staff a strategic initiative quickly is tantamount to ceding the field to your rivals. The reactive model inherently accepts this staggering opportunity cost as a standard part of doing business, which is a strategic failure of the highest order.

The Quality vs. Speed Dilemma: The High Price of "Good Enough"

This constant pressure cooker environment leads directly to the quality versus speed dilemma. The urgency to stop the bleeding from a vacancy forces a compromise between hiring quickly and hiring the right person. The truth is, the A-player you dream of is rarely unemployed and actively looking for a job the exact moment your requisition opens. They are a passive candidate, happily employed elsewhere, and can only be engaged through proactive, long-term relationship building.

Reactive recruiting, therefore, almost always results in hiring the "best available" candidate from a limited pool of active seekers. This leads to the curse of the "good-enough" hire. I remember a time we hired a sales director under immense pressure. He was fine. He hit about 85 percent of his quota, his team didn't complain much, and the board was placated. But he was an operational manager, not an inspirational leader. He maintained the status quo. Two years later, a competitor hired a true A-player in the same role, someone we had identified but who wasn't "looking" at the time. She rebuilt their sales methodology, inspired her team to new heights, and took significant market share. Our "good-enough" hire cost us millions in growth we never realized. The U.S. Department of Labor famously estimates that the cost of a bad hire can be at least 30 percent of their first-year earnings, but I'd argue the cost of a mediocre hire in a critical role is infinitely higher—it's the delta between the business you have and the business you could have built.[2]

A Powerful Engine for Diversity, Equity, and Inclusion

I am convinced that building talent communities is the single most powerful and authentic strategy for achieving meaningful DEI goals. So many well-intentioned organizations treat diversity as a reactive sourcing problem. When a senior role opens, a frantic search begins to ensure a "diverse slate" is presented. This last-minute approach often feels transactional and can be perceived as tokenism by the very candidates you are trying to attract. It does little to address the systemic issues of trust and belonging.

The community approach is fundamentally different. It allows for intentional, thoughtful, and long-term relationship building with professionals from a wide range of backgrounds, particularly those from underrepresented groups. By creating content that speaks to their interests, hosting events in partnership with organizations like the National Society of Black Engineers or Women Who Code, and providing genuine mentorship and networking opportunities, you build trust over time. You are creating a space of belonging long before a job is ever discussed. When a role does become available, you are not scrambling to "find" diverse candidates, you are turning to the trusted, respected, and diverse members of your established community. This approach directly tackles the "pipeline problem" myth by demonstrating a long-term commitment. It aligns perfectly with extensive research from firms like McKinsey & Company, which has consistently shown that diverse companies are more likely to outperform their less diverse peers, not just in profitability but in innovation and employee satisfaction.[3] This is how you shift your focus from the tactical goal of "finding diverse candidates" to the strategic one of "building a diverse and inclusive community."

The "How-To": Core Strategies for Building Your Talent Community

Shifting from a reactive recruiter to a proactive community builder requires a new set of skills and a commitment to new habits. It's a move from being a hunter to being a farmer. This is the practical, hands-on playbook I've used to build and scale successful talent communities from scratch, turning TA functions from cost centers into strategic assets.

Discipline 1: Talent Mapping as Community Design

The entire process begins with a discipline I consider non-negotiable: talent mapping. But in this new paradigm, we reframe it as community design. We're not just identifying targets, we're designing the blueprint for the community we want to build.

- *Step 1: The strategic dialogue.* This cannot be a simple email exchange. I schedule dedicated, 60-minute workshops with business leaders. The agenda isn't about current open roles, it's about their three-year strategic plan. I ask specific, forward-looking questions: "What skills will our team need to master to stay ahead of the competition in 2027?" "If we were to build a 'dream team' for your division, what companies would we recruit from?" "Who are the top five thinkers or influencers in your field that we should be following?" The answers provide the raw material for our community blueprint.
- *Step 2: Intelligence gathering.* We take the insights from that dialogue and go broad. We use tools like LinkedIn Talent Insights, of course, but we go deeper. We use platforms like Zippia or Craft.co to analyze competitor org charts and identify reporting structures. We scrape the speaker lists from the last three major industry conferences. We identify the authors of the most-cited papers or popular trade publications. This isn't about finding people who are "open to work", it's about identifying the nodes of influence and expertise in our target domain.

- *Step 3: Developing a rich community persona.* A job description is not a persona. For each critical talent segment, we build a rich, detailed persona. Let's imagine we're building a community for "AI Ethics Specialists." Our persona might look like Table 6.1.
- *Step 4: Creating a living map.* A static spreadsheet is useless. We use our CRM to tag individuals according to these personas. For a more visual approach, I've used tools like Kumu to create dynamic network maps, showing how different individuals in the community are connected. This "living map" is our guide for every subsequent action.

Discipline 2: The Evergreen Requisition as a Community Gateway

The evergreen requisition is the practical tool for capturing interest, but its true power is realized when you frame it as the "front door" to your talent community. I implemented this after seeing countless great candidates slip through the cracks simply because our timing was off. The language of the posting itself must change. Instead of "Software Engineer Needed," it becomes, "Join Our Software Engineering Talent Community."

TABLE 6.1 Community persona

Category	Description
Name	Dr. Evelyn Reed
Background	PhD in Philosophy or Sociology, with a post-doc in technology policy. Currently an Associate Professor or a Senior Researcher at a major tech firm's research lab.
Watering Holes	Attends conferences like FAccT (Conference on Fairness, Accountability, and Transparency). Active on academic Twitter, follows and interacts with specific ethics think tanks. Reads publications like the *AI Ethics Journal*.
Motivations	Driven by mission and impact, not just salary. Wants to solve complex, ambiguous problems. Values academic freedom and the ability to publish. Wary of "ethics-washing."
How to Engage	Do not send a standard InMail. Share a thoughtful critique of a recent paper. Invite her to a private, moderated roundtable discussion with our own head of research. Offer a platform, like our tech blog, to share her work.

The description shouldn't list a litany of requirements for a specific, non-existent job. Instead, it should describe the mission of the engineering team, the interesting problems they are solving, and the culture of learning and growth. It should explicitly state: "Even if we don't have the perfect role for you today, we invite you to join our talent community. As a member, you'll receive exclusive access to our tech talks, research papers, and updates from our engineering leaders." This sets a clear expectation of a long-term, value-based relationship. Behind the scenes, the workflow is critical. Applications to this req must be routed to a dedicated community manager or recruiter who immediately begins the nurturing process, ensuring no one who walks through the front door is left standing in the foyer.

Discipline 3: Content and Events as the Lifeblood of Community

This is where you truly earn the right to be a community leader. The biggest mistake I see teams make is creating a "pipeline" and then only communicating with it when they have a job to fill. That's not a community, it's a mailing list that people will quickly abandon. You must consistently provide value that is independent of a job offer.

I push my teams to think like media editors and event producers. We develop a simple content calendar for each major talent community. For our Data Science community, a quarterly plan might look like Table 6.2.

TABLE 6.2 Quarterly content and engagement plan

Month	Content and Engagement Activities	
Month 1	Technical Blog Post	A deep-dive from a senior data scientist on a new ML model they deployed.
		"Meet the team" video: Introducing the data science leadership and their vision.
		Curated newsletter: An email with links to three fascinating, recent data science articles from around the web.

(continued)

TABLE 6.2 (Continued)

Month	Content and Engagement Activities	
Month 2	Exclusive webinar	An invitation to a virtual event on "The Future of Causal Inference in Business," hosted by the Head of Data. Downloadable asset: A whitepaper or case study showcasing a major project success. Employee spotlight: A Q&A with a junior data scientist about their career path and experience.
Month 3	Live Q&A Session	An "Ask Me Anything" (AMA) live Slack session with a panel of our data scientists. Company announcement: Sharing the news of a new open-source tool the team is releasing to the public. Personalized outreach: A one-on-one note pointing a community member to a specific part of the recent webinar relevant to their profile.

Events are the tentpole moments that bring the community together. We use a mix of formats:

- *The virtual tech talk*: These are low-cost, high-reach events that establish our expertise and provide genuine learning opportunities.
- *The invite-only roundtable*: For more senior talent, we host small, virtual roundtables (8–10 people) on a specific, high-level topic. We invite a respected external moderator and our own internal expert. The exclusivity and high-level discourse make this incredibly valuable for top-tier talent.
- *The open house and workshop*: Once or twice a year, we host a hybrid open house. We stream the main presentation but also invite local community members to our office for food, networking, and hands-on workshops. This gives people a tangible feel for our culture and workspace.

Discipline 4: Referrals as Community Invitations

Finally, this proactive ethos can transform your employee referral program. I've always found that standard referral programs are too transactional. I work to create a culture where our employees are our best community ambassadors. We shift the question from, "Who do you know that's looking for a job?" to "Who is the best product manager you have ever worked with that we should invite into our community?"

We change the incentive structure to match. We offer a small bonus or recognition for a qualified introduction that leads to a new community member, and a separate, larger bonus if that person is eventually hired. We use dedicated tools like ERIN or Gem to make it incredibly easy for employees to share content and make introductions. This turns the entire workforce into a community-building engine. Studies have consistently shown that referred employees are hired faster and stay longer, and I believe that's because they already have a trusted connection to the community from day one.[4]

Real-World Examples from the Field

These strategies come to life when you see them in action. I've seen them work time and again, but two examples stand out.

The first was at a SaaS company that needed to hire 20 senior software engineers. We didn't just build a pipeline, we built the "Innovatech Engineering Community." The head of engineering was skeptical at first. "I need engineers, not pen pals," he told me. I asked for one quarter to prove the model. We used their existing "Code & Coffee" sessions as our anchor content. Our recruiters became community managers, engaging their mapped list with personal invitations and thoughtful questions. In six months, we had a thriving community of over 500 engineers who regularly attended our events and engaged in our private Slack channel. When hiring needs arose, we posted them to the community first. We filled all 20 roles two months ahead of schedule, with 70 percent of the hires coming from the heart of our new community. The head of engineering became my biggest advocate.

The second was a healthcare system facing a chronic shortage of oncology nurses. The burnout was palpable. They stopped just hunting for talent and started the "Carewell Nursing Community." They forged deep partnerships with nursing schools and created mentorship programs pairing senior nurses with students. They ran a content campaign celebrating the stories of their current nurses—not the polished corporate version, but the raw, authentic stories of why they chose this difficult but rewarding work. All these initiatives funneled into their community. Within a year, their time-to-hire dropped from 120 days to just 40, because they were hiring trusted members of their community, not cold contacts from a job board.

Nurturing Your Talent Community

Sourcing a list of names is a simple task. The real, sustained work—and where most initiatives fail—is in the nurturing required to turn that list into a vibrant, engaged community. A community is a living ecosystem that requires consistent care, attention, and value. My guiding principle here is simple: community management is about building trust and credibility by giving, not taking. It is a long-term investment in relationships.

This is why a dedicated Candidate Relationship Management (CRM) tool is non-negotiable, though I prefer to think of it as a CRM platform. It is the central nervous system of your operation, the single source of truth for every member and every interaction. But the platform itself is just a database, its power is unlocked through sophisticated segmentation. I insist that my teams move beyond simplistic tags. We create a multi-layered segmentation strategy:

- *Demographic/firmographic*: Skill set, years of experience, current company, geographic location. This is the basic layer.
- *Behavioral*: How do they interact with us? We create tags like attended_webinar_Q2, opened_last_5_emails, and clicked on tech blog link. This tells us what they are interested in.

- *Psychographic/tiered*: This is the most advanced layer. We create conceptual tiers for our community members:
    - *Tier 1: The Champions*. These are our super-users. They attend every event, share our content, and refer others. We treat them like VIPs, giving them early access to news and inviting them to exclusive roundtables.
    - *Tier 2: The Engagers*. These members consistently open emails and attend events. They are our core audience. Our goal is to provide them with so much value that they convert into Champions.
    - *Tier 3: The Lurkers*. These are often high-potential individuals who are busy and passive. They signed up but rarely engage. The strategy here is not to bombard them, but to use highly targeted, high-value outreach to re-activate them, perhaps with a personal note from a senior leader.

This segmentation allows for a thoughtful nurture cadence, which is the rhythm of your community communication. The cardinal rule I teach is the "90/10 rule": 90 percent of your communications must provide value to the community, while only 10 percent can be a direct ask about a job. You have to earn the right to present opportunities.

Let's make this tangible. Here are the first three emails in the nurture stream for Alex, our new software engineer community member.

Email 1 (Day 1, The Welcome):

- **Subject** Welcome to the Innovatech Engineering Community!
- **Body** "Hi Alex, Thanks so much for joining our engineering community. We're excited to have you. My name is [recruiter's name], and I'm the community manager here. My only job is to make sure you get value from being a part of this group. To start, I thought you might find this recent post from our tech blog interesting—it's about how our team solved a tricky database scaling issue: [link]. No strings attached. We'll be in touch soon with some exclusive content and event invites. Welcome aboard! –[name]"

Email 2 (Day 30, The Value Add):

- **Subject** An invite for our community members
- **Body** "Hi Alex, Hope you're having a great month. I'm writing to personally invite you to a live virtual tech talk we're hosting exclusively for our community members next Thursday: 'Scaling Microservices for High-Traffic Applications,' led by our Principal Architect. Given your background, I thought it might be right up your alley. You can register here: [link]. Hope to see you there. –[name]"

Email 3 (Day 75, The Personal Touch):

- **Subject** Thought of you
- **Body** "Hi Alex, I saw on your profile that you have experience with Python and just remembered this part of our tech talk Q&A where our architect discussed our Python framework. The timestamp is 42:15 if you want to jump right to it: [link]. Just thought you'd find it particularly relevant. Cheers, –[name]"

Notice, we haven't mentioned a single job. We have only given, given, given. It is this patient, value-driven approach that builds the trust necessary for a strategic recruiting conversation down the line. It is this level of personalization that shows you are a dedicated community facilitator, not just a recruiter. It is this investment that turns a community member into a transformative hire.

The Enablers: Technology, AI, and Analytics

A community strategy at scale is impossible without a modern technology stack and a rigorous commitment to data. As a leader, it's my job to advocate for these tools and to use the data they provide to prove our value to the business. Today, this conversation must include a thoughtful approach to artificial intelligence, moving beyond the hype to practical application.

The foundational tech stack starts with CRM. When choosing a platform, I prioritize features specifically for community building: advanced tagging and segmentation, email campaign builders with robust analytics (open rates, click-through rates), and native integration with event platforms like Luma or Eventbrite. The CRM must seamlessly integrate with your Applicant Tracking System (ATS) so you can track the full journey from community member to applicant to hire. This is complemented by sourcing tools that help identify potential community members, and analytics platforms like Tableau or Looker Studio that can create a holistic view of your community's health.

The Rise of AI in Proactive Recruiting

Layered on top of this traditional tech stack is the transformative power of AI. I'll admit I was skeptical at first, viewing it as a potential source of bias. However, when used responsibly, AI is a powerful partner that can supercharge community building.

I've seen its most immediate impact in intelligent sourcing, helping us identify ideal members for our communities based on nuanced profiles rather than simple keywords. But the real game-changer for my teams has been personalization at scale. Generative AI tools, now being integrated into our CRMs, can help our community managers draft first-pass, hyper-personalized outreach and nurture content based on a member's profile. This saves hours and allows us to have more high-quality, individual touchpoints. We are also using AI-powered predictive analytics to forecast which content topics will be most valuable to the community, and AI chatbots to act as community concierges, answering FAQs and guiding new members.

However, a word of caution is essential. AI is a tool, not a replacement for human judgment. We have a strict policy that AI is used to augment our recruiters, not automate relationships. We regularly audit our AI tools for potential bias and ensure that every critical decision is made by a human. The goal of AI in our function is to free up human time for more meaningful, high-touch community management, not to remove humanity from the process.[5]

Measuring What Matters

With this technology in place, we can measure what truly matters. I have to be able to tell a compelling story to my leadership team, and I do it with data. We've moved beyond simple metrics like time-to-fill and developed a "Community Health Score," a composite metric that includes:

- *Growth rate*: The net growth of new community members month-over-month.
- *Engagement rate*: A blended score of email opens, clicks, event attendance, and content downloads.
- *Sentiment analysis*: Using tools to track the tone of conversations in community forums or social media mentions.
- *Member-sourced referrals*: The number of new members referred by existing members.

Ultimately, these health metrics allow me to prove our return on investment. The KPI I lead with is Source of Hire, showing what percentage of new hires come from within our established talent communities. I present side-by-side comparisons showing our dramatically lower time-to-hire for community-sourced roles (often 30–50 percent faster). I work with HR business partners to connect our data to quality of hire metrics, proving we don't just hire faster, but *better*. Finally, I can point to a hard number: the reduction in agency spend. This is the data that transforms talent acquisition from a cost center into an undeniable strategic advantage.

Building a Sustainable Talent Advantage

We began this chapter with a painful memory of a strategic failure born from a reactive recruiting model. That reality, I hope I have shown, is a choice, not an inevitability. I've spent my career advocating for and building an alternative path, a strategic framework based not just on proactive processes, but on the rich, rewarding work of building vibrant talent communities.

Throughout this chapter, I've shared my playbook. We've dismantled the traditional model and presented community building as a strategic imperative for any company that wants to win the war for talent. We've walked through the core disciplines of community design, creating gateways for new members, and providing relentless value through content and events. We've focused on the crucial art of nurturing relationships, because a pipeline is a list, but a community is a living, breathing asset. We've also explored the technology, including the responsible use of AI, and the analytics that are essential for execution and for proving your immense value.

Adopting this model is a commitment to building long-term, sustainable organizational resilience. In a world of constant change, being the center of gravity for a thriving community of top talent is the ultimate competitive advantage. A talent community is an appreciating asset, one that pays dividends in agility, innovation, and market leadership long after you've filled the roles you need today.

The journey from reactive recruiter to community builder can feel daunting, but it starts with a single step. So, here is my challenge to you: Start small. Pick one critical talent segment. Commit to building a three-month community for them. Map the talent, create valuable content, and start two conversations a day that are not about a job, but about building your community. Measure the difference. The transformation begins not with a new requisition, but with a single, proactive conversation. Go have that conversation today.

Reflections

Reading is passive, but change is active. As you close this chapter, take a few quiet moments to bridge the gap between theory and action. Begin with an honest assessment. If you were to place your team on a scale from 1 (purely reactive firefighting) to 10 (proactive community building), where would you land? Be honest with yourself about that number, and then consider the cultural barriers—a resistance to change, a perceived lack of time, a gap in technology—that are holding you there.

With that reality in mind, start building your case for the future. Think about a critical role that was recently difficult to fill in your company. How could you articulate the true, full cost of that vacancy to a skeptical leader? This pain point is your leverage for change. Use it to identify the one critical talent segment you could choose for a pilot project, proving the value of this community model on a small, manageable scale. Who is the business leader you would need as your champion?

Success will ultimately depend on the value you provide. So, ask yourself, what unique knowledge, connections, or culture exists inside your organization that you could share? What would make a group of talented professionals *want* to be part of a community you facilitate, even if they never apply for a job? Finally, bring it back to yourself. What is one habit you can change or one action you can commit to *next week* to personally dedicate more of your time to these community-building activities? Change, after all, begins with that single, personal step.

Notes

1 SHRM (2024) The True Cost of a Bad Hire, Society for Human Resource Management. (While a specific 2024 report with this exact title may be illustrative, SHRM frequently publishes on this topic, and the principle is a well-established HR metric).

2 U.S. Department of Labor (n.d.) The Cost of a Bad Hire. This is a widely cited statistic in the HR industry, often attributed to the DOL, highlighting the significant financial impact of poor hiring decisions.

3 Hunt, V., Layton, D., and Prince, S. (2015) Diversity Matters, McKinsey & Company. This foundational report was one of the first to draw a clear statistical line between ethnic and racial diversity in corporate leadership and better financial performance. Subsequent reports from McKinsey have reinforced these findings.

4 Zao-Sanders, M. (2017) How to Boost Employee Referrals Without Spending a Dime, *Harvard Business Review*. This article outlines the strategic benefits of referral programs, noting they are a top source of quality hires.

5 Gartner (2025) Top HR Technology Trends for 2025, Gartner, Inc. Gartner's annual reports on HR technology trends consistently highlight the growing adoption and practical application of AI in talent acquisition, from sourcing to candidate experience.

7

Leveraging Technology and AI for Seamless Integration

The Great Divide: Introduction

Maria, a senior sourcer at a rapidly growing fintech firm, felt a familiar surge of pride. After weeks of meticulous research and careful outreach, she had done it. She had engaged with a candidate that she called "The Unicorn"—a senior backend engineer with rare experience in both high-frequency trading systems and quantum computing. He was passively happy in his current role, but intrigued by Maria's persistent, value-driven approach. She had built a genuine rapport, sharing industry articles and company news over several weeks before ever mentioning a specific role. Finally, the perfect senior position opened up. She logged her detailed notes, conversation history, and the candidate's resume into her team's designated sourcing spreadsheet and sent a triumphant email to the recruiting team lead. "He's ready for a conversation," she wrote. "This is our guy."

A month passed. The role was still open. Puzzled, Maria checked in with the recruiter, who looked bewildered. "I never saw him," the recruiter admitted, scrolling through hundreds of applicants in the Applicant Tracking System (ATS). "Was he an applicant?" It turned out Maria's email had been buried, her spreadsheet note unseen. Two weeks later, the ultimate gut punch arrived: The Unicorn updated his LinkedIn profile with a new title—at their biggest competitor. He hadn't even been contacted. The competitor launched a new algorithmic trading feature three months later—a feature Maria's company had planned to build with the team this role was meant to lead. The cost of this process failure wasn't just a lost candidate, it was a tangible loss of market opportunity, a multi-million dollar delay in their product roadmap directly attributable to a broken internal process.

This isn't a rare horror story, it's a daily reality in countless organizations, a silent tax on innovation and growth. It's the inevitable outcome of a "siloed tech stack," a common ailment in talent acquisition where vital information is trapped in disconnected systems. Sourcers live in LinkedIn Recruiter and spreadsheets, while recruiters operate almost exclusively within the ATS. The bridge between them is a rickety, manual path of emails, Slack messages, and copy-pasting. This digital divide leads to duplicated efforts, invisible candidate pipelines, a catastrophic candidate experience, and a fundamental lack of shared data. It creates friction, fosters blame, and turns the talent acquisition process into a series of disjointed, inefficient handoffs.[1] The cost is staggering, with studies suggesting that the time it takes to fill a job has increased by over 50 percent in the last decade, and the negative business impact of an unfilled critical role can exceed the role's salary several times over.[2]

The solution is to move beyond a mere collection of tools and build a Unified Talent Operating System, powered by artificial intelligence. This is not just an integrated ecosystem where data flows seamlessly, it is an intelligent system where AI provides the predictive and analytical horsepower to make the entire process proactive. AI acts as the central nervous system, transforming a connected set of tools into a finely tuned orchestra with a conductor that can anticipate the music. Without AI, an integrated system is like a body with all its limbs connected but no brain to direct them. With AI, the system can learn, adapt and predict, turning reactive processes into proactive strategies.

By strategically integrating key technologies and infusing them with AI, talent acquisition teams can eliminate friction, foster true collaboration, and create a seamless, predictive process that enhances both efficiency and the candidate experience. This chapter will provide the blueprint for that transformation. We will dissect the anatomy of a modern, AI-powered recruiting tech stack, map out the critical integration points, and explore the human-centric strategies required to turn a collection of disparate tools into a powerful, intelligent engine for acquiring top talent.

Anatomy of a Modern Recruiting Tech Stack

To build a unified system, we must first understand its components. A modern talent acquisition tech stack is not a monolithic platform but a constellation of specialized tools working in concert, with AI as the connective tissue. Each has a distinct purpose, and its value is magnified exponentially when it communicates effectively with the others. The goal is not to have the most tools, but the most intelligent and connected tools.

The System of Engagement: Candidate Relationship Management (CRM)

If the talent acquisition process is a funnel, the CRM is its wide, welcoming, and intelligent mouth. This is the top-of-funnel engine, the system designed for proactive, long-term relationship building. It is the organization's long-term talent memory, a living database of every promising individual your company has ever interacted with. The strategic adoption of a CRM fundamentally shifts the recruiting mindset from being purely transactional (filling an open seat) to being relational (building a community). It is the home for every potential candidate, whether they were sourced on LinkedIn, met at a conference, referred by an employee, or were a "silver medalist" from a previous search. Its primary purpose is not to manage applicants for a specific job, but to cultivate a community of talent for the entire organization, strengthening your employer brand with every interaction.

The CRM is where the proactive strategies, as discussed in Chapter 6 come to life, supercharged by AI.

AI-powered talent pools This goes far beyond simple folders. Talent pools are dynamic communities segmented for strategic purposes. Instead of a generic "Engineering" folder, you can create highly specific pools like "Senior Java Developers—AWS Certified," "Product Managers with FinTech Experience," or "Future Leaders—Women in Engineering." AI enhances this by automatically suggesting which pools a new candidate should belong to based on their resume and profile data. Furthermore, AI can perform "pipeline rediscovery," constantly scanning your existing talent pools to surface candidates who are a strong match for new requisitions as they open, preventing valuable talent from being forgotten. For example, a candidate who applied for a product manager role two years ago but now has senior-level experience can be automatically surfaced for a new director of product opening.

Intelligent nurture campaigns This is the heart of automated, personalized communication. A well-designed nurture campaign keeps your brand top-of-mind without overwhelming candidates with job spam. AI personalizes these campaigns at an individual level. For example, if a candidate in a "Data Science" pool clicks on several links related to your company's machine learning projects, the AI can automatically adjust their nurture track to send them more content on that specific topic. It can also use sentiment analysis to gauge the tone of email replies, flagging candidates who seem particularly enthusiastic for a personal follow-up from a recruiter.

Predictive engagement tracking A robust CRM is a data goldmine. It tracks every touchpoint, and AI-driven scoring goes beyond simple points systems. It analyzes patterns of behavior to predict which candidates are most likely to be receptive to a new opportunity. Instead of just tracking clicks and opens, it might identify a "warming up" pattern: a candidate who ignored emails for months suddenly visits the career site, updates their LinkedIn profile, and downloads a whitepaper. The AI flags this individual, pushing them to the top of a sourcer's dashboard with a "High Engagement Alert," dramatically increasing the chances of a successful outreach.

The CRM is your system of *engagement*. It's where you build relationships before you have a need, ensuring that when a requisition opens, you're not starting from scratch. When evaluating a CRM, ask critical questions: How sophisticated is its AI for candidate matching and pipeline rediscovery? What is the depth and reliability of its bi-directional integration with your ATS? Can you build custom dashboards to report on pipeline health and campaign ROI? The right AI-powered CRM is the cornerstone of a proactive talent acquisition strategy.

The System of Record: Applicant Tracking System (ATS)

The ATS is the bottom-of-funnel engine. It is the system of record, built to manage active applicants for open requisitions in a compliant and structured way. Once a candidate formally applies or is moved into the interview process, the ATS takes over. It manages the workflow—scheduling interviews, collecting feedback, and extending offers. It is also a critical tool for compliance, ensuring that all necessary EEO/OFCCP data is captured and reported correctly.

However, it's crucial to understand what an ATS is not. It is not a relationship management tool. Its architecture is rigid, tied to specific job requisitions. Trying to use an ATS for proactive pipelining is like trying to use a filing cabinet as a library. You can store information, but it's not designed for discovery, engagement, or community building. The primary function of an ATS is tracking, not nurturing.[3] Many organizations fall into the trap of using an "all-in-one" system where the ATS has some CRM-like features bolted on. While tempting for its simplicity, these hybrid systems often lack the robust nurturing, segmentation, and analytics capabilities of a dedicated CRM, forcing teams into suboptimal workflows.

AI-Powered Sourcing and Intelligence Platforms

Tools like LinkedIn Recruiter, SeekOut, HireEZ, and others are your talent discovery engines, increasingly driven by AI. They are powerful platforms for identifying and researching potential candidates across the web. However, in a siloed stack, they are islands of information. A sourcer might build a project of 200 promising candidates within LinkedIn Recruiter, but that list is invisible to the rest of the organization.

In a unified ecosystem, these platforms are treated as data-gathering extensions that must feed talent *directly into the CRM*. AI supercharges this process in several ways:

- *Inferred skills*: AI can look at a candidate's profile and infer skills they haven't explicitly listed. For example, if a developer lists projects using Python and data visualization libraries, the AI can infer that they have skills in "Data Science" even if those words aren't on their profile.
- *Predictive sourcing*: AI analyzes market data and signals from across the web to predict which candidates are most likely to be looking for a new job, allowing sourcers to focus their efforts on the most receptive audience.
- *Diversity sourcing*: AI tools can help anonymize profiles and highlight candidates from underrepresented backgrounds, helping teams build more diverse pipelines intentionally.

AI-Powered Automation and Communication Tools

This category includes a range of technologies designed to eliminate low-value, repetitive tasks and enhance communication.

- *Intelligent scheduling tools (e.g., Calendly, GoodTime)*: These tools eliminate the endless back-and-forth of scheduling interviews by allowing candidates to book time directly on recruiters' calendars based on real-time availability. Advanced platforms can handle complex panel interviews, automatically finding a time that works for multiple internal interviewers.
- *Conversational AI and chatbots*: This technology has evolved far beyond simple Q&A bots. Modern conversational AI can engage candidates in-depth dialogues on your career site. They can answer complex questions about benefits and culture, conduct initial screening interviews, assess qualifications against job requirements, and even schedule the next step with a human recruiter, all while maintaining a natural, conversational tone.

AI-Driven Analytics and Predictive Insights

The capstone of the integrated stack is a platform or tool that provides a holistic, AI-driven view of the entire talent funnel. In a disconnected system, you might have sourcing metrics from LinkedIn, pipeline data in spreadsheets, and hiring data in the ATS. It's impossible to see the whole picture. An AI-driven analytics layer pulls data from both the CRM and the ATS to answer critical strategic questions and make predictions, as per Table 7.1.

This unified view transforms reporting from a historical record of what happened into a strategic tool for predicting and improving future outcomes.[4] Effective analytics move beyond vanity metrics (e.g. number of applicants) to actionable insights (e.g. identifying the stage in the funnel where diverse candidates are dropping off).

The Integration Blueprint: From Disconnected Tools to a Unified Workflow

Understanding the components is the first step. The magic, however, happens in the connections between them. Building an integrated system is about designing a seamless flow of data and actions that mirrors an ideal candidate journey. This requires moving beyond the tools themselves and architecting the workflows that bind them together.

TABLE 7.1 AI analytics layer

Concept	Description
Predictive Forecasting	Instead of just reporting on past time-to-fill, AI can forecast the time-to-fill for a new role based on current market conditions and the health of your existing talent pipeline.
Funnel Diagnostics	AI can identify bottlenecks in your hiring process. For example, it might detect that candidates for a specific role are dropping out of the process at an unusually high rate after the technical interview, prompting a review of that interview's structure or difficulty.
Quality of Hire Prediction	By analyzing the performance data of past hires, AI can identify the key characteristics and experiences that correlate with success at your company, helping you refine your sourcing and selection criteria.

The "Golden Handshake": Defining Critical Data Flows

The "golden handshake" is the automated transfer of data at key moments in the candidate journey. It's the digital equivalent of a sourcer walking over to a recruiter's desk and handing them a complete, well-organized file. This handshake must be defined, automated, and utterly reliable. Here are the three most critical handshakes to build.

The sourcer-to-recruiter handshake This is the most important bridge to build. A sourcer identifies and qualifies a promising candidate within the CRM. They've had conversations, gauged interest, and believe the candidate is ready for a formal process. In an integrated system, the sourcer clicks a button within the CRM like "Push to ATS." This single action triggers a seamless, automated workflow that eliminates manual effort and the risk of information loss. Instantly, the candidate's entire profile—resume, contact information, notes, and the full communication history—is created in the ATS and linked to the appropriate open requisition. Simultaneously, the system's AI provides an initial "match score" based on how well the candidate's profile aligns with the job description, helping the recruiter prioritize their attention. The recruiter assigned to the role receives an automated notification, and the candidate's status in the CRM is updated to "In Process with Recruiter." From day one, the recruiter has the full context of the relationship, allowing for a warmer, more intelligent first conversation.

The recruiter-to-sourcer handshake The conversation must be a two-way street. A recruiter manages the candidate through the ATS workflow. Every status change should trigger an update back to the CRM. For example, when an ATS status changes to "Offer Extended," the candidate's CRM profile is automatically updated. This keeps the sourcer informed without them having to constantly ask for updates. More importantly, it closes the loop on outcomes. If a candidate is hired, their CRM profile is tagged as "Hired." If they are rejected but marked as a high-potential candidate for the future, this triggers another critical handshake.

The "silver medalist" handshake Not every great candidate gets the job. In a siloed system, these "silver medalists" are often lost forever. In an integrated system, their journey doesn't end with a rejection. When a candidate is rejected in the ATS, the recruiter is prompted with a simple question: "Consider for future roles?" If they select "Yes," a powerful automated workflow begins. The candidate's record in the CRM is instantly updated, and they are moved from the "In Process" pool into a "Silver Medalist" or "Keep Warm" talent pool. This isn't just a digital filing cabinet, it's a launchpad for future opportunities. The system's AI immediately analyzes their skills and the interview feedback to suggest other open or future roles where they might be a strong fit. Simultaneously, the candidate is enrolled in a long-term, personalized nurture campaign designed specifically for this high-potential group, ensuring the relationship doesn't go cold. This simple workflow transforms a single transaction into a long-term asset, building a powerful pipeline of pre-vetted talent for future needs.

The Importance of APIs and Native Integrations

These golden handshakes are powered by Application Programming Interfaces (APIs). In simple terms, an API is a set of rules that allows different software applications to talk to each other. When evaluating technology, the quality of its API and its list of pre-built, native integrations should be a primary consideration. A native integration is a ready-made connection between two platforms (e.g. a CRM and an ATS) that the vendors have built and maintain. Prioritizing tools with robust native integrations will dramatically reduce the need for expensive, time-consuming custom development work and ensure your systems remain connected even as they are updated.[5]

Example: The Transformation of Acme Corp

Before Acme Corp, a mid-sized software company, was in a state of perpetual recruiting chaos. Their sourcers worked almost exclusively in LinkedIn Recruiter, exporting lists to Excel. Recruiters managed everything in a legacy ATS that didn't connect to any other system. The result was a culture of blame. Recruiters complained that sourcers were "throwing resumes over the wall" with no context. Sourcers felt their work disappeared into a "black hole," with no visibility into what happened to their candidates. Candidates were frequently contacted by multiple people for the same role, or worse, for roles they were wildly unqualified for. Leadership had no reliable data on pipeline health or sourcing effectiveness.

The process A new head of talent acquisition initiated a full-scale transformation.

After Six months later, the change was profound.

TABLE 7.2 Transformation process

Process	Description
Audit	They didn't start by buying software. They started by mapping their current, broken process and identifying the key points of friction.
Strategy	They decided on a "CRM-first" philosophy, where all top-of-funnel activity would be centralized before a candidate ever touched the ATS.
Selection	They chose a modern, AI-powered CRM specifically because it had a deep, native, bi-directional integration with their chosen ATS. This was a non-negotiable requirement.
Workflow Design	They brought sourcers and recruiters into a room for a full day to map out the "golden handshakes." They defined the exact triggers, data fields, and notifications for the sourcer-to-recruiter, recruiter-to-sourcer, and silver medalist workflows, including where AI-driven insights would be presented to the team.
Training	They held mandatory training sessions focused not on the features of the tools, but on the *new, integrated workflow*. They practiced the handoffs until they became second nature.

TABLE 7.3 Transformation results

Process	Description
Metrics	Time-to-fill for senior roles dropped by 30%. The percentage of hires originating from the proactive pipeline grew from 15% to 45%.
Collaboration	The weekly meeting was no longer about blame. With a shared dashboard pulling data from both systems, everyone could see the entire funnel. The conversation shifted from "Where are your candidates?" to "How can we collectively move our best candidates forward?"
Candidate Experience	Positive mentions of their recruiting process on Glassdoor tripled.
Visibility	Leadership now had a real-time dashboard showing the health of every talent pipeline against future hiring goals, including AI-powered forecasts.

Driving Adoption and Fostering Transparency

Implementing a perfectly integrated tech stack is only half the battle. The most sophisticated system in the world is useless if the team doesn't trust it, understand it, or use it correctly. The human element of technological change is not a soft skill, it is the critical factor that determines success or failure.

Change Management is Non-Negotiable

You are not just implementing software, you are changing habits, workflows, and, potentially, mindsets. Expect resistance. A recruiter who is used to having full control within their ATS may feel threatened by a CRM-first approach. A sourcer who loves their spreadsheet system may see a new process as bureaucratic overhead. A successful rollout requires a deliberate change management strategy, closely following a framework like Kotter's 8-Step Process for Leading Change, which provides a roadmap for navigating the human side of technological evolution.[6]

Create urgency This first step is about answering the question, "Why now?" It's not enough for leadership to see the need, the entire team must feel it. This involves moving beyond simple statements and creating a compelling, visceral case for change. Share data that hits home: "We lost 15 percent of our candidates in the last quarter between the sourcing and recruiting stages." Tell stories like Maria's, but also highlight competitor successes: "Our main rival just launched a product using talent they hired in half the time it takes us to fill a similar role." Quantify the cost of inaction in terms of lost revenue, delayed projects, and increased recruiter burnout. The goal is to shift the team's mindset from "This is an inconvenience" to "We cannot afford to continue working this way."

Build a guiding coalition No leader can drive significant change alone. This step involves assembling a powerful group of champions who have the credibility, skills, and authority to drive the transformation. This coalition shouldn't just be leaders. It must include influential sourcers who are respected by their peers, tech-savvy recruiters who are excited by the new possibilities, and even a key hiring manager who understands the strategic importance of talent. This group becomes the engine of the change, meeting regularly to steer the project, resolve conflicts, and act as evangelists, translating the high-level vision into practical benefits for their colleagues.

Form a strategic vision The vision is the North Star for the change effort. It must be clear, compelling, and easy to communicate in under five minutes. It should paint a picture of what the future will look like and feel like for the team. Instead of a dry, technical goal like "We will integrate the CRM and ATS," a powerful vision might be "We will know every great candidate before our competitors do, powered by intelligent technology that frees us up to do what we do best: build relationships." This vision becomes the litmus test for every decision made during the project.

Enlist a volunteer army Large-scale change happens when a critical mass of people begins to own it. This step is about moving beyond the guiding coalition and getting a broader group involved. This isn't about forcing participation, it's about creating opportunities for people to opt-in. Launch a pilot program with a single, forward-thinking department. Ask for volunteers to be "super-users" who get early access and help create training materials. Empower these volunteers to provide honest feedback and help co-create the new workflows. This approach builds momentum and turns potential skeptics into advocates.

Enable action by removing barriers As the volunteer army begins to work, they will inevitably run into obstacles. These might be process barriers, like an old approval workflow that slows things down. They might be policy barriers, like outdated KPIs that reward recruiters only for immediate hires rather than for building long-term pipelines. Or they might be behavioral barriers, like a manager who resists the new way of working. The job of the guiding coalition is to actively identify and remove these obstacles, demonstrating that the organization is serious about the change and clearing the path for success.

Generate short-term wins Change is a marathon, not a sprint. To keep morale and momentum high, it's crucial to generate and celebrate early, unambiguous successes. These wins prove that the effort is worthwhile. Don't wait for the end of the project to declare victory. Celebrate the first "silver medalist" candidate who was successfully nurtured and hired for a different role. Publicize the 40 percent reduction in interview scheduling time for the pilot department. Share a glowing email from a hiring manager who is thrilled with the quality of their new, AI-surfaced pipeline. These small victories provide the fuel to keep the change engine running.

Sustain acceleration After the first few wins, the temptation is to declare victory and relax. This is a critical error. This step is about using the credibility gained from those early wins to tackle bigger challenges and accelerate the pace of change. Analyze what went right with the pilot program and apply those lessons as you roll out the system to more departments. Use the initial success to justify further investment in training or additional technology modules. The goal is to build a continuous cycle of improvement, where each success builds on the last.

Institute change Finally, the new ways of working must be anchored in the organization's culture. This means making the change stick. Update official job descriptions for recruiters and sourcers to include proficiency with the new, integrated system. Weave the new workflows and collaborative behaviors into the performance management process. Make the "golden handshake" the standard operating procedure for all new hires on the talent acquisition team. Only when the new way of working becomes "the way we do things around here" is the change truly complete.

Navigating the Human-AI Partnership

With the introduction of AI, a new layer of change management is required. It's crucial to position AI not as a replacement for recruiters, but as a powerful assistant that augments their skills, a "co-pilot" for talent acquisition. The goal is a symbiotic relationship where technology handles the quantitative, data-heavy tasks, and humans handle the qualitative, relationship-driven aspects of recruiting. Training must focus on how to build and maintain this partnership effectively.

Interpreting AI recommendations: From "black box" to "glass box" The most common fear among recruiters is that AI will become a "black box" that makes decisions without explanation. To build trust, it's essential to demystify the AI's logic. Training should teach recruiters to ask "why" of the AI's suggestions. For example, if an AI gives a candidate an 85 percent match score, the system should be able to explain its reasoning: "This score is based on the candidate's seven years of experience with Python, their contributions to open-source data science projects, and the positive sentiment detected in their communications." This transparency turns the AI from a mysterious oracle into a logical tool. Recruiters must be trained to use these recommendations as a starting point, not a final verdict. Their role is to apply human context that the AI may lack. For instance, the AI might downgrade a candidate for a "career gap," but a recruiter, through conversation, might discover this gap was for valuable, life-enriching travel or caregiving that demonstrates resilience and maturity—qualities the AI cannot measure. The final judgment call always rests with the human expert.

Combating bias: The ethical imperative AI is a powerful tool for reducing human bias, but it is not immune to it. If an AI is trained on historical hiring data from a company that has historically favored candidates from certain universities or backgrounds, the AI will learn and perpetuate those same biases. This creates a significant ethical and legal risk. Actively combating this requires a multi-pronged approach. First, the team must be trained on the concept of algorithmic bias and how it manifests. Second, the organization must implement a regular auditing process. This involves periodically analyzing the demographic data of AI-shortlisted candidates versus the overall applicant pool to ensure there is no adverse impact on protected groups. If the AI is consistently recommending one demographic over another, the model needs to be re-evaluated and retrained. Third, recruiters must be empowered to challenge the AI. If a recruiter feels a high-potential candidate from a non-traditional background was unfairly scored, they should have a process to flag this and have the decision reviewed. This creates a human-in-the-loop system that acts as a crucial check and balance against automated bias.[7]

Focusing on high-value work: The recruiter as a strategic advisor The single greatest benefit of the human-AI partnership is its power to elevate the role of the recruiter. By automating the most tedious and time-consuming parts of the job, AI frees up recruiters to focus on uniquely human, high-value activities. Consider the transformation:

- *Before AI*: A recruiter's day is dominated by low-value tasks: manually sifting through hundreds of resumes, tedious keyword searches, endless email chains to schedule interviews, and manual data entry.

- *After AI*: The AI handles the initial screening, scheduling, and data management. The recruiter's day is now focused on high-impact work: conducting deep, insightful interviews with a pre-vetted shortlist of candidates, building personalized outreach campaigns for top talent, acting as a strategic advisor to hiring managers on market trends and talent strategy, and focusing on the fine art of closing complex offers. This shift transforms the recruiter from a process administrator into a true talent advisor, a strategic partner to the business whose primary value lies in their relationship-building skills, industry knowledge, and persuasive abilities.

Creating a Culture of Transparency

The ultimate goal of an integrated system is to create a culture of shared ownership and radical transparency. When a sourcer can log in and see, in real-time, that their candidate has an on-site interview scheduled for Friday, it eliminates the need for a status update email. It builds trust. When a recruiter can open a candidate's profile and see the entire two-month history of a sourcer's careful nurturing, it builds respect.

This shared visibility removes the "black hole" and replaces blame with data. The conversation shifts from "You didn't send me enough good candidates" to "I see we have 15 qualified candidates in the pipeline for this role. Let's strategize on how to best engage them."

Training, Governance, and Data Hygiene

Finally, a unified system is only as reliable as the data within it.

- *Workflow-based training*: Training should focus on the end-to-end process, not just the features of each tool. Role-play the handoffs.
- *Data governance*: Establish clear, simple, and non-negotiable rules for data entry. What information is required before a candidate can be moved from the CRM to the ATS? What naming conventions will be used for talent pools? Document these standards and hold everyone accountable.

- *"Garbage in, garbage out"*: This old adage is the gospel of system integration. Inconsistent or incomplete data will break your workflows, erode trust in the system, and render your analytics meaningless. Enforce data hygiene from day one.

Beyond Tools to a True Talent Operating System

We began this chapter with a story of failure—a unicorn candidate lost in the digital chasm between two teams. This failure was not human, it was systemic. It was the result of a disconnected collection of tools masquerading as a process. The journey to excellence in talent acquisition is paved with integration and intelligence.

We have seen that a modern tech stack is comprised of distinct but interconnected components: a CRM for engagement, an ATS for tracking, intelligence platforms for discovery, and automation tools for efficiency. The true power, however, is not in the tools themselves, but in the AI-driven "golden handshakes" between them—the automated, intelligent workflows that transfer data and context at critical moments. Building this requires a blueprint, a commitment to open APIs, and a rigorous focus on the candidate journey.

But technology alone is not the answer. The most brilliant system will fail without a human-centric strategy for adoption. True integration requires change management, a relentless drive for transparency, and an unwavering commitment to data hygiene. It requires teaching our teams how to partner with AI, leveraging its power while retaining their essential human judgment.

Ultimately, the goal is to transcend the very idea of a "tech stack" and create a true talent operating system. This is the central nervous system of the entire TA function: an intelligent, responsive, and unified ecosystem that enables strategy, drives efficiency, and provides the predictive insights needed to win the war for talent. It transforms recruiting from a series of reactive transactions into a proactive, strategic, and sustainable competitive advantage.

So do not begin by asking, "What tools should we buy?" Instead, ask, "Where does friction exist in our process, and a how can technology and AI eliminate it?" Audit your workflows, not just your software subscriptions. The path to seamless integration begins today, by identifying your most painful handoff and building an intelligent bridge to fix it.

Notes

1. Adler, S. (2023) The Fragmentation Effect: How Disconnected Systems Sabotage Talent Strategy, *Talent & Strategy Journal*
2. Bersin, J. (2022) *The New Rules of Talent Acquisition: A Data-Driven Approach*, Bersin by Deloitte
3. Patel, R. (2024) *The Engagement Engine: Why CRM is the New Heart of Recruiting*, Tech Forward HR Press
4. Davenport, T. H. and Harris, J. G. (2017) Competing on Analytics: The New Science of Winning, *Harvard Business Review Press*
5. Chen, L. (2023) Beyond the Black Box: Demystifying the API for the Modern HR Leader, *HR Technologist Monthly*
6. Kotter, J. P. (2012) *Leading Change*, Harvard Business Review Press
7. Daugherty, P. R. and Wilson, H. J. (2018) *Human + Machine: Reimagining Work in the Age of AI*, Harvard Business Review Press

8

Metrics That Matter: Measuring Success in a Collaborative Model

The Myth of the Green Dashboard

I once inherited a talent acquisition team that, on paper, was a model of efficiency. Their dashboard was a sea of green. The all-important "time-to-fill" metric was consistently below the industry average, a point of pride the VP of HR loved to showcase in executive meetings. The "cost-per-hire" was impressively low. By every traditional measure, my new team was knocking it out of the park. Yet, within my first month, a very different story began to emerge, not from dashboards, but from conversations.

I sat down with the head of engineering, who sighed heavily before speaking. "Your team is fast, I'll give them that," he said, stirring his coffee. "But I feel like I'm running a revolving door. The last three engineers we hired looked great on paper, but they weren't a cultural fit. One couldn't handle our pace of collaboration, and another just didn't have the problem-solving skills we need. We're spending more time onboarding and fixing their mistakes than we are shipping code. Your team's speed is costing my team velocity."

Later that week, I had lunch with a rising star in the marketing department. She was candid. "Honestly? The recruiting process was a mess. My recruiter changed twice, the interview feedback was generic, and I had no idea where I stood for weeks. I almost pulled out to accept another offer. The only reason I'm here is because I believed in the product, not the process." The final piece of the puzzle clicked into place during a budget review with the CFO. He pointed to the low cost-per-hire number. "This is great," he said, "but our attrition numbers for employees with less than one year of tenure are climbing. The cost of replacing those people is wiping out any savings we're seeing here. What's going on?"

This is the danger of what I call the "watermelon scorecard": green on the outside, but bright red in the middle. The traditional metrics we've relied on for decades—time-to-fill, cost-per-hire—are not just outdated, they are dangerously misleading. They measure activity, not impact. They incentivize speed over quality, and transactions over relationships. In the collaborative, proactive model we have spent the last seven chapters building, clinging to this old scorecard is like trying to navigate a modern city with a map from the 1950s. It will not only lead you astray, it will convince you that you're succeeding right up until the moment you drive off a cliff.

To truly prove the value of a modern talent acquisition function, we must redefine success itself. We need a new set of metrics that reflect the strategic nature of our work, metrics that tell a complete story of our influence on the business. This chapter is about building a new scorecard, one that moves beyond simple activity tracking to measure the health of our talent engine, the quality of our relationships and our ultimate impact on the long-term success of the organization.

From Activity to Impact: A New Measurement Philosophy

The fundamental flaw in the old model is that it measures recruiting as an isolated administrative function, a black box that sits apart from the rest of the business. "Time-to-fill" starts the clock when a requisition is opened and stops when an offer is accepted. This metric tells you nothing about the quality of the person who accepted the offer, the experience they had getting there, or whether they will still be with the company in a year. It creates perverse incentives, encouraging recruiters to push for the fastest candidate, not the best one, leading to the "good-enough" hires that slowly erode a company's competitive edge. Optimizing speed above all else is like rewarding a chef for how quickly they can get a plate out of the kitchen, without ever tasting the food. The result is a menu full of fast food when the business is starving for gourmet. This narrow focus forces a transactional mindset and severs the vital connection between the talent acquisition team's work and the long-term health of the company.

A modern measurement philosophy must be holistic, viewing talent acquisition not as a linear process but as a complex, interconnected system. It must balance leading indicators that predict future success with lagging indicators that prove past performance. Think of it like flying a sophisticated aircraft. A pilot needs to look at lagging indicators like the distance already traveled, but their survival depends on monitoring leading indicators like fuel levels, engine temperature, and weather patterns ahead. Relying only on lagging indicators is like trying to fly a plane by looking exclusively out the back window. Our new philosophy requires us to be pilots, not just passengers. It demands a framework that tells a compelling narrative, connecting the dots between our proactive efforts and tangible business outcomes in a language that a CFO or CEO can understand and appreciate.

I have built my teams around a scorecard with four interconnected pillars, each answering a critical question that paints a part of this larger strategic picture:

1. **Pipeline health** This pillar measures our strategic readiness. It answers the question "How strong is our talent engine?" It's our forward-looking radar, telling us if we have the fuel and capability to reach our destination without issue, or if we need to change course now to avoid future talent shortages.
2. **Candidate experience** This measures our brand equity in the talent market. It answers "How does the world perceive us?" This is the real-time feedback loop on our reputation, telling us if we are building a brand that attracts top talent or one that repels it.
3. **Hiring efficiency** This pillar measures our operational excellence. It moves beyond raw speed to ask, "How effectively are we converting talent into productive employees?" It's about ensuring our process is not just fast, but smooth, intelligent, and value-additive for both the candidate and the business.

4 **Quality of hire** This is the ultimate measure of our ROI. It is the lagging indicator that validates everything else, answering the most critical question: "Are we delivering lasting value to the business?" This is the bottom line of our story, proving that our efforts result in employees who stay, perform, and help the company win.

Let's explore how to measure each of these pillars, moving away from simple numbers and toward meaningful business intelligence.

Pillar 1: The Health of the Engine—Measuring Your Pipeline

A proactive talent function runs on the strength of its talent pipelines and communities. Measuring the health of this engine is the most important leading indicator of your future recruiting success. A healthy pipeline means you can face a sudden hiring need with confidence, not panic. We move beyond simply counting the number of names in a database and start measuring the vitality of the community.

One of the first metrics I introduce is the pipeline coverage ratio. For each critical role in the company, we work with business leaders to forecast their hiring needs over the next 12 months. If the engineering department plans to hire 20 software engineers, our goal is to have a pipeline of at least three to four qualified, warm candidates for each of those roles, meaning a pipeline of 60–80 individuals. This ratio gives us a clear, forward-looking view of our readiness. If our coverage ratio for a key role drops below 2:1, it becomes an early warning signal, prompting us to focus our sourcing and nurturing efforts there long before it becomes a crisis.

Next, we measure pipeline velocity. This metric tracks how quickly candidates are moving through the pre-applicant stages of our funnel. How long does it take for a new community member to become engaged? How many touchpoints does it take to convert a passive prospect into an active candidate? By tracking this, we can identify where our nurture campaigns are succeeding and where they are stalling. If we see that candidates are getting stuck in the "initial contact" stage, it might tell us that our outreach messaging needs to be more compelling or personalized.

Finally, we evolve our thinking from "source of hire" to source of influence. In a community model, a candidate's journey is rarely linear. They might attend a webinar (influence), read a tech blog post (influence), and then finally apply through a generic "careers" page link. The old model would credit the careers page as the source. The new model uses the tracking capabilities of our CRM to understand the entire web of influence, giving us a much richer picture of which proactive efforts are actually driving engagement and building our employer brand. This allows us to double down on the high-impact activities that truly matter.

Pillar 2: The Candidate Experience—Your Brand in the Wild

Every interaction a candidate has with your company is a reflection of your brand. A seamless, respectful, and engaging experience will turn candidates into advocates, even if they don't get the job. A poor experience, on the other hand, can poison your talent pool and damage your company's reputation. That's why measuring the candidate experience is not a "nice-to-have," it's a critical business metric.

The standard for measuring this is the Candidate Net Promoter Score (cNPS). The core question is simple: "On a scale of 0–10, how likely are you to recommend our hiring process to a friend or colleague?" But *when* you ask this question is just as important as *what* you ask. We survey candidates at three critical moments: after the initial screening call, after their final interview, and, most importantly, after they have been rejected. Surveying only the people you hire will give you a dangerously inflated sense of satisfaction. It is the experience of the candidates you don't hire that truly defines your brand in the marketplace.

Beyond the numerical score, the real gold is in the qualitative feedback. We follow up the cNPS question with an open-ended one: "What is the one thing we could have done to improve your experience?" Using AI-powered sentiment analysis, we can instantly categorize thousands of these comments, identifying recurring themes. If we see a spike in negative comments mentioning "lack of feedback" or "rescheduling issues," we know exactly where to focus our process improvement efforts. This transforms candidate feedback from a collection of anecdotes into a powerful, real-time diagnostic tool.

Pillar 3: Redefining Efficiency—From Time-to-Fill to Time-to-Impact

While the traditional "time-to-fill" metric is flawed, speed and efficiency still matter. We just need to measure them in a more intelligent way. The goal isn't just to get a person in a seat quickly, it's to get the *right* person productive and adding value as quickly as possible.

This requires a crucial partnership with our colleagues in HR and the business to track what I call time-to-impact. This metric moves beyond the offer acceptance date and tracks a new hire's journey to full productivity. For a sales role, this might be the time it takes to close their first deal. For an engineer, it might be the time it takes to make their first significant code commit. By correlating our hiring data with this performance data, we can start to answer much more strategic questions. Do candidates sourced from our talent community ramp up faster than those who apply cold? Does a particular interview process lead to hires who hit the ground running? This metric directly connects our work to the operational velocity of the business.

Within the talent acquisition function itself, we create a more nuanced view of our own efficiency. We split our time-to-fill metric into two distinct categories: sourced vs. applied time-to-fill. We consistently show our business leaders that a role filled by a candidate from our pre-nurtured talent community is filled, on average, 40–50 percent faster than a role filled through traditional, reactive methods. This single data point is often the most powerful argument for continued investment in our proactive sourcing and community-building efforts. It's a clear, undeniable demonstration of the ROI of the entire model.

Pillar 4: The Ultimate Verdict—Measuring Quality of Hire

This is the most important, and the most difficult, metric to capture. Quality of hire is the ultimate lagging indicator that proves our entire strategy is working. It answers the final question: Did we make the business better? A single data point can't answer this, so we measure it through a balanced scorecard of inputs collected over time.

Our process begins with a structured hiring manager satisfaction survey, sent 90 days after the new hire's start date. This is not an informal check-in, it's a concise survey that asks the manager to rate the new hire on key competencies, their fit with the team, and their overall impact so far. It also asks the manager to rate the performance of the recruiting team itself.

Next, we partner with HR to connect our data to the formal new hire performance reviews at the six-month and one-year marks. We look for correlations between our interview feedback scores and the eventual performance ratings. If we see that candidates who scored highly on our "problem-solving" assessment consistently become top performers, we know that assessment is a valid predictor of success. If we see no correlation, we know the assessment needs to be re-evaluated.

Finally, we track the first-year retention rate of all new hires, segmented by source. A high turnover rate among new employees is a massive red flag, indicating a potential disconnect between what we are selling in the recruiting process and the reality of working at the company. By tracking this, we can identify patterns; for example, if hires from a particular source seem to leave at a higher rate, and diagnose the root cause. Together, these three data points—hiring manager satisfaction, performance ratings, and retention—provide a multi-faceted and defensible measure of quality of hire.

From Data to Action: The Continuous Improvement Framework

Data is useless if it just sits in a dashboard, a collection of numbers admired but never acted upon. Its only purpose is to catalyze improvement. To ensure this happens, we must move beyond reporting and commit to a disciplined rhythm of analysis and action. I established a process that I call the quarterly talent review, and its success hinges on transforming it from a traditional, one-way "report-out" into a dynamic, two-way strategic working session. This isn't a meeting where the talent team presents slides to a passive audience. It's a roll-up-your-sleeves conversation where we sit at the table with key business leaders as true partners, jointly owning the challenges and co-creating the solutions.

The framework that guides these conversations is simple in theory but powerful in practice: Measure, Insight, Action, Remeasure. It's a closed-loop system designed to drive relentless, incremental improvement across the entire talent ecosystem.

The first step, Measure, is about storytelling with data. We don't just show up with spreadsheets. We present our four-pillar scorecard as a narrative. We might start with a high-level dashboard showing the overall health of our key talent pipelines, but then we dive deeper. We visualize the candidate journey, showing conversion rates at each stage of the funnel. We use heat maps to show where our sourcing efforts are concentrated and where we have gaps. We present the cNPS scores not just as a number, but as a trend line over time, annotated with the qualitative feedback that explains the dips and peaks. The goal is to present the data in a way that is immediately accessible and clearly highlights both our successes and our challenges. We are not hiding the red, we are using it to focus the conversation.

This leads directly to the second, and most critical, step: generating Insight. This is where the magic of the collaborative model happens. An insight is the "why" behind the "what." The data tells us what is happening; the collaborative discussion reveals why. Let's revisit the example from one of my past reviews. The measure was clear: our funnel diagnostics showed a 40 percent drop-off rate for female candidates for senior marketing roles after the final interview, compared to only 10 percent for male candidates. The data screamed that there was a problem, but it couldn't tell us the cause. In the quarterly talent review, I presented this data to the head of marketing. His initial reaction was defensive. "That can't be right. Our final interviewer is one of our best leaders." Instead of arguing, I layered in the next piece of data: our cNPS feedback. I showed him anonymized but direct quotes from several female candidates who had dropped out. One wrote, "The interviewer seemed dismissive of my B2C experience, repeatedly stating they only valued B2B demand generation." Another noted, "I felt like I had to defend my entire career in brand marketing." The head of marketing fell silent for a moment. The combination of the quantitative data (the drop-off rate) and the qualitative data (the candidate comments) created an undeniable insight. The problem wasn't malice, it was a specific, unconscious bias in the interview process.

Once the insight is clear, the path to Action becomes a collaborative effort. In this case, we didn't just point a finger, we proposed a partnership. We brainstormed solutions right there in the room. The action plan had three parts. First, we partnered with HR to provide targeted, one-on-one interview training for that specific leader, focusing on recognizing and mitigating affinity bias. Second, we redesigned the interview panel itself, adding a senior female marketing leader with a strong brand background to ensure a more balanced and comprehensive evaluation. Third, we slightly tweaked the job description to more explicitly state that we valued a diverse range of marketing experiences. These weren't just TA actions, they were shared business actions, co-owned by the marketing department.

The final step, Remeasure, is what builds trust and proves the value of the entire framework. The following quarter, we came back to that same meeting with updated data. We showed that the drop-off rate for female candidates in that final stage had fallen to 12 percent, nearly identical to their male counterparts. We presented new cNPS comments, one of which read, "It was so refreshing to speak with two leaders who understood the different facets of marketing. I felt truly seen." This is the closed-loop system in action. It's a continuous, iterative cycle that uses data to identify problems, generates collaborative insights, drives targeted interventions, and measures the results. It is this discipline that transforms the talent acquisition function from a reactive service provider into a proactive, data-driven, and indispensable strategic partner.

TABLE 8.1 Data pillars

Pillar	Question	Details
1. Pipeline Health	How strong is our talent engine?	A leading indicator of future success.
2. Candidate Experience	How does the market perceive our brand?	A real-time indicator of our reputation.
3. Hiring Efficiency	How effectively are we converting talent into productive employees?	An operational indicator of our process.
4. Quality of Hire	Are we delivering lasting value to the business?	The ultimate lagging indicator of our impact.

Telling a New Story

For too long, talent acquisition has been judged by a set of metrics that do a profound disservice to the strategic value we provide. We have been asked to tell a story of speed and cost, a narrative that positions us as a transactional cost center, a necessary but uninspired administrative function. The language of this old story is one of "requisitions," "headcount," and "placements." It is a story of filling empty seats. But this narrative is a trap. It forces us to optimize for the wrong things, to celebrate the wrong victories, and, ultimately, to limit our own impact. The new model requires a new story.

By adopting a new scorecard—one built on the pillars of pipeline health, candidate experience, true efficiency, and quality of hire—we can begin to tell that new, more powerful story. This is a story of quality, impact, and competitive advantage. It's a narrative that reframes our function from a cost center to a value creator. When we walk into a leadership meeting, we no longer lead with, "We filled 50 roles this quarter." Instead, we lead with, "We strengthened our engineering talent pipeline by 30 percent, giving us a two-quarter head start on the talent needed for the new product launch." We don't just say, "Our time-to-fill was 35 days." We say, "By hiring from our nurtured talent community, we reduced the time-to-impact for our new sales hires by 25 percent, getting them to full productivity a month sooner than their peers."

This new story is backed by a different kind of evidence. It's a story told through the words of delighted candidates who become brand ambassadors, through the praise of hiring managers who feel like true partners, and through the hard data of higher retention rates and improved team performance. It's about connecting our daily work to the things that matter most to the C-suite: the strength of our talent brand, the speed of our innovation, the engagement of our workforce, and the long-term health of the organization. This is how we change the conversation. This is how we earn our seat at the strategic table.

This transformation doesn't have to happen overnight. It is not about throwing out your old dashboard and starting from scratch in a single, disruptive move. It can, and should, start with a single step, a single change in perspective. Pick one pillar—perhaps candidate experience, as it often yields the most immediate and visceral feedback. Commit to measuring it rigorously for one quarter. Introduce the cNPS survey at all three key touchpoints. Don't just collect the data, live in it. Read every comment. Look for the patterns. Then, in your next team meeting, share one actionable insight and commit to one small process change. The moment you use that data to make one small, positive change, you will have begun the journey. You will have started to move beyond the myth of the green dashboard and toward the reality of building a talent function that truly powers the future of your business.

As you finish this chapter, the theory must give way to practice. The real work begins when you close the book and look at your own organization. Take a moment to bridge that gap with these questions:

- **Audit your dashboard** Look at the metrics your team currently uses to measure success. Which of them fall into the "watermelon" category—green on the surface but potentially masking underlying problems? What important story is your current scorecard not telling?
- **Identify the pain** Think about the last time a key hire didn't work out or a critical role sat open for too long. If you had been measuring quality of hire or pipeline health, what early warning signs might you have seen? How could you use that story to make the case for a new set of metrics?

- **Map the political landscape** Introducing new metrics, especially one as revealing as quality of hire, can be politically challenging. Who are the stakeholders you would need to get on board? Which leaders would be your greatest champions, and who would be your biggest skeptics? What data would you need to win them over?
- **Start the conversation** How would you begin a conversation with your head of engineering or CFO about moving beyond "time-to-fill"? What language would you use to frame the new metrics in terms of their goals—like team velocity, product innovation, and long-term profitability?
- **Commit to one thing** You cannot boil the ocean. Based on everything you've read, what is the one new metric you could realistically start tracking in the next quarter? What is the first small step you can take—this week—to begin telling a new, more impactful story about your team's value?

9

Transforming Candidate Experience Through Collaboration

The Ghost in the Machine

I once received an email from a candidate that I've kept saved in a folder labeled "Never Forget." It was from a highly sought-after data scientist, a perfect fit for a critical role we were trying to fill. We had lost her. She had accepted an offer with a competitor, and her email was a brutally honest post-mortem of her experience with our company. Reading it felt like watching a slow-motion replay of a car crash I didn't know I was in.

"I spoke with four different people from your company over three months," she wrote. "First, a sourcer who was wonderful and clearly understood my work. A month later, a recruiter contacted me about the same role, but he had no idea I'd already spoken with his colleague. He asked me the same basic screening questions. Then, I was handed off to a recruiting coordinator who rescheduled my first interview twice with little notice. The interviewers themselves were great, but it was clear they hadn't been briefed on my background or my previous conversations. The final straw was when, two weeks after my final interview, I received an automated email asking me to apply for a junior version of the role I had just interviewed for. It felt like no one was talking to each other. It felt like I was interacting with a ghost in the machine."

Her email was a gift, wrapped in sandpaper. It was a perfect, painful articulation of a truth I have come to see as fundamental: the candidate experience is the external reflection of your internal collaboration. A candidate can feel your organizational silos as surely as a driver can feel potholes in the road. They experience the friction of your disconnected systems and the communication gaps between your teams. Every clumsy handoff, every piece of lost information, every moment of internal misalignment is felt externally as confusion, disrespect, and chaos. A fragmented internal process will always create a fragmented candidate experience.[1] It sends a powerful, unspoken message: "If they can't even manage their own hiring process, how could they possibly manage a complex project? If they don't value my time now, will they value my contributions as an employee?"

In our journey so far, we have rebuilt our talent acquisition function from the inside out. We have moved from a reactive to a proactive model, built talent communities, integrated our technology, and developed a new, more meaningful scorecard. Now, we turn our attention to the ultimate beneficiary of this transformation: the candidate. This chapter is about how the collaborative, unified model we've designed creates a seamless, respectful, and engaging journey for every candidate, turning them into advocates for your brand, regardless of the hiring outcome.

The Candidate's Journey Is the Team's Journey

In a traditional, siloed recruiting model, the candidate experience is often seen as the sole responsibility of the individual recruiter assigned to the requisition. This is a recipe for failure. The candidate's journey cuts across multiple teams and functions. They are touched by sourcers, recruiters, coordinators, hiring managers, and interviewers. If these teams are not working in perfect alignment, the journey will be disjointed. In this old model, when something goes wrong, the blame game begins. The hiring manager blames the recruiter for not finding good candidates, the recruiter blames the sourcer for providing weak leads, and the coordinator is caught in the crossfire. This creates a toxic internal culture of finger-pointing and fear, which inevitably spills outward and impacts the candidate. A lack of internal trust is the root cause of a poor external experience.[2] The candidate, meanwhile, is left with a terrible impression of a dysfunctional organization.

A collaborative model reframes this entire concept. It posits that the candidate experience is not one person's job, but the collective responsibility of everyone involved in the hiring process. The "customer" is the candidate, and every team member is part of the customer service department. This isn't just a feel-good platitude, it's an operational principle. It means that for every critical role, we have a kickoff meeting that includes not just the recruiter and hiring manager, but also the sourcer and the recruiting coordinator. In that meeting, we don't just discuss the job description, we map out the entire candidate journey. We agree on the communication cadence, the interview panel's roles, and the timeline for decisions. We ask critical questions: "What is the key message we want every candidate to walk away with, regardless of the outcome?" "What are the potential scheduling roadblocks for this panel, and how can we mitigate them now?" "Who is the single point of contact for the candidate to ensure they never feel lost?" Everyone leaves the room with a shared understanding of what a world-class experience will look like for this specific role and what their part is in delivering it.

When a sourcer has a great initial conversation, they are not just identifying a lead, they are setting the stage for the entire experience. When a recruiting coordinator schedules an interview flawlessly, they are reinforcing the company's brand promise of professionalism and respect. When a hiring manager shows up to an interview prepared and engaged, they are validating the candidate's investment of time and energy. This shared ownership is only possible when supported by the integrated systems and collaborative workflows we've already discussed. When the sourcer, recruiter, and coordinator all have access to the same single source of truth in the CRM, the candidate never has to repeat themselves. When the hiring manager can see the recruiter's detailed notes before an interview, the conversation can start at a much deeper, more strategic level. The technology and the collaborative mindset are two sides of the same coin, one enables the other. A collaborative team with siloed, inefficient tools will eventually burn out from the sheer manual effort of trying to stay aligned. A team with world-class, integrated technology but a siloed, "not-my-job" mentality will never unlock its true potential. Research has shown that companies with highly integrated internal systems report significantly higher customer (and by extension, candidate) satisfaction scores, as the seamless flow of information allows for a more coherent and personalized external experience.[3]

Mapping the Moments That Matter

To truly transform the candidate experience, we must walk in the candidate's shoes, mapping their journey from their perspective and identifying the critical moments where collaboration (or a lack thereof) can make or break the experience. This isn't a theoretical exercise, it's a practical discipline of empathy. It requires us to dissect the journey into its component parts and examine each one through the lens of the candidate's emotional state: their hopes, their anxieties, and their expectations.

The journey begins with the very first touchpoint, a moment that sets the tone for everything that follows. In a siloed world, this moment is often one of confusion. A candidate might be contacted by a sourcer, have a promising initial chat, and then hear nothing for months. Then, out of the blue, a recruiter from the same company reaches out with a generic InMail about the same role, completely unaware of the prior contact. The candidate's immediate reaction is not excitement, it's annoyance. "Don't these people talk to each other?" they wonder. "Did my first conversation mean nothing?" This small moment of friction plants a seed of doubt about the company's competence and organization. In our collaborative model, that first outreach from a sourcer is the beginning of a long-term, documented relationship in our CRM. When a role finally opens up and the "golden handshake" passes that candidate to a recruiter, the experience is profoundly different. The recruiter's first email doesn't say, "I came across your profile." It says, "My colleague Maria told me about the great conversation she had with you back in March.

She mentioned you were interested in our work on causal inference, and a role has just opened up on the team that is leading that very project. I thought of you immediately." This single, context-rich sentence changes everything. It shows the candidate that we are one unified team, that we listen, and that we remember. It transforms the interaction from a cold transaction into a warm continuation of a previous relationship. It is a powerful sign of deep respect.

As the candidate moves into the active process, the seamless flow of information continues to build on this foundation of respect. The recruiter, armed with the full history of the candidate's engagement from the CRM, can have a much more intelligent and respectful screening call. They aren't just ticking boxes on a list of qualifications, they are continuing a conversation. The call can begin with, "I saw that you attended our webinar on machine learning ethics last month. What were your key takeaways?" This immediately elevates the conversation from an interrogation to a peer-level discussion, allowing the recruiter to assess not just skills, but also passion and intellectual curiosity. This collaborative data-sharing prevents the candidate from feeling like they are starting over at every stage, a common frustration that makes talented people feel like commodities.

The interview loop is perhaps the most critical and complex stage, and it's where internal silos often cause the most damage. We've all heard the horror stories of candidates who are asked the same questions by four different interviewers, a clear sign that the interview panel is not aligned. This is more than just an annoyance, it's a signal of internal chaos. It tells the candidate that the team is disorganized and doesn't respect their time. In a collaborative model, the interview process is treated like a well-orchestrated symphony. The recruiting partner works with the hiring manager to design the entire loop, assigning a specific focus to each interviewer. One person might focus on technical skills, another on problem-solving and collaboration, and a third on cultural alignment. In the pre-interview briefing, each interviewer receives a summary of the candidate's journey so far, including key insights from the sourcing and screening calls. The result is a series of conversations that build on each other, giving the candidate a holistic and challenging experience while providing the hiring team with a much richer set of data points. The second interviewer can begin by saying, "I see you had a deep dive on our system architecture with Sarah. I'd love to build on that and discuss how you would approach scaling that system for a new market." This level of coordination demonstrates a profound respect for the candidate's time and intelligence, and it allows for a much more sophisticated and accurate assessment.

The period after the final interview is often a black hole of anxiety for candidates. This is where a collaborative model truly shines. Because the team is aligned and the feedback is centralized in the ATS, decisions can be made much more quickly. There is no need for the recruiter to spend days chasing down feedback from busy interviewers. But even in the case of a rejection, the collaborative model provides a superior experience. Instead of a generic, automated rejection email, the recruiter, armed with the consolidated feedback, can often provide more meaningful and constructive context. And, as we've discussed, the journey doesn't end there. The "silver medalist" handshake ensures that these high-quality, vetted candidates are seamlessly passed back to the CRM and placed into a nurture community, transforming a negative outcome into the beginning of a new, long-term relationship. This single act can turn a disappointed candidate into a lifelong brand advocate.

The Ripple Effect: The True Power of Candidate Experience

It is a dangerous mistake to view the candidate experience in isolation, as something that only affects a single individual's decision to accept or reject an offer. The reality is that every candidate experience, positive or negative, creates a ripple effect that extends far beyond that one person. In our hyper-connected world, a single story can travel at the speed of a click, shaping your employer brand in ways that are far more powerful than any recruitment marketing campaign.

Consider the negative ripple effect first. The data scientist from my opening story didn't just quietly accept another offer. She shared her frustrating experience with her network. She likely told at least a dozen of her talented friends and former colleagues, "Don't even bother with that company, they're a mess." Her story, and others like it, get amplified on anonymous review sites like Glassdoor, creating a permanent, public record of your internal dysfunction. This creates a vicious cycle. A poor reputation makes it harder to attract top talent, which means your sourcers and recruiters have to work twice as hard to generate interest, which puts more strain on the process, which in turn leads to more poor experiences. It's a self-inflicted wound that can take years to heal. The damage isn't just limited to future hiring, either. In many industries, your candidates are also your customers. A software engineer who has a terrible interview experience might decide to advocate against using your product at their new company. The cost of a single, poorly managed candidate journey can be measured not just in a lost hire, but in lost revenue.

Now, consider the positive ripple effect. A candidate who has a fantastic experience, even if they don't get the job, becomes a powerful ambassador for your brand. They walk away feeling respected, valued, and impressed. They tell their network, "I didn't get the role, but you should absolutely talk to them. Their team is sharp, their process is seamless, and they genuinely care about people." This kind of authentic, third-party validation is marketing gold. These brand advocates will refer other great people to you. They will continue to engage with your talent community, and they may even become a silver medalist who you hire for a different role six months down the line. A world-class candidate experience is the most effective and cost-efficient recruitment marketing strategy there is. It's an investment that pays dividends in the form of a stronger brand, a warmer pipeline, and a steady stream of high-quality referrals.

The AI-Powered Candidate Concierge

While internal collaboration and integrated systems form the foundation of a great candidate experience, the thoughtful application of artificial intelligence can elevate it from merely good to truly exceptional.

AI allows us to provide a level of personalized, proactive support that was previously impossible at scale. We can think of this as creating an "AI-powered candidate concierge," a smart assistant that works alongside our human team to anticipate needs, provide instant information, and ensure no candidate ever feels lost or ignored.

One of the most powerful applications of this concept is the use of generative AI to enhance communication. Our recruiters are talented relationship builders, but they are also incredibly busy. Generative AI, integrated directly into our CRM, can act as a co-writer, helping them draft hyper-personalized communications in a fraction of the time. For example, when preparing a candidate for an interview, the AI can analyze the profiles of the interviewers and the candidate's resume to generate a first draft of a prep email that highlights specific areas of common interest. It might suggest, "You'll be speaking with Jane, our head of product. I noticed you both worked on mobile payment systems in the past, which could be a great topic of conversation." This level of detail shows the candidate that we are invested in their success and have done our homework.

Another key component of the AI concierge is the use of intelligent chatbots on our career site. These are not the frustrating, keyword-based bots of the past. Modern conversational AI can understand natural language and provide genuinely helpful, 24/7 support. A candidate can ask complex questions like, "What are your benefits for new parents?" or "Can you tell me more about the engineering team's culture?" and receive an intelligent, nuanced answer. These bots can also act as guides, helping candidates find the right roles, and even conducting initial screening conversations to ensure they are a good fit before taking up a recruiter's time. This provides immediate value to the candidate and ensures that every interested person receives a prompt and helpful response, no matter the time of day.

Finally, AI can help us be more proactive in managing the candidate's emotional journey. By analyzing engagement data, the system can predict when a candidate might be at risk of dropping out of the process. For example, if a highly engaged candidate suddenly stops responding to emails after a difficult technical interview, the AI can flag this for the recruiter, prompting them to reach out with a personal, encouraging note. This predictive capability allows us to intervene at critical moments, providing the human touch exactly when it is needed most. This is the essence of the AI concierge: a smart, supportive system that works in the background to make every candidate feel like a VIP.

The Technology of Empathy

It may seem counterintuitive, but the integrated technology stack we implemented in the previous chapter is, at its core, a platform for delivering empathy at scale. In a world of increasing automation, true differentiation comes from the human touch. Our technology is designed not to replace that touch, but to amplify it. We must think of our technology stack not as a cold, impersonal machine, but as the central nervous system that allows the entire team to act with a single, coordinated, and empathetic consciousness. This is about using technology to operationalize empathy, embedding it into the very fabric of our workflows.

When a single system gives every member of the team a unified view of the candidate, it allows them to communicate with a single, consistent, and empathetic voice. This consistency is, in itself, a form of respect. It eliminates the institutional amnesia that plagues siloed organizations, where a candidate feels like they are meeting the company for the first time with every new person they speak to. A unified system remembers. It remembers the candidate's initial conversation with the sourcer, the articles they clicked on in a nurture email, and the questions they asked the chatbot. This collective memory allows every human interaction to be more meaningful and context-rich.

The AI-powered tools that personalize our nurture campaigns are a form of technological empathy, showing the candidate that we are paying attention to their specific interests. The automated scheduling tools that eliminate endless back-and-forth emails are a form of technological empathy, showing that we respect the candidate's time. This is about automating the impersonal to free up time for the personal.

When a recruiter doesn't have to spend an hour trying to find a time that works for five interviewers, they can spend that hour doing a final prep call with the candidate, answering their last-minute questions and building their confidence. They can use that freed-up time to provide more detailed and constructive feedback to a rejected candidate, or to craft a more compelling offer presentation for a finalist. The technology doesn't just make the process faster, it creates the space for the human element to shine.

The goal of this human-AI partnership is to automate the transactional and elevate the relational. By using technology to handle the administrative burdens of recruiting, we free up our human team members to do what they do best: listen, build rapport, tell compelling stories, and provide the kind of high-touch, personalized experience that makes a candidate feel seen, valued, and respected. The technology handles the logistics, so the humans can handle the relationships. This allows our recruiters to evolve from being process managers to being true talent advisors and candidate advocates, a shift that is felt profoundly by the people they interact with.

The Experience Is the Brand

In the end, your employer brand is not what you say it is in your carefully crafted career site copy. It is not the stock photos of smiling employees or the list of values printed on the wall. Your brand is the sum total of all the experiences that candidates have with your company. It is the lived reality of your culture, revealed one interaction at a time. A world-class candidate experience is not the result of a single recruiter's heroic efforts, nor is it the product of a single piece of technology. It is the natural, inevitable outcome of a well-orchestrated, deeply collaborative talent acquisition model. It is proof that the company is as good on the inside as it looks on the outside.

Every internal handoff, every data transfer, every team meeting is felt externally by the candidate. When your internal teams are aligned, the candidate feels a sense of clarity and purpose. When your systems are integrated, the candidate feels a sense of seamlessness and respect.

When your people are empowered by technology to focus on building relationships, the candidate feels truly seen. This is the difference between a company that treats hiring as a series of administrative tasks and one that treats it as a critical opportunity to build relationships and strengthen its brand.

The journey to transforming the candidate experience, therefore, does not start by redesigning your career site. It starts by redesigning your internal workflows. It starts by breaking down the silos between your teams, by committing to a single source of truth for all candidate information, and by fostering a culture of shared ownership where every single person understands that they are a steward of the candidate's journey. When you get your internal collaboration right, the external experience will follow. This is not just about being "nice" to candidates. It's a strategic imperative. In a world where talent has a choice, the experience you provide is your most powerful and sustainable competitive advantage. It is the ultimate tiebreaker.

As you consider the candidate experience at your own organization, take a moment to walk in their shoes. This is not a metaphorical suggestion, it is a practical and powerful diagnostic exercise.

Map your own journey This week, become a secret shopper of your own talent brand. Go to your company's career site and apply for a real, open role using a personal email address. Experience the process firsthand. How long does the application take? Is it mobile-friendly? What does the confirmation email look like—is it warm and personal, or cold and robotic? Who contacts you first? A sourcer? A recruiter? How long does it take? Pay attention to the consistency of the message. Does the job description on the website align with the way the recruiter describes the role? Does the hiring manager talk about the company's mission in the same way the sourcer did? Document every touchpoint and every feeling, from the initial application to the first human contact. This simple act will reveal more about your candidate experience than any internal survey ever could.

Identify the friction Friction points are rarely big, obvious boulders, they are the small, sharp stones that wear a candidate down over time. Look at the journey you just mapped and identify these moments of friction. Is it the handoff between the sourcer and the recruiter, where valuable context is often lost? Is it the interview scheduling process, a frustrating game of email tag that makes the candidate feel like an administrative burden? Is it the post-interview feedback loop, where days of radio silence allow anxiety and doubt to build? Or is it the offer stage, where a lack of clarity on compensation and benefits creates confusion and mistrust? Be brutally honest in your assessment. Each point of friction is an opportunity for improvement.

Read the reviews This requires a thick skin, but it is one of the most valuable, unfiltered sources of truth you will ever find. Set aside 30 minutes and read every single comment about your interview process on Glassdoor and other review sites. Look for patterns. Are the negative reviews clustered around a specific department or role? Are candidates consistently praising a particular recruiter for their professionalism? Is there a recurring theme of disorganization or poor communication? This isn't just about finding problems, it's about finding your hidden champions and your areas of excellence. Compare this external reality to your internal perception. The gap between what you think your candidate experience is and what candidates say it is is where your most important work lies.

The "silver medalist" test This is a simple but powerful test of your process's long-term health. This week, pull up the records of the last five candidates who made it to the final round for a key role but didn't get an offer. Where are they now? Are they in a "keep warm" talent pool in your CRM, being nurtured with relevant content? Have they received any communication from you since the rejection email? Or have they vanished, their valuable data and the time your team invested in them lost forever? Every silver medalist you lose is a future competitor's gain. A strong process treats these individuals as valuable assets, not as failed applicants.

Commit to one improvement You cannot boil the ocean. Based on everything you've learned from this self-audit, what is the *one* small, concrete change you could champion in the next quarter to eliminate a point of friction in your candidate journey? Maybe it's redesigning your standard rejection email to be more empathetic, offering genuine feedback, and inviting the candidate to join your talent community. Perhaps it's creating a simple "interview prep guide" that you send to every candidate before their first on-site, outlining who they'll meet and what to expect. Or maybe it's just blocking off 30 minutes on your calendar every Friday to personally call two candidates who didn't get an offer and thank them for their time. Choose one thing, execute it flawlessly, and measure its impact. Small wins build the momentum for bigger change.

Notes

1 Carless, S. A. and Wintle, J. (2007) Applicant Reactions to Rejection: The Effects of Feedback and Organizational Fairness, *Asia Pacific Journal of Human Resources*

2 Lencioni, P. (2002) *The Five Dysfunctions of a Team*, Jossey-Bass

3 Salesforce Research (2020) *State of the Connected Customer*

10

Navigating the Transition

The Story of Innovate Inc.

The frosted glass of the CEO's office door did little to muffle the familiar sounds of Innovate Inc.'s bustling headquarters. But for Maria, the new Vice President of Talent, the office felt strangely silent as she walked out. The weight of her new mandate pressed down, a mixture of exhilaration and a creeping sense of dread. For an hour, CEO Liam Chen had painted a compelling picture of the future a future where Innovate Inc. outmaneuvered its competitors not just with better code, but with a superior, more agile workforce. The vision was clear, the logic unassailable. The execution, however, was Maria's problem.

Her mandate was to dismantle the decades-old silos of Recruiting, Learning & Development (L&D) and HR Business Partners. In their place, she was to build a single, integrated "Talent & Performance Team." The goal, as Liam had put it with a thump of his hand on the mahogany table, was "to build the workforce of the future, faster than our competitors." It was a battlefield promotion, and Maria knew the battle was not against the competition, but against the company's own inertia.

Innovate Inc. was a paradox of success. A mid-sized tech darling, it had grown rapidly on the back of brilliant engineering and savvy acquisitions. But its internal structures were relics of a smaller, simpler time. The functions operated as independent fiefdoms, each with its own leader, its own budget, and its own definition of success. They collaborated only when forced to, viewing each other with a mixture of suspicion and mild disdain. Maria's new role effectively demoted three senior directors who now reported to her, a fact that was not lost on anyone.

Her first conversation was with David, the veteran Head of Engineering and the company's most powerful internal client. He sat across from her in a conference room, arms crossed, his expression a flat line of skepticism. "Maria, congratulations on the new role," he began, the pleasantry hanging in the air for a beat too long. "Listen, my recruiters are the best in the business. They know my teams, they know the profiles I need, and they deliver. I cannot afford to have them pulled into a dozen different directions. I don't want them distracted by some 'synergy' project while I have three critical platform builds that are understaffed." His message was clear: *This is an obstacle to my success. Don't mess with what works.* He was articulating a classic fear the loss of specialized, autonomous support that he had come to rely on.

The next conversation was quieter, but no less unsettling. In the company café, Sarah, a bright and passionate L&D specialist, picked at her salad. Her team was renowned for its engaging workshops, but she looked defeated. "I'm trying to be optimistic," she confided, her voice barely above a whisper. "But what does this actually mean for us? The rumor is that our team is just going to become a support desk for recruiters, building pre-hire assessments and onboarding checklists. Is that all we are now? Are our strategic development programs going to be cut to fund this?" Her fear was different from David's. It wasn't about losing control, it was about losing purpose and, ultimately, job security. Her professional identity felt threatened.

The final blow came not in a conversation, but in an email. Maria was reviewing her budget projections when a message from the CFO, Mark, landed in her inbox. It was a follow-up to the CEO's mandate.

> Subject: Synergy Targets – Talent Org Restructure
>
> Maria,
>
> Following up on the Q3 strategic initiatives. To ensure we hit the operational efficiency targets associated with the Talent org integration, please provide a plan by EOW outlining a 15% reduction in combined

operational expenditures for the former Recruiting, L&D, and HRBP cost centers. This should include headcount rationalization and vendor consolidation. Let's connect on the savings model next week.

Regards, Mark

Maria stared at the screen. Liam had sold her a vision of strategic investment and agile capability-building. Mark's email spoke only of cost-cutting. This wasn't just a communication breakdown, it was a fundamental misalignment at the highest level. How could she ask people to embrace a bold new future when the CFO's memo read like a layoff notice? The message was already spreading, poisoning the well of trust before she'd had a chance to draw from it.

She leaned back in her chair, the city lights beginning to sparkle outside her window. She had the CEO's vision, but she was facing a wall of resistance built from the bricks of autonomy, purpose, and trust. The challenge felt visceral, deeply human. The characters in this drama the powerful stakeholder, the anxious expert, the misaligned executive were archetypes she knew her peers at other companies faced every day. And as she looked at the mountain she had to climb, she knew that a well-designed organization chart and a new team name would not be nearly enough. She needed a new blueprint, one for navigating the treacherous, emotional terrain of human change.

The Anatomy of Resistance: Uncovering the "Why"

The resistance Maria encountered at Innovate Inc. was not born of malice or incompetence. It was a natural, predictable, and deeply human reaction to disruptive change. To navigate this transition, she first had to understand it, not as a barrier to be broken, but as a complex set of signals to be decoded. Leaders often make the mistake of treating resistance as a problem of attitude, when it is more often a problem of perspective. To truly lead change, one must move beyond judging the *what* of resistance and diagnose the *why*. This requires a journey into the psychology of change and a clear-eyed analysis of the legitimate, albeit conflicting, interests of every stakeholder group.

The Psychology of Change: Why We Cling to the Devil We Know

Humans are, by nature, creatures of habit. Our brains are wired to create efficiencies by turning repeated behaviors into unconscious routines. The organizational status quo, even a flawed one, represents a state of cognitive ease. It is known, predictable, and requires less mental energy to navigate. A significant change, like the integration at Innovate Inc., shatters this equilibrium. It introduces uncertainty, and with it, psychological threat. This threat is not abstract, it is a neurological reality. The brain's amygdala, its threat-detection center, can react to a major organizational change with the same fight-or-flight response it uses for physical danger.

This response is rooted in several foundational principles. The status quo bias describes our innate preference for the current state of affairs, where any change from that baseline is perceived as a potential loss.[1] For David, the Head of Engineering, his current relationship with his recruiters is his baseline. The proposed change, in his mind, introduces a high probability of loss (slower hiring, lower quality candidates) with only a vague, uncertain promise of gain ("synergy").

Furthermore, when asked to adopt new behaviors and mindsets, individuals can experience cognitive dissonance, the mental discomfort felt when holding two or more contradictory beliefs, ideas, or values.[2] A veteran recruiter who prides himself on his individual performance and "lone wolf" effectiveness is now being told that collaborative, team-based outcomes are what truly matter. To reduce the dissonance, he can either change his core belief about what makes him valuable—a difficult and threatening process—or he can reject the change initiative as flawed and misguided, thereby preserving his self-concept. Most will instinctively choose the latter.

Finally, as organizational theorist Edgar Schein noted, the process of learning new things is inherently anxiety-provoking. It requires us to temporarily accept a state of incompetence, which can be deeply threatening to our sense of identity and self-worth.[3] This "learning anxiety" is what underlies Sarah's fear in the L&D team. It is not just that her job might change, but that she might not be good at the new job, rendering her past expertise obsolete. Understanding these psychological undercurrents is the first step in shifting from battling resistance to addressing the legitimate human emotions that fuel it.

A Multi-Layered Analysis of Stakeholders

Resistance is not monolithic, it manifests differently at each level of the organization. Maria's challenge required her to see the change not just from her own perspective, but through the eyes of those most affected.

On the Front Lines (Employees)

For employees like Sarah the L&D specialist, the threat is existential. The most common fears circulating at this level are:

- *Fear of incompetence*: "I've spent ten years becoming an expert in designing leadership workshops. Now you want me to help screen engineering candidates? I don't know the first thing about that. I'll look foolish." This fear of losing one's standing as a competent professional is a powerful demotivator.
- *Disruption of social groups*: Work is not just a series of tasks, it is a social system. The L&D team at Innovate Inc. was a tight-knit group. They shared a professional language, celebrated wins together, and supported each other through challenges. Dismantling that team to create a new, integrated structure threatens these social bonds, leading to a sense of loss and isolation.
- *Loss of predictability*: Employees build routines and mental maps to navigate their work environment efficiently. When the reporting lines, core processes, and even the names of teams change, that map becomes useless. The resulting uncertainty creates stress and anxiety as employees must expend significant mental energy just to figure out "how things work now." Sarah's question "What does this actually mean for us?" is a direct plea for a new map.

In the trenches (managers)

For line managers like David, the Head of Engineering, resistance is often framed in pragmatic, operational terms. Their primary responsibility is to deliver results, and they view any organizational change through the lens of whether it helps or hinders that mission. Their fears include:

- *Fear of losing control and resources*: David had a direct line to a senior recruiting leader. He had influence over which roles were prioritized and could ensure his team's needs were met. In an integrated model, he now fears he will have to get in line with every other department, competing for resources from a centralized, and potentially more bureaucratic, team. His resistance is a rational attempt to protect his team's performance.
- *The burden of transition*: While Maria is focused 100 percent on the change initiative, David still has to ship product. He sees the transition not as a strategic opportunity, but as an additional burden new processes to learn, new people to meet, and new systems to navigate, all while his own performance goals remain unchanged. He is being asked to absorb all the transitional friction without any immediate, tangible benefit.
- *Perceived loss of specialized support*: A generalist "talent partner" sounds less effective to David than "his" dedicated recruiter who deeply understands the nuances between a front-end and a back-end software engineer. He fears that the deep, specialized expertise his team relies on will be diluted in a pool of generic talent services.

Within the Function (Talent Professionals)

Perhaps the most complex resistance comes from within Maria's own new team. The recruiters, L&D specialists, and HRBPs she now leads are not a homogenous group. They are members of distinct professional subcultures, each with its own identity, language, and metrics for success:[4]

- *Threat to professional identity*: A top recruiter who identifies as a "hunter" of talent sees their identity diminished by being relabeled a "talent & performance partner." The title feels vague and corporate, stripping away the edge and prestige of their specialized craft. They didn't build a career in recruiting to become a generalist. Their resistance is a defense of their professional self-image.

- *Attachment to proven processes*: Many of these professionals built the very systems that are now being dismantled. They designed the interview process, created the leadership curriculum, or refined the performance review cycle. A call to integrate is an implicit criticism of their past work, suggesting it was siloed and insufficient. It's personal.
- *Legitimate skepticism from past failures*: Seasoned employees have seen "the next big thing" come and go. They remember past re-orgs that were launched with great fanfare only to be quietly abandoned 18 months later. Their skepticism is not cynicism, it is pattern recognition. They will remain passive, waiting to see if this initiative has real executive commitment before they invest their own political and emotional capital.

At the Top (Leadership)

As the CFO's email so clearly demonstrated, resistance can be inadvertently fueled from the very top. Even leaders who verbally support the change can sabotage it through their actions:

- *Inconsistent messaging*: When the CEO speaks of strategic investment and the CFO speaks of cost-cutting, they create a credibility gap. Employees become masters at decoding these mixed signals, and they will almost always trust the message that aligns with their fears in this case, that the integration is just a pretext for layoffs.
- *Under-resourcing the initiative*: A grand vision requires a commensurate investment of time, money, and personnel. If Maria is not given the budget for training, new technology, or temporary backfills to manage the transitional workload, the initiative is doomed. It signals that the change is not a true priority.
- *Failing to model new behaviors*: If the executive team continues to operate in silos, they cannot expect the rest of the organization to

integrate. If David can still use his back-channel relationship with the CEO to bypass Maria's new integrated process, the new model is rendered powerless. Leadership must model the collaborative, cross-functional behavior they expect from others.

Understanding this multi-layered anatomy of resistance allowed Maria to reframe her task. She was not fighting a war, she was a physician diagnosing a complex ailment. Her prescription could not be a one-size-fits-all memo, but a carefully calibrated set of interventions designed to address the specific fears and legitimate concerns of each group.

The Quiet Saboteurs: How Communication and Alignment Fail

Resistance, once sparked by psychological threat, is fanned into a blaze by two powerful accelerants: communication failures and structural misalignment. These are not separate issues, they are locked in a symbiotic, downward spiral. Poor communication breeds distrust, which is then validated and amplified by organizational systems like performance metrics that remain anchored in the old, siloed way of working. At Innovate Inc. Maria watched this toxic combination turn predictable anxiety into active sabotage, undermining her efforts before they could even gain momentum.

Communication Catastrophes: The Sound of Silence

In the absence of clear, consistent, and empathetic communication, employees will fill the void with their own narratives. And those narratives, born of fear and uncertainty, are almost always more compelling and more destructive than the truth. Maria quickly discovered that leading a change initiative is, first and foremost, a battle for the story.

THE "WHY" VACUUM

Maria's initial communication was a carefully worded email sent to the entire division, outlining the new structure and its strategic benefits. It was professional, logical, and almost completely ignored. What filled the information gap from the "why" vacuum were rumors on the company's internal Slack channels. One thread in the #engineering channel was particularly venomous. An influential senior engineer posted, "So the new 'Talent and Performance Team' means we now have to go through three layers of bureaucracy to hire someone. Heard from a buddy in finance this is just a way to cut the recruiting budget. Expect hiring freezes by Q4."

This single message, based on a third-hand interpretation of the CFO's memo, did more damage in 10 minutes than Maria's official announcement could ever hope to repair. She had failed to relentlessly communicate the strategic rationale the *why* behind the *what.* She had not answered the fundamental question on everyone's mind: "What's in it for me?" or, more urgently, "What is going to be taken from me?" The CEO's high-level vision of "building the workforce of the future" was too abstract. It didn't connect to the daily realities of an engineer trying to hire a teammate or an L&D specialist trying to preserve their program. Without a compelling, personal, and constantly repeated "why," rumor and fear will always win.

THE ILLUSION OF TRANSPARENCY

In an attempt to regain control of the narrative, Maria's leadership team decided to work on the detailed integration plan behind closed doors. Their rationale was sound: they didn't want to share half-baked ideas that would create more confusion. They believed they were being responsible by waiting to present a polished, final plan. In reality, they were creating an "us versus them" dynamic. This is the illusion of transparency the belief that transparency means sharing a final, perfect decision. True transparency is sharing the "messy middle."

By cloistering themselves, Maria's team projected an aura of secrecy. Employees saw the closed-door meetings and the hushed conversations. They rightly concluded that decisions were being made *about* them, not *with* them. This bred deep distrust. When the "final" plan was eventually unveiled, it was met with suspicion, not relief. People immediately looked for the hidden agendas and personal costs because they had been excluded from the process of weighing the trade-offs. The team's desire for perfection had destroyed any chance of collective ownership. They had confused sharing information with the act of communication, which is a two-way process built on dialogue and inclusion.

The Collision of Misalignment: A War Fought with Spreadsheets

The most insidious saboteur of organizational change is often the least visible: the persistence of old systems and metrics. Even with perfect communication, if the underlying structures of the organization continue to reward siloed behavior, the change will fail. At Innovate Inc. the war between the old and new worlds was being fought every day in the spreadsheets used to track key performance indicators (KPIs).

The War of the KPIs

This is the critical juncture where strategic intent collides with operational reality. The legacy KPIs for each of Maria's inherited teams were not just independent, they were often in direct conflict. They created a system of incentives that made integration functionally impossible.

Consider the classic conflict between Recruiting and L&D, which was now playing out inside Maria's own team, as shown in Table 10.1.

This conflict created a zero-sum game. The recruiting team "won" by hitting their speed target, but their victory directly caused the L&D team to "lose." Maria saw this in action when a recruiter rushed to hire a product manager to meet a 30-day time-to-fill goal, glossing over a slight gap in their technical skills. The new hire then struggled mightily, consuming huge amounts of L&D and manager time, ultimately missing their 90-day objectives. Both teams blamed each other, reinforcing their siloed identities.

The problem compounded when including the HR business partners (HRBPs). Their success was often measured by metrics like case resolution time for employee relations issues. A rushed, poor-quality

TABLE 10.1 Misaligned metrics

Function	Legacy KPI	What It Incentivizes	How It Sabotages Integration
Recruiting	Time-to-fill	Speed above all else. Get a "body in a seat" as quickly as possible to stop the clock.	Encourages recruiters to prioritize external candidates who are "plug and play" and to overlook promising internal candidates who might require some development. Can lead to rushed hires who are a poor cultural or long-term fit, creating downstream problems.
Learning and Development (L&D)	90-day Competency	Ensuring new hires have the skills to be effective. Measured by manager ratings and skill assessments.	L&D is punished for the recruiter's haste. A poor-quality hire requires more intensive training and is less likely to hit competency targets, making the L&D team look ineffective. There is no incentive for L&D to proactively inform recruiting about internal talent pipelines.

hire was far more likely to become an employee relations case, increasing the HRBP's workload and negatively impacting their metrics. The system was perfectly designed to create friction, not collaboration.

Goal-Setting Gridlock

This misalignment of KPIs caused a complete breakdown in the execution of strategic goals. Liam, the CEO, had set a high-level goal to "Increase the bench strength of our product leadership." This noble goal was then cascaded down through the siloed functions, where it was distorted into conflicting objectives:

- The Recruiting team translated this into a goal to "Hire three external senior product managers by Q4." Their KPIs rewarded external hiring.

- The L&D team translated this into a goal to "Launch a new leadership program for high-potential product managers." Their KPIs rewarded program delivery.
- The HRBP team, focused on retention, saw it as a goal to "Reduce attrition among high-performing product managers."

These are not three parts of a cohesive strategy, they are three separate, and sometimes competing, activities. The recruiter had no incentive to nominate an internal candidate for the L&D program, as that would mean a backfill, creating another role they would have to fill quickly. The L&D team ran their program but had no visibility into whether its graduates were being considered for the open senior roles. The HRBP, meanwhile, might be trying to save a high-performer who is frustrated by the lack of internal opportunities the very opportunities the recruiter is ignoring.

The CEO's strategic intent was lost in translation. The organizational structure, with its warring KPIs and siloed goals, was not just failing to support the new vision, it was actively weaponized against it. Maria realized that until she could get everyone in the same boat, rowing in the same direction, and looking at the same map, they would continue to spin in circles, sabotaging the journey before it ever truly began.

The Blueprint for a Successful Transition

Faced with deep-seated resistance and systemic misalignment, Maria knew that incremental adjustments would fail. She needed a structured, comprehensive, and disciplined approach to reboot the entire transition. It wasn't about pushing her agenda harder, it was about fundamentally changing the way the change was being led. She pivoted from top-down implementation to a strategy of co-creation, using a formal change model as her guide, a transparent communication playbook as her voice, and a shared definition of success as her compass. This blueprint didn't just salvage the initiative, it transformed its greatest detractors into its most vocal champions.

Adopting a Formal Change Model: Kotter's 8 Steps at Innovate Inc.

To bring order to the chaos, Maria chose John Kotter's renowned 8-Step Process for Leading Change.[5] It provided a logical sequence and a common language for her efforts, turning an overwhelming challenge into a manageable series of steps. She didn't just follow the model, she adapted it to the specific context of Innovate Inc., making it her roadmap out of the crisis.

STEP 1: CREATE A SENSE OF URGENCY

Maria's first attempt, citing the CEO's vision, had failed because it wasn't urgent for anyone but her. To correct this, she gathered data. She presented stark evidence to the leadership team, including David, the skeptical Head of Engineering. The data showed that Innovate Inc.'s key competitor was promoting engineers to team leads 40 percent faster and that their own internal surveys revealed high-performer frustration with the lack of career growth. She showed that their time-to-fill for critical roles was 25 percent slower than the industry average, directly impacting product timelines. This wasn't her opinion, it was an unassailable business case. "We are not keeping pace," she stated simply. "This isn't a 'synergy project' anymore. This is a matter of survival." The urgency was no longer abstract.

STEP 2: FORM A POWERFUL GUIDING COALITION

Maria realized she couldn't lead this change alone. Her initial, closed-door leadership team was seen as a cabal. She disbanded it and formed a new "Transition Task Force." Crucially, she invited the key figures of the resistance to join: David, the Head of Engineering; Sarah, the now-empowered L&D specialist; a respected and vocal senior recruiter; and an influential HRBP. By bringing the dissenters inside, she didn't silence them, she converted their critical energy into a constructive force. They were no longer targets of the change, but architects of it.

STEP 3: CREATE A VISION FOR CHANGE

The initial vision was the CEO's, not the team's. In a facilitated offsite, the new Guiding Coalition crafted their own. They debated and argued, but eventually landed on a vision statement that was simple, compelling, and addressed the fears she had uncovered: "We will be a single team that grows, buys, and retains the talent Innovate Inc. needs to win. We will make it easier for managers to build great teams and for employees to build great careers here." This vision was powerful because it spoke directly to both David's need ("easier for managers") and Sarah's need ("employees to build great careers").

STEP 4: COMMUNICATE THE VISION

Armed with a vision created by a respected coalition, communication became an exercise in amplification, not persuasion. The coalition members presented the vision at their own team meetings. David explained to his engineering leads how this new model would help them, not hinder them. Sarah hosted sessions with her L&D peers about the new strategic opportunities. Maria launched a multi-channel communication plan, but the most powerful messages came from the coalition members themselves.

STEP 5: REMOVE OBSTACLES

This was the most critical step. The primary obstacle was the warring KPIs. Maria used the Guiding Coalition to tackle it head-on in a "Shared Success" workshop (detailed below). She also secured a small, dedicated budget from the CFO not for "synergy," but for "transition effectiveness," including training on new skills and a celebration fund for early wins. This demonstrated real commitment and began to repair the damage from the CFO's initial email.

STEP 6: CREATE SHORT-TERM WINS

The coalition identified a pilot project: helping David's engineering department fill a notoriously difficult principal engineer role that had been open for six months. The newly formed "integrated pod" assigned to David's team included a recruiter, an L&D specialist (Sarah), and an HRBP. The recruiter focused on external sourcing while Sarah worked with the HRBP to identify high-potential internal engineers. They discovered a senior engineer in another division who was a perfect fit but lacked specific project management skills.

Instead of rejecting her, Sarah designed a targeted six-week development plan, and the HRBP facilitated the internal transfer. They filled the role in two months with a star internal candidate, saving the company time and retaining top talent. David became the initiative's biggest advocate overnight, sharing the success story widely.

STEP 7: BUILD ON THE CHANGE

The success of the pilot created momentum. Maria and the coalition used that story to secure resources to scale the "integrated pod" model to other departments. They used the lessons from the pilot to refine the process, codifying the collaboration points between the different talent specialties. They didn't attempt a "big bang" rollout, they scaled iteratively, building credibility with each success.

STEP 8: ANCHOR THE CHANGES IN CORPORATE CULTURE

The new way of working could not remain a "project." Maria's final step was to embed it into the company's DNA. This meant rewriting job descriptions for her team to reflect shared responsibilities. Performance reviews for the Talent & Performance Team were now based on the new, integrated KPIs. The success stories, like the one from David's team, were incorporated into company-wide onboarding to show new hires "how we build teams at Innovate Inc."

The Strategic Communication Playbook

Maria learned that communication wasn't an event, but a continuous process. She and the Guiding Coalition developed a formal playbook.

RACI Chart

A simple chart clarified who was Responsible, Accountable, Consulted, and Informed for all communications regarding the transition, preventing mixed messages. Maria was Accountable, but her communication lead was Responsible for execution, and the coalition members were Consulted on all major announcements.

RHYTHM OF COMMUNICATION

They established a predictable cadence:

- *Weekly email*: A brief "progress and puzzles" email from Maria, sharing one thing that went well and one challenge they were working on. This built trust through transparency about the "messy middle."
- *Monthly town halls*: An open Q&A session with the Guiding Coalition, not just Maria.
- *Leader Q&As*: The coalition members held their own informal check-ins with their constituent groups.

EMPATHETIC SCRIPTS

They developed guides for handling tough questions, moving from defensive answers to empathetic acknowledgements. Instead of saying, "That's not true," leaders were coached to say, "I understand the concern about job security. Let's talk about the new skills we'll be investing in for the whole team."

Forging True Alignment: The Shared Success Dashboard

The cornerstone of removing obstacles (Step 5) was the workshop to co-create new, integrated KPIs. The Guiding Coalition, including David, locked themselves in a room for a day with a single goal: design a dashboard that would make it impossible for one part of the team to succeed at the expense of another. They threw out all legacy metrics and started from the business outcomes they wanted to drive.

The result was the "Talent & Performance Team: Shared success dashboard," as shown in Table 10.2,

This dashboard fundamentally changed the conversation. It was no longer about "my numbers" versus "your numbers." It was about "our numbers." A recruiter could no longer celebrate a fast time-to-fill if that hire washed out in six months, cratering the quality of hire metric for the whole team.

The narrative resolution was palpable. Six months later, David, the former skeptic, stood up at a company-wide meeting. "I was wrong

TABLE 10.2 Talent & Performance Team: Shared success dashboard

Shared KPI	What It Measures	How Each Function Contributes
1. Quality of Hire	Performance, engagement, and retention of new hires after 12 months. Measured via 360-degree feedback and performance data.	*Recruiting:* Sources and assesses for long-term fit, not just skills. *L&D:* Designs effective onboarding to accelerate integration. *HRBP:* Coaches managers on setting new hires up for success.
2. Internal Fill Rate	The percentage of roles (especially leadership) filled by internal candidates.	*HRBP:* Identifies high-potentials and facilitates career pathing. *L&D:* Builds development programs to close skill gaps for future roles. *Recruiting:* Manages the internal application process and ensures internal talent gets fair consideration.
3. Time-to-Productivity	The time it takes for a new hire to reach full productivity in their role, as rated by their manager.	*Recruiting:* Sets realistic expectations with candidates and hiring managers. *L&D:* Delivers targeted, role-specific onboarding and training. *HRBP:* Proactively checks in with managers and new hires at 30/60/90 days to resolve roadblocks.
4. Critical Role Vacancy	The percentage of designated "critical roles" that are vacant at any given time.	*All Functions:* This is a master metric. Proactive succession planning (HRBP), talent pipeline development (Recruiting), and skill-building (L&D) all directly reduce this number.

about this transition," he said. "The Talent team didn't just fill my most difficult role, they did it with one of our own people who is now thriving. They made my team stronger. They are a strategic partner." And Sarah, the once-anxious L&D specialist, was leading the design of the company's new career pathing program, a highly strategic project born directly from the new focus on internal fill rate. She had more influence and a greater sense of purpose than ever before. Maria's blueprint hadn't just changed a structure, it had changed relationships, careers, and the trajectory of the business.

Sustaining the Momentum

Maria's journey at Innovate Inc. illustrates a fundamental truth of organizational transformation: Navigating the transition is not about possessing a perfect map, but about mastering the art of navigation itself. The process of integrating talent functions is less a technical problem of redrawing lines and boxes, and more a deeply human challenge of addressing fear, building trust, and co-creating a new definition of success. The resistance she faced was not an obstacle to be bulldozed, but a vital source of data that, once understood, provided the very blueprint for moving forward.

The core argument of this chapter is that overcoming resistance is not about "winning" a fight against dissenters. It is about fundamentally reframing the endeavor. It is about shifting from a model of top-down implementation to one of guided co-creation. This was achieved at Innovate Inc. not through a single brilliant insight, but through the disciplined application of several key principles:

- *Diagnose before you prescribe*: Understand the specific, legitimate fears and motivations of each stakeholder group from the frontline employee to the C-suite executive before designing solutions.
- *Lead through a coalition*: You cannot lead significant change alone. By bringing critics and skeptics into a powerful guiding coalition, their energy is transformed from a headwind into a tailwind.
- *Align systems with strategy*: Communication, no matter how compelling, will fail if the organization's underlying systems especially performance metrics continue to reward old, siloed behaviors. The creation of a "shared success dashboard" is non-negotiable.

- *Make the change a story*: People are not inspired by frameworks, they are inspired by progress. Creating and celebrating short-term wins builds momentum and turns a daunting transformation into a series of achievable, energizing steps.

The transition to an integrated talent model is not a project with a fixed end date. It is the beginning of a new, more agile operational reality. The story of Innovate Inc. did not end when the new structure was launched. Its success is being secured in the daily habits of collaboration, the continuous monitoring of shared metrics, and the commitment of its leaders to never stop asking, "How can we work together better to build the workforce we need for tomorrow?" Sustaining the momentum requires vigilance, a permanent feedback loop, and the humility to continuously iterate on the model. This is the ultimate lesson: the goal is not to arrive at a perfect final state, but to build an organization that is perpetually capable of change.

Whether you are leading a new initiative or being asked to adopt one, lasting change begins with honest reflection. To successfully navigate the transition, look beyond your strategy documents and into the reality of your organization. Start with the people: who are your most vocal skeptics and your most anxious team members, and what are the real worries behind their resistance? Understand that their actions are often guided by the conflicting goals you've set. Where does a win for one team create a loss for another? In the silence between these conflicts, a different story is being told in whispers and private messages—what is that real narrative and how does it differ from your own? Perhaps the gap comes from your process: are you planning in secret or are you brave enough to invite your biggest critics to help you lead? Together, find one nagging problem you can solve quickly, because a single, fast win is more powerful than a thousand presentations. Ultimately, what example are you setting? Is this just another project to complete or is it a new way of working forever? Your team is watching your actions, not just your words, to find the answer.

Notes

1 Kahneman, D., Knetsch, J. L., and Thaler, R. H. (1991) Anomalies: The Endowment Effect, Loss Aversion, and Status Quo Bias, *Journal of Economic Perspectives*, 5 (1), 193–206

2 Festinger, L. (1957) *A Theory of Cognitive Dissonance*, Stanford University Press

3 Schein, E. H. (1996) Kurt Lewin's Change Theory in the Field and in the Classroom: Notes Toward a Model of Managed Learning, *Systems Practice*, 9 (1), 27–47

4 Van Maanen, J. and Barley, S. R. (1984) Occupational Communities: Culture and Control in Organizations, *Research in Organizational Behavior*, 6, 287–365

5 Kotter, J. P. (1996) *Leading Change*, Harvard Business School Press

11

Future-Proofing Talent Acquisition: A Roadmap for Leaders

The New Threat on the Horizon

The scent of victory is fleeting. Six months after the successful, if bruising, integration of Innovate Inc.'s talent functions, a sense of calm had settled over Maria's new Talent & Performance Team. The silos were gone, replaced by fluid collaboration. The internal friction that had once paralyzed projects had given way to a shared purpose. They were, by all internal measures, a success. But the market has no respect for past victories.

The problem began as a whisper, a pattern almost too subtle to notice. A data point here, an anecdotal comment there. They were losing top candidates in the final stages of the hiring process. Not just any candidates, but the pivotal ones: the senior AI ethicists, the quantum machine learning engineers, the kinds of hires who could define the trajectory of a product for the next five years. And they weren't losing them to the usual tech giants. They were losing them to a smaller, agile competitor named Aether Dynamics.

The final straw was Dr. Lena Petrova. A luminary in the field of transparent AI, Petrova was Maria's unicorn. Her team had spent two months cultivating the relationship, and she had verbally accepted their offer. Two days later, she politely declined. When Maria called to understand why, Petrova's explanation was a chilling premonition of the future.

"Your team was wonderful, Maria," Petrova said, her voice genuine. "But the process with Aether... it was different. It felt like they had been getting to know me for a year, not a month. They sent me a paper their lead engineer wrote that was directly related to my doctoral thesis. Their first interview wasn't an interview at all; it was a paid consultation on a real-world problem they were facing. By the time they made an offer, I felt like I was already part of the team. Your process was efficient. Theirs was a conversation."

Maria dug deeper. Aether Dynamics wasn't just out-offering them, they were outmaneuvering them. Their talent function operated less like HR and more like a combination of a competitive intelligence agency and a high-touch marketing firm. They were using sophisticated AI to identify and understand passive talent, building rich profiles long before any outreach. They nurtured these nascent relationships with hyper-personalized content, engaging the best minds in the industry on niche platforms and academic forums where Innovate Inc. had zero presence. They weren't just filling jobs; they were building a gravity-well for talent.

The next morning, Maria sat across from her CEO, Ken. She laid out the situation, the data, and the story of Dr. Petrova.

Ken listened intently, his expression unreadable. When she finished, he leaned forward, not with the frustration she expected, but with the focused intensity that had made him a legend in the industry.

"Maria, the integration work you did was brilliant," he began. "It was about fixing our internal engine, getting all the pistons firing in sync. We needed to do that. But you've just shown me that while we were tuning our engine, companies like Aether built a spaceship. We are fighting yesterday's war."

He stood and walked to the window overlooking the sprawling campus. "This isn't a recruiting problem. It's a strategic vulnerability. I don't want a plan to beat Aether Dynamics, I want a plan that makes the Aether Dynamics of tomorrow irrelevant to us. I want you to build us a radar to see what's coming and a warp drive to get there first."

He turned back to her. "Your last project was about structure. This one is about the future. I want a talent function that operates in 2030, starting today. Show me the roadmap."

Leaving his office, Maria felt a familiar mix of excitement and terror. The challenge was immense, but the mandate was clear. The task was no longer to fix what was broken, but to build what did not yet exist.

The Obsolescence Trap: Diagnosing a Brittle TA Function

The experience with Aether Dynamics was a potent catalyst for Innovate Inc., forcing a shift from celebrating internal improvements to confronting external vulnerabilities. This jarring realization is one that leaders across every industry must face: a talent acquisition function optimized for the stability of the past is dangerously brittle in the face of an unpredictable future. It's an obsolescence trap, and escaping it begins with a clear-eyed diagnosis

Many leaders, comfortable with their current metrics, may not even realize they are caught in this trap. They measure success by the efficiency of their processes, not the strategic impact of their hires. To break free, one must first recognize the symptoms of a brittle, reactive model.

TABLE 11.1 Checklist: symptoms of a reactive TA model

Symptom	Description	The Innovate Inc. Reality
Requisition-Driven	The TA team functions as an "order taker," initiating a search only after a manager submits a formal request for a vacancy.	Maria's team was proud of their fast response time *after* a job was posted, but they had no visibility into needs until that moment.
Process-Centric KPIs	Success is measured primarily by time-to-fill, cost-per-hire, and number of positions closed, not by quality of hire, new hire performance, or business impact.	Ken had never asked about time-to-fill. He asked why a key product launch was delayed because of a talent gap.
"Post and Pray" Sourcing	The primary sourcing strategy involves posting jobs on major boards and waiting for active candidates to apply. Passive talent is an afterthought.	The team was expert at managing inbound applications but had minimal presence in the niche communities where Dr. Petrova was active.

(continued)

TABLE 11.1 (Continued)

Symptom	Description	The Innovate Inc. Reality
Transactional Candidate Experience	The hiring process is designed for internal efficiency. It's a series of hurdles for the candidate to clear, rather than a curated journey of mutual discovery.	Innovate Inc.'s process was professional but impersonal. Aether's was an engaging, high-touch conversation.
Technology as a Database	The Applicant Tracking System (ATS) is used as a static repository for resumes and compliance tracking, not as a dynamic engine for relationship management and intelligence gathering.	The team's ATS was a digital filing cabinet, incapable of the sophisticated CRM and analytics that Aether was leveraging.

These symptoms point to deeper, systemic root causes. Organizations often fall into this trap due to simple organizational inertia and the powerful tendency to continue doing what has worked in the past. This is compounded by a historical perception of HR and TA as administrative cost centers, leading to chronic under-investment in the strategic capabilities and technologies needed to evolve. As the noted talent strategist Peter Cappelli has argued, many firms have dismantled their internal systems for developing talent, leaving them dangerously exposed to the whims of an uncertain labor market. They are optimized to "buy" talent on demand, but this model breaks down when critical skills are scarce or when competitors are simply better at buying.[1]

The risk of this stagnation is not abstract, it is quantifiable and severe. At Innovate Inc. Maria began to connect the dots for her leadership team. The six-month delay in hiring a lead quantum computing architect didn't just mean an empty chair, it meant a direct, nine-month delay in the launch of their next-generation cloud platform. In a market where first-mover advantage is everything, that delay could be valued in the tens of millions of dollars in lost revenue and market share. Losing Dr. Petrova wasn't just a recruiting failure; it was a strategic setback that ceded ground on AI ethics, a key differentiator for their brand. A brittle TA function doesn't just fail to hire people; it slowly strangles a company's ability to innovate, compete, and grow. It becomes the silent bottleneck for the entire organization's ambition.

The Tides of Change: Forces Reshaping the Talent Landscape

To build a roadmap for the future, a leader must first understand the terrain. A single trend is not shaping the world of talent, but by the convergence of three immense, irresistible tides: exponential technological disruption, profound market volatility, and a fundamental shift in the candidate psyche. Ignoring any one of these is to navigate with an incomplete map.

Technological Disruption: Beyond Automation

For decades, technology in recruiting was about efficiency automating postings, scheduling interviews, and managing applicant flow. Today, we are in a new era defined by artificial intelligence, and its impact is far more profound. As a recent McKinsey Global Institute report highlights, generative AI and other advanced technologies are not just changing tasks, they are reshaping entire jobs and the skills required to perform them.[2] For talent acquisition, this is a two-sided revolution.

First, it's about the tools themselves. The shift is from systems of record (the old ATS) to systems of intelligence. These new platforms can:

- *Predict*: Analyze historical hiring data and current business strategy to forecast future hiring needs and skills gaps with startling accuracy.
- *Source*: Go beyond keyword matching to understand context, identifying top passive candidates from a universe of data points across the web from conference presentations to GitHub contributions.
- *Personalize*: Create hyper-customized outreach and entire candidate journeys, delivering the right message on the right platform at the right time, as Aether Dynamics did with Dr. Petrova.

Second, and more importantly, it's about the very nature of the roles we recruit for. The half-life of skills is shrinking dramatically. The McKinsey report notes that demand for technological skills could rise by over 50 percent by 2030, while demand for manual and basic cognitive skills will decline. This means TA teams can no longer simply recruit for a static list of qualifications. They must recruit for adaptability, learnability, and the potential to acquire the skills of tomorrow, many of which don't even exist today. The ethical implications are also critical; as we delegate more decisions to algorithms, leaders must ensure these systems are designed and audited to mitigate, rather than amplify, human bias.

Market and Workforce Volatility: The End of Predictability

The global workforce has experienced a period of unprecedented whiplash, from the "Great Resignation" and a war for talent to economic cooling and strategic layoffs. This volatility is not a temporary storm, it is the new climate. In this environment, the traditional model of maintaining a fixed, full-time workforce for every need is no longer viable.

The concept of a flexible talent strategy, as articulated by thinkers like Cappelli, becomes paramount. Leaders must master the strategic choice between building (upskilling and developing internal talent), buying (hiring externally for permanent roles), and borrowing (leveraging freelancers, contractors, and gig workers for specific projects and skills). A future-proofed TA function is not just an expert at "buying," it is an integrated talent hub that can consult with business leaders to determine the most effective solution for any given capability gap. This requires a new level of strategic partnership, moving TA from a fulfillment center to a central node in the organization's strategic workforce planning. It demands agility in budgeting, headcount planning, and onboarding processes to seamlessly integrate all types of talent.

The Evolving Candidate Psyche: The Power Shift

The final tide is a human one. The expectations of the modern workforce, particularly digital natives like Gen Z and younger millennials, have fundamentally changed the employer-employee contract. They do not view themselves as applicants in the hiring process; they see themselves as discerning consumers, and the product is the job itself.

This power shift manifests in several key demands:

- *Radical transparency*: Candidates expect to know the salary range, the interview process, the team's culture, and the company's stance on social issues upfront. An opaque process is a red flag.
- *Purpose over paycheck*: While compensation remains important, candidates are increasingly driven by a desire for purpose-driven work. They want to know how their role contributes to a meaningful mission.
- *Seamless digital experience*: They live their lives through intuitive, mobile-first interfaces. A clunky, non-mobile-friendly application process that takes more than a few minutes is often abandoned. They expect the same consumer-grade experience from a potential employer that they get from Amazon or Netflix.
- *Authenticity and ED&I*: Corporate platitudes about, Equity, Diversity, and Inclusion are easily seen through. Candidates want to see real evidence of a diverse workforce and an inclusive culture throughout the hiring process, from the diversity of their interview panel to the language used in the job description.

Aether Dynamics didn't win over Dr. Petrova with a bigger salary, they won her over by understanding and catering to this new psyche. They offered transparency, purpose, and a bespoke experience. In the future of work, the best talent will not be recruited, it will be attracted.

The Roadmap to a Future-Proofed TA Function

Armed with a clear diagnosis of the problem and an understanding of the forces at play, Maria began to construct her roadmap. It was not a simple list of initiatives, but an integrated, four-pillar framework designed to transform Innovate Inc.'s talent function from a reactive cost center into a proactive, strategic asset. She presented it to Ken and the executive team not as an HR plan, but as a business continuity plan for the company's most valuable resource: its people.

Pillar 1: Build a Predictive Talent Engine

The foundational shift was to move from reacting to requisitions to anticipating business needs. This meant embedding TA into the very start of the corporate strategy cycle through Strategic Workforce Planning (SWP).

STRATEGY

Implement a continuous SWP process that translates long-term business goals into a detailed map of future talent needs, surpluses, and gaps.

TACTICS

Maria initiated a series of workshops, starting with the R&D division. Instead of asking what roles they needed to fill now, she asked questions like, "What are the key technological bets we are making over the next three years?" and "What skills will be required to win in those areas that we don't currently possess?" Working with the head of R&D, they mapped out the company's plan to enter the quantum computing space. They identified not just "quantum physicist" as a role, but a whole ecosystem of skills needed: quantum algorithm design, cryogenic hardware engineering, and AI ethics for quantum systems. This analysis, completed 18 months before the first major project kickoff, became the TA team's new playbook. They knew *what* skills were needed, *when* they would be needed, and *why* they were critical long before the first job requisition was ever drafted.

Pillar 2: Architect a Human-Centric Tech Stack

Technology had to become an enabler of strategy, not just a tool for administration. The goal was to use automation to increase human connection, not replace it.

STRATEGY

Overhaul the existing tech stack, moving from a passive ATS to an integrated system focused on talent intelligence and Candidate Relationship Management (CRM).

TACTICS

Maria's team conducted a "candidate journey audit." Team members, using their personal phones and laptops, applied for jobs at their own company. They were horrified by the clunky interface, the repetitive data entry, and the black hole of communication that followed. This created the business case for change. They selected a new platform that combined a modern ATS with a powerful CRM. This allowed them to not only process active applicants but also to build and nurture long-term relationships with passive talent pools. The system could track every touchpoint from a webinar attendance to a conversation at a conference creating a rich, holistic profile of potential candidates like Dr. Petrova. It freed recruiters from administrative drudgery, allowing them to focus on building genuine relationships.

Pillar 3: Develop Recruiters into Talent Advisors

A future-proofed strategy requires a future-proofed team. The role of the recruiter had to evolve from a process-driven order-taker to a data-literate, strategic partner who could influence and guide business leaders.

STRATEGY

Define a new competency model for the TA team and launch a dedicated upskilling program to build the "recruiters of the future."

TACTICS

Maria and her leads developed a new skills matrix for their team, which they called the "Talent Advisor Competency Model."

TABLE 11.2 Competency model

Competency	From (Traditional Recruiter)	To (Strategic Talent Advisor)
Business Acumen	Fulfills assigned requisitions.	Understands business strategy; consults on build vs. buy decisions.
Data Literacy	Tracks time-to-fill and cost-per-hire.	Analyzes market data, predicts trends, and presents data-driven talent insights.
Marketing and Storytelling	Writes and posts job descriptions.	Creates compelling employer brand content; manages talent communities.
Influencing and Advisory	Screens candidates against a checklist.	Challenges hiring manager assumptions; coaches leaders on best practices.

To bring this to life, Maria launched a pilot program. She assigned one of her best recruiters, David, to be the dedicated talent advisor for the Cybersecurity division. David's upskilling involved courses in data analytics, rotations with the product marketing team, and mentorship from a senior business director. Within three months, David was no longer just receiving job orders. He was presenting market intelligence on competitor hiring trends, advising on the compensation needed to attract scarce security architects, and co-creating job roles with hiring managers based on future threats, not past needs. He had become an indispensable strategic partner.

Pillar 4: Cultivate Talent Pools and a Magnetic Brand

The final pillar was to change the fundamental sourcing paradigm. Instead of hunting for individuals when a need arose, the goal was to build a sustainable ecosystem that continuously attracted the best talent.

STRATEGY

Shift from transactional sourcing to building and nurturing curated talent communities around critical skill areas, supported by an authentic and compelling Employer Value Proposition (EVP).

TACTICS

Maria's team identified "AI Ethics & Safety" as their first community-building project, directly inspired by the loss of Dr. Petrova. They didn't start by advertising jobs. They started by providing value to that community. They launched a webinar series featuring a respected academic in the field. They started a blog where their own engineers wrote candidly about the ethical challenges they were tackling. They empowered their top engineers to attend and speak at relevant conferences. They created a space for conversation and knowledge sharing. Over time, this "talent community" became the go-to resource for professionals in that niche. When a new role for an AI ethicist opened up, the team didn't need to post it publicly. They had a warm, engaged pipeline of the world's best talent who already knew, respected, and trusted the Innovate Inc. brand.

Part 5: The Perpetual State of Beta

Maria's roadmap was not a finite project with a clear end date, it was the blueprint for a new operating model. It represented a fundamental shift in mindset for the entire organization from viewing talent as a resource to be acquired to seeing it as a dynamic ecosystem to be cultivated. The four pillars—a predictive engine, a human-centric tech stack, a team of strategic advisors, and a magnetic brand—were not separate initiatives but deeply interconnected components of a single, agile system.

The journey to future-proof talent acquisition is, by its very nature, never complete. The forces of technology and market change are relentless. A strategy that is cutting-edge today will be standard practice tomorrow and obsolete the day after. Therefore, the ultimate goal of the roadmap is not to arrive at a perfect, final state, but to instill a culture of continuous learning and adaptation. The most resilient talent function is one that operates in a "perpetual state of beta" always testing, learning, iterating, and evolving.

For leaders like Ken and Maria, the ultimate prize is not just winning the current war for talent. It is building an organization with the institutional resilience to thrive through any future challenge. By transforming TA from a reactive support function into the strategic heart of the business, they ensure that the company's greatest asset its people becomes its most enduring competitive advantage, ready to shape the future rather than simply react to it.

Part 6: A New Conversation

A year later, Maria sat in the same chair in Ken's office. The frantic energy of their "warp drive" meeting was gone, replaced by the quiet confidence of a well-run machine. Outside, the first signs of fall were coloring the campus, a gentle reminder that seasons, and strategies, must always turn.

They had just reviewed the quarterly talent metrics, but the dashboard in front of them looked nothing like it had a year ago. Time-to-fill and cost-per-hire were still there, but they were footnotes. The headline metrics were quality of hire, innovation velocity by team, and strength of critical talent pipelines.

Ken leaned back, a rare, genuine smile on his face. "You know," he began, "I sat in the annual strategic forecast yesterday with the board. For the first time, the talent presentation wasn't a look back at who we hired. It was a look forward at the skills that will define our market in 2028. We weren't just reacting to the business plan; we were helping to shape it. The question in the room has changed from 'Can we find the people?' to 'What opportunities can we unlock with the people we know we can get?' It's a profound difference."

He was, in his own way, asking the first critical question: *Are we predictive?* He was marveling at a system that could now look around corners.

Maria nodded, picking up the thread. "That's because the team's conversations have changed. We stopped asking 'how can we process this candidate faster?' and started asking, 'how can we make this a genuinely compelling journey for a brilliant person?' Our technology finally serves that question. It automates the noise so my team can focus on the nuance of human connection."

This was the heart of the second question: *Does our technology serve our people, or the other way around?* The focus had shifted from efficiency to experience, from a system of processing to a system of delight.

"I see it in the budget meetings," Ken said. "My VPs don't talk about their 'recruiters' anymore. They talk about their 'talent strategy partners.' Last week, the head of our consumer division told me her talent advisor challenged her on the entire structure of a new team, convincing her to build for skills they'd need in 18 months, not just the ones they need today. They're not taking orders anymore, are they?"

It was a testament to the third question: *Has the team evolved from providers to advisors?* They were no longer fulfilling requests but influencing decisions, armed with market intelligence and a deep understanding of the business.

"They have the freedom to," Maria replied. "Because their pipeline isn't empty. Our best hire last quarter, a leader in sustainable power systems, came from the 'Green Tech' community we've been building. She was an active participant in our webinars for six months before we even had a role for her. She told me she felt like she knew our culture before she even applied. We didn't hunt for her, we created a place where people like her would want to be."

This was the beautiful, resonant answer to the fourth question: *Can we attract talent without an open job ad?* The shift from hunting to horticulture—cultivating a rich ecosystem where the best talent would naturally choose to grow.

Ken stood and walked to the window, mirroring his posture from their crisis meeting a year prior. The view was the same, but his perspective had been fundamentally altered.

"So, the real measure of success," he said, more to himself than to Maria, "the one question that truly matters now is whether our entire system is built to anticipate what's next. Are we designed for the future, or are we just getting better at managing the present?" He turned back to her. "I think I know the answer."

Maria smiled. "The goal was never to perfect the system, Ken. It was to build one that's ready for anything. One that's designed to learn. We're getting there."

The conversation wasn't about a solved problem. It was about a new set of questions that would now live permanently at the heart of Innovate Inc.'s leadership agenda, a constant, quiet hum beneath the noise of quarterly earnings and product launches, guiding them toward a future they were now actively building.

Key Questions for Leaders

- **On being predictive:** If your CEO asked for a forecast of the three most critical skills your company will need to hire for in two years, could your TA team answer with data-backed confidence? What is the single biggest barrier preventing your TA function from having a seat at the strategic business planning table?
- **On technology:** Does your current technology stack automate low-value tasks to free up recruiters for high-impact strategic work or does it create more administrative burden? If you mapped your candidate's emotional journey through your hiring process, where would technology create moments of frustration versus moments of delight?
- **On team capabilities:** Beyond filling roles, how does your TA team provide tangible value and market intelligence to hiring managers? Are they perceived as service providers, or as strategic advisors who can confidently challenge assumptions and influence talent decisions?
- **On brand and community:** If you had to stop posting jobs publicly for one month, could your team still generate a pipeline of qualified candidates from your existing talent communities and brand reputation alone? What value are you providing to your talent network before you ever ask them to apply for a job?
- **On overall readiness:** Looking at your entire talent acquisition function today, is it fundamentally designed to react to the past or anticipate the future? What is the one, most courageous decision you could make this quarter to begin tilting the balance toward the future?

Notes

1 Cappelli, P. (2008) *Talent on Demand: Managing Talent in an Age of Uncertainty*, Harvard Business Press

2 McKinsey Global Institute (2023) *Generative AI and the Future of Work in America*, McKinsey & Company

12

The AI Revolution in Talent Acquisition

My goal in this book was not to write about artificial intelligence. It was to lay out a blueprint for a fundamental, human-centric shift in how we approach talent acquisition moving from a fragmented, reactive function to an integrated, proactive, and strategic partner to the business. We have journeyed through rethinking our roles, our processes, our metrics, and our very definition of success. Throughout these pages, we have dismantled the siloed, firefighting model of recruiting and drawn the blueprint for a more agile, intelligent, and value-driven alternative. However, to close this book without addressing the single most powerful catalyst for this transformation would be a profound disservice. The revolution we have been discussing the move toward an intelligent, unified talent function is being supercharged by AI.

Therefore, this final chapter will serve as a capstone, revisiting the core tenets of our journey through the lens of artificial intelligence. AI is not a separate topic to be bolted on, it is the connective tissue, the central nervous system that makes the vision laid out in the preceding chapters not just possible, but scalable and predictive. It is the force that will ultimately separate the talent functions that thrive from those that merely survive. We will explore the different facets of AI impacting our field, and then revisit each stage of our transformation to see how this revolutionary technology provides the engine for our new model.

Understanding the AI Toolkit for Talent Acquisition

Before we can effectively leverage AI, we must understand its different forms. For a talent acquisition leader, "AI" is not a single entity but a toolkit of different technologies, each suited for a specific challenge. Grasping this distinction is the first step in moving from hype to practical, strategic application.

Predictive AI: The Forecaster

At its core, predictive AI is about using historical and current data to identify patterns and forecast future outcomes. This is the cornerstone of moving from a reactive to a proactive stance. For TA leaders, it is the crystal ball, grounded in data science, that allows for strategic planning rather than constant reaction. As Jordan Morrow, world leader in data literacy, says "Don't forget about the world of predictive analytics. With all going on in generative AI, there is still power in predictive analytics."[1]

How it Works

Predictive models analyze vast datasets hiring histories, employee performance data, labor market trends, even company financial projections to make statistical predictions. These algorithms can identify which employees are at high risk of attrition, forecast hiring needs for a new product line six months in advance, or predict a candidate's likelihood of success in a specific role.

Strategic Use for TA Leaders

WORKFORCE PLANNING

Use predictive analytics to get ahead of hiring needs. Instead of waiting for a manager to open a requisition, the AI can flag that the data science team has a 60 percent probability of needing three new machine learning engineers in the next quarter based on project roadmaps and historical growth patterns. This insight allows your team to start building the pipeline now.

CANDIDATE SCORING AND PRIORITIZATION

Predictive models can score and rank inbound applicants or sourced candidates based on their predicted quality of hire, allowing recruiters to focus their energy on the most promising individuals first. This moves beyond simple keyword matching to a nuanced assessment of potential.

RETENTION INSIGHTS

By identifying flight risks within the current workforce, predictive AI enables HRBPs and managers to intervene proactively, reducing attrition and, by extension, the need for reactive backfills.

Generative AI: The Creator

This is the form of AI that has captured the world's attention. Generative AI, as its name suggests, creates new, original content. It learns from existing data (text, images, code) and generates novel outputs that mimic the patterns it has learned. For talent acquisition, it's a powerful tool for communication and content creation at scale.

How it Works

Large language models (LLMs) are trained on trillions of words from the internet, books, and other sources. When given a prompt, they can generate human-like text, from emails and job descriptions to entire reports.

Strategic Use for TA Leaders

ENHANCING OUTREACH

Use generative AI to draft hyper-personalized outreach emails. By feeding the AI a candidate's profile and the job description, it can create a first draft that connects the candidate's specific experience to the unique challenges of the role, saving hours of manual work. This transforms a recruiter's capacity for personalized communication.

For example, the AI can analyze an interviewer's profile and a candidate's resume to suggest specific points of common interest, such as past work on similar systems.

OPTIMIZING JOB DESCRIPTIONS

Generative AI can write compelling, inclusive job descriptions that are optimized to attract the right candidates. It can analyze the text for language that might discourage certain demographics and suggest alternatives, directly supporting ED&I goals.

INTERNAL COMMUNICATION

Use it to draft internal communications, status reports for leadership, or even first drafts of candidate prep materials, ensuring consistency and quality in your team's messaging.

Conversational AI: The Concierge

Conversational AI is designed to understand and respond to human language in a natural way. It powers the chatbots and virtual assistants that are revolutionizing the front end of the candidate experience.

How it Works

Using Natural Language Processing (NLP) and Natural Language Understanding (NLU), these systems can interpret a user's intent whether spoken or typed and provide intelligent responses or perform tasks. These are not the frustrating, keyword-based bots of the past but modern AI that can handle complex queries.

Strategic Use for TA Leaders

24/7 CANDIDATE SUPPORT

Deploy an intelligent chatbot on your career site to answer candidate questions about benefits, culture, or application status at any time of day. This provides immediate value and ensures no potential applicant is left without an answer.

AUTOMATED SCREENING AND SCHEDULING

Advanced chatbots can conduct initial screening conversations, asking basic qualifying questions, assessing fit, and, if the candidate is qualified, integrating with scheduling tools like Calendly to book an interview with a human recruiter. This automates the top of the funnel, freeing up recruiter time for more meaningful conversations.

INTERNAL HELPDESKS

Use conversational AI internally to answer recruiter or hiring manager questions about TA processes, policies, or the status of their requisitions.

A mature TA strategy does not choose one of these, it blends them. A predictive model forecasts a need, a generative AI drafts the outreach to potential candidates, and a conversational AI handles their initial inquiries. This intelligent workflow is the core of the modern talent operating system.

AI and the Unified Front: A New Look at Chapter 1

In Chapter 1, we began with the story of a chaotic and disjointed talent acquisition team, where well-meaning professionals worked against each other in a state of fragmentation and confusion. The core challenge was the existence of deep operational and communication silos. The solution, I argued, was integration a unified approach where teams collaborate toward a shared vision.

AI accelerates this integration from a strategic goal to an operational reality. It acts as the ultimate "shared brain" for the entire talent function. In a traditional setup, data is trapped in separate systems a sourcer's spreadsheet, a recruiter's ATS, a manager's inbox. This digital divide fosters blame and turns the talent acquisition process into a series of inefficient handoffs. The story of "The Unicorn" candidate lost to a competitor because of an email buried in an inbox is a direct consequence of this fragmentation.

AI-powered platforms break down these walls by creating a single, intelligent source of truth.

Data Unification

AI engines can ingest and understand data from multiple sources. Using NLP, an AI can parse a recruiter's interview notes, a sourcer's outreach emails, and a candidate's resume, and consolidate this unstructured information into a single, unified candidate profile. Every team member sees the same complete picture, eliminating the institutional amnesia that forces candidates to repeat themselves.

Intelligent Workflow Management

AI doesn't just centralize data, it acts on it. It powers the "golden handshakes" between systems, as we discussed in Chapter 7. When a sourcer qualifies a candidate in the CRM, an AI-driven workflow can instantly create a profile in the ATS, notify the recruiter, and provide an initial match score, eliminating the manual friction that causes delays and dropped leads. This automated, intelligent transfer of data and context is the antidote to the process failures that cost companies top talent.

Breaking Down Human Silos

When everyone is working from the same data and the same set of AI-driven insights, collaboration becomes the path of least resistance. The conversation shifts from "Where are the candidates you promised me?" to "The AI has surfaced five high-potential candidates from our existing community, let's strategize together on the best way to engage them." It provides the objective, shared foundation that a culture of collaboration requires.

The future promised by a unified model is one of seamless teamwork, and AI is the engine that drives it, turning a collection of separate functions into a truly integrated ecosystem.

From Proactive to Predictive: A New Look at Chapters 2 and 6

Chapters 2 and 6 laid out the critical shift from a reactive, requisition-based recruiting model to a proactive one centered on building strategic talent pipelines and nurturing vibrant talent communities. We contrasted the "firefighting" model of filling seats as they become vacant with the strategic approach of cultivating relationships with talent long before a need arises. The goal, as Chapter 6 argued, is to become a "center of gravity" for that talent in our industry, ensuring you are never starting from zero.

AI takes this proactive model and makes it *predictive*. It transforms talent pipelining from an art based on experience into a science based on data.

Predictive Workforce Planning

Instead of relying solely on conversations with business leaders to forecast needs, AI analyzes a confluence of data streams. It can integrate with the company's financial planning software, project management tools, and HRIS. By analyzing internal data (like promotion velocity and attrition rates) and external market data (like competitor hiring trends and skill demand from platforms like LinkedIn Talent Insights), it can predict future talent gaps with remarkable accuracy. It can flag that a team is at high risk of losing its senior engineers in the next six months, prompting the talent team to build a pipeline for that role *before* the resignations happen. This is the ultimate fulfillment of the proactive promise laid out in Chapter 2.

Intelligent Community Management

Building and nurturing a talent community requires consistently providing value that is independent of a job offer. AI personalizes this engagement at scale. Based on a community member's behavior, the articles they read on your tech blog, the virtual workshops they attend, the links they click in a newsletter, an AI-driven CRM can tailor the content they receive, ensuring every interaction is relevant and valuable. As discussed in Chapter 9, AI-powered chatbots can act as 24/7 community concierges, answering questions and guiding new members, providing the immediate value that builds trust. Furthermore, AI-powered sentiment analysis can monitor the health of the community, flagging potential issues or waning engagement before they become significant problems.

Pipeline Rediscovery and Automation

One of the greatest failures of a siloed system is "lost" candidates—the "silver medalists" who were great but not hired for a specific role and then forgotten. AI-powered CRMs solve this problem definitively. They constantly scan your existing talent pools to surface past applicants or community members who are a perfect fit for new roles as they open. A candidate who applied two years ago and was too junior can be automatically surfaced for a senior role now that their LinkedIn profile shows the requisite experience. This intelligent automation turns your talent community into an appreciating asset that pays continuous dividends, ensuring that the time your team invested is never lost forever.

With AI, we are no longer just preparing for the future we can see, we are preparing for the future the data predicts. We move from building pipelines to cultivating intelligent talent ecosystems.

The AI Co-Pilot: A New Look at Chapters 3, 4, and 5

Our journey through Chapters 3, 4, and 5 was about redefining the very identity of our teams. We broke down the traditional, siloed roles of "sourcer" and "recruiter" and reimagined them as integrated "talent partners" and "talent researchers". This new model calls for a broader, more consultative skill set, where sourcers understand the business context and recruiters are sourcing-savvy. It requires deep, cross-functional collaboration built on shared ownership and empathy. The bridge to this new way of working, as outlined in Chapter 5, is built through deliberate cross-training, joint projects, and skill sharing.

AI acts as a powerful co-pilot, accelerating this evolution of roles and skills. The goal of AI in our function is to automate the transactional to free up time for the relational and strategic the very skills we've identified as critical for the future. It makes the aspirational roles of "talent partner" and "talent researcher" pragmatically achievable. "One wonderful thing about the world of AI is now, not everyone needs to be a technical AI engineer, but we get to utilize AI as our co-pilot, bring our own unique creativity to it and be augmented."[2]

Augmenting the Talent Researcher (Sourcer)

AI supercharges the research process. It uses inferred skills and predictive analytics to identify not just candidates with the right keywords, but those most likely to be receptive to outreach. Generative AI can then draft first-pass personalized outreach messages based on a candidate's profile and the detailed persona co-created with the recruiter and hiring manager. This frees the sourcer from hours of manual searching and generic messaging, allowing them to focus on the human-centric work of strategic market mapping, building genuine initial rapport, and acting as a true talent advisor the core of the modern "talent researcher" role.

Empowering the Talent Partner (Recruiter)

AI automates the most tedious parts of a recruiter's day: manually sifting through hundreds of resumes, the endless email chains to schedule complex panel interviews, and manual data entry to keep systems updated. This administrative liberation is profound. It allows recruiters to fully step into the "talent partner" role. Their time is reallocated to high-value work: conducting deep, strategic interviews with a pre-vetted shortlist of candidates, providing consultative advice to hiring managers on market trends and talent strategy, and focusing on the art of closing complex offers. They transition from process managers to trusted advisors, a shift felt profoundly by the candidates they interact with.

A Shared Foundation for Collaboration

When both sourcers and recruiters use the same AI-driven platform, the technology itself becomes a powerful tool for cross-functional learning, as advocated in Chapter 5. A recruiter can see the data-driven sourcing strategies the AI is suggesting and the resulting engagement rates. A sourcer can see the AI's analysis of which candidates are progressing through the interview pipeline and the consolidated feedback from interviewers. This shared intelligence fosters the mutual empathy and understanding that Chapter 5 identified as the bedrock of a cohesive team, making joint intake meetings and strategy sessions vastly more productive.

AI doesn't replace the need for skilled professionals, it elevates them, allowing them to operate at the top of their license as strategic, human-centric advisors.

The Ethical Imperative: Navigating AI Bias and Ensuring Fairness

As we embrace the power of AI, we must do so with a profound sense of responsibility. AI is a tool, and like any tool, it can be used to build or to break. The single greatest risk of deploying AI in talent acquisition is the potential for it to perpetuate and even amplify human biases at an unprecedented scale. If an AI is trained on a company's historical hiring data, and that data reflects decades of biased decision-making (e.g. favoring candidates from certain universities, backgrounds, or demographics), the AI will learn those biases and apply them with ruthless efficiency. The cautionary tale of Amazon's abandoned AI recruiting tool, which learned to penalize resumes containing the word "women's," serves as a stark reminder of this danger.

A TA leader's role is not just to be an implementer of AI, but a steward of its ethical use. This is non-negotiable. Building a fair and equitable AI-powered talent function requires a deliberate framework.

Rigorous Vendor Due Diligence

Before purchasing any AI tool, you must become a skeptical interrogator. Ask vendors hard questions: What data was your model trained on? How do you audit for and mitigate algorithmic bias? Can you explain how your AI reaches its conclusions (is it a "glass box" or an unexplainable "black box")? Partnering with vendors who prioritize transparency and ethical AI is the first line of defense.

Continuous Auditing and Monitoring

Implementation is the beginning, not the end. You must establish a regular cadence for auditing your AI's impact. This involves analyzing the demographic data of AI-shortlisted candidates versus the overall applicant pool to ensure there is no adverse impact on protected groups. If the AI is consistently recommending one demographic over another, the model must be investigated, challenged, and retrained.

The Human-in-the-Loop

The most critical safeguard is ensuring that AI augments human decision-making, it does not replace it. Your process must always have a "human-in-the-loop." Recruiters and hiring managers must be trained and empowered to challenge and override AI-generated recommendations. Their human context and judgment are irreplaceable. For instance, an AI might flag a candidate's resume for a six-month employment gap, but a human recruiter can discover that the gap was for a valuable, skill-building volunteer experience that the AI cannot comprehend.

Transparency with Candidates

A growing area of best practice is transparency with candidates. Informing them when and how AI is being used in the evaluation process builds trust. Providing a channel for them to appeal or ask questions about an automated decision is a key part of a respectful and fair process.

Ethical AI is not a feature, it is the foundation. Without it, all the efficiency gains are meaningless and expose the organization to significant legal and reputational risk.

The Transparent Scorecard and the AI-Driven Narrative: A New Look at Chapters 8, 9, and 10

A recurring theme in the latter half of this book has been the critical importance of measurement, experience, and change management. In Chapter 8, we dismantled the "watermelon scorecard" and its dangerously misleading metrics like time-to-fill, which incentivize speed over quality. We proposed a new model focused on pipeline health, candidate experience, hiring efficiency, and, the ultimate arbiter, quality of hire. Chapter 9 argued that this internal machinery is felt externally, as the candidate experience is the direct reflection of your internal collaboration. And Chapter 10 provided a blueprint for navigating the human side of this transition, using Kotter's 8-step model to address the resistance that inevitably arises when you try to change the system.

AI provides the analytical horsepower to make this new vision a reality, transforming how we measure, how we are perceived, and how we lead change.

Measuring What Truly Matters

Traditional metrics were simple because the data was hard to collect and connect. AI makes tracking sophisticated metrics possible at scale. It can correlate pre-hire assessment data with post-hire performance reviews, sales quotas, or code commits to create a true, data-driven quality of hire score. It can analyze thousands of open-ended candidate survey comments using NLP to instantly identify the root causes of a poor candidate experience, pinpointing recurring issues like "scheduling delays" or "lack of feedback." AI transforms measurement from a historical report card into a real-time, predictive diagnostic tool that allows for continuous improvement.

Powering a World-Class Candidate Experience

A seamless candidate experience, as we discussed in Chapter 9, is built on personalization and respect. AI delivers this at a scale humans cannot. It ensures every candidate receives timely updates and powers chatbots that provide instant answers 24/7. Generative AI can help recruiters draft personalized interview preparation materials that reference a candidate's specific past projects and connect them to the interviewer's expertise. By automating the frustrating, impersonal parts of the process like scheduling, it frees up human time for the high-touch, empathetic interactions that truly define a great experience.

Making the Objective Case for Change

Overcoming resistance, as Maria discovered in Chapter 10, requires a clear, data-backed case for urgency. AI provides this in spades. It can quantify the business impact of slow hiring in terms of lost revenue or calculate the true cost of attrition from poor-quality hires, providing the objective data needed to win over skeptical stakeholders like the CFO or a pragmatic head of engineering. It turns the argument for change from a subjective opinion into an irrefutable, data-driven business case, providing the fuel for the entire change management process.

A Final Caution: The Soul of the Machine Is Human

Throughout this chapter, we have celebrated the transformative power of AI. It is the engine of efficiency, the master of personalization at scale, and the seer of predictive insights. The allure for a TA leader, under pressure to reduce costs and accelerate hiring, is to see AI as a panacea a way to automate the entire talent acquisition process from end to end. This is a powerful temptation. It is also a fatal trap. "Remember, we are engineering intelligence: data/AI + the human. We are here to be augmented by AI and allow it to truly be our partner in our career."[3]

The most critical strategic decision a leader will make in the age of AI is not which tools to buy, but where to draw the line between automation and human connection. The integration of the human touch is what makes AI powerful. Removing it is what makes AI dangerous.

Think back to the core principles of this book. We aim to build talent communities, not just databases. We want to forge empathetic partnerships between sourcers and recruiters. We aspire to create a candidate experience so positive that even rejected candidates become brand advocates. None of these goals are achievable through automation alone. They are deeply, fundamentally human endeavors.

What AI Cannot Replace

True Empathy

An AI can be programmed to say, "I understand this must be a difficult time," but it cannot truly comprehend a candidate's anxiety after a layoff. It cannot share in the genuine excitement of a candidate discussing a passion project. The human ability to connect emotionally, to listen with compassion, and to build rapport is the bedrock of trust.

Strategic Persuasion and Complex Negotiation

Closing a top-tier, passive candidate is rarely a matter of simply meeting their salary expectations. It involves the art of storytelling, of selling a vision, of addressing unspoken fears, and of building a relationship where the candidate trusts you as their advocate. The final, critical conversations that convince a "unicorn" candidate to take a leap of faith are a human-to-human interaction.

Nuanced Cultural Assessment

An AI can screen for skills and experience with incredible accuracy. But assessing whether a candidate will truly thrive within a specific team's unique sub-culture its communication style, its approach to conflict, its sense of humor requires human intuition. It's the "vibe" that a sourcer in Chapter 5 couldn't ascertain from a req, and it's a gap that only human interaction can fill.

Ethical Judgment

As discussed, AI models can have biases. The final defense against an unfair or biased outcome is a human leader, recruiter, or hiring manager who can apply context, question a recommendation, and make a values-based decision.

The Augmentation Framework: The Human + AI Partnership

The healthiest and most effective approach is to think of AI not as a tool for *replacement*, but for *augmentation*. A TA leader must be ruthless in automating low-value, transactional tasks to liberate human time for high-value, relational work.

When you remove the human element, you are left with a cold, efficient, but brittle process. Candidates feel like data points in a system; hiring managers feel disconnected. Your employer brand becomes known for its robotic precision, not its human connection. In a world where talent has a choice, the experience you provide is the ultimate tiebreaker. The companies that win will be those that use technology to become more efficient, yes, but fundamentally, more human.

TABLE 12.1 Automation framework

Automate This (Low-Touch)	So Humans Can Do This (High-Touch)
Initial resume screening against basic qualifications.	Conducting deep, behavioral interviews with a pre-vetted shortlist of top candidates.
Scheduling interviews and sending reminders.	Personally calling a candidate before a final interview to answer last-minute questions and build their confidence.
Answering frequently asked questions via a chatbot.	Acting as a strategic talent advisor to hiring managers, providing market intelligence and consultative guidance.
Sending mass newsletter updates to a talent community.	Writing a personal, one-to-one note to a high-potential community member referencing a specific article you think they would find interesting.
Entering data and updating records between CRM and ATS.	Building a relationship of trust with a "silver medalist" candidate, keeping them warm for the next perfect opportunity.

A Final Reflection: The Human-AI Partnership

The future of talent acquisition is not a contest of human versus machine. It is a partnership. The integrated, proactive, and strategic model we have architected throughout this book relies on uniquely human skills: empathy, strategic thinking, relationship-building, and ethical judgment. AI, when used responsibly, does not diminish these skills, it unleashes them.

By automating the mundane, predicting future needs, and connecting the disparate pieces of our ecosystem, AI frees us to do the work that truly matters. It allows us to move from being process administrators to strategic talent advisors. It gives us the tools to build vibrant talent communities, to deliver exceptional candidate experiences, and to prove our value in the language of business outcomes.

The journey we have taken is one of transformation. It begins with a single, courageous step: the decision to challenge the status quo, to break down the silos, and to build a better way. The principles in this book provide the blueprint. And now, AI provides the accelerator. The revolution is here. Let's get to work.

Your Turn to Lead the Revolution

As you close this final chapter, the theories and case studies within these pages must now give way to the reality of your own organization. The hum of your office, the glow of your team's monitors, the unopened emails in your inbox this is where the real work begins. Before you are pulled back into the relentless current of the day-to-day, take a quiet moment. Look at the reflection of your own leadership in the screen before you, and ask the questions that will shape your future.

Start with the honest truth of today. Look at your team's current dashboard, at the metrics you celebrate. Is it a true measure of impact, or is it a "watermelon scorecard" green on the outside, but hiding a sea of red problems within? What critical story, whispered in the hallways or on Glassdoor, are your current metrics failing to tell? Now, think of your team itself. Are they firefighters, exhausted from running from one requisition crisis to the next? Or are they fireproofers, confidently building the talent pipelines for tomorrow? If you were to map your team's time, how much is spent on low-value, administrative tasks that an AI could handle, versus the high-value, human-centric work that truly wins talent?

With that picture in mind, turn your gaze to the future. What is the single most compelling, data-driven story you could tell your CEO or CFO to create a true sense of urgency for this change? How would you articulate the cost of inaction, not in HR jargon, but in the language they understand market share, product velocity, and long-term profitability? What would your vision for an AI-augmented talent function look like? Not the vendor's sales pitch, but your own authentic vision one that empowers your people, not replaces them. Who would you need in your guiding coalition to make this vision a reality, and how would you recruit your most vocal skeptics to become its chief architects?

Then, bring the focus to the most human element of all: the experience. If a candidate were to go through your hiring process tomorrow, from first click to final decision, would they describe it as seamless and respectful or as interacting with a "ghost in the machine"? Where are the points of friction where your internal silos become their external frustration? As you plan to implement these powerful AI tools, how will you govern them? What is your personal commitment to ensuring the AI you deploy is audited for bias and used as a force for equity, not just efficiency? What conversations must you lead to ensure your organization never takes the seductive but dangerous path of replacing its human soul with a purely automated engine?

Finally, bring it back to yourself. This kind of transformation is not just a project to be managed, it is a change to be led. What is the one small, courageous step you can take *next week* to begin this journey? Will you personally secret-shop your own candidate experience? Will you schedule a workshop to dismantle your warring KPIs? Or will you simply sit down with your most promising recruiter and ask them: "If we could remove all the administrative noise from your job, what amazing things could you accomplish with that time?"

The path forward is not about having all the answers. It is about having the courage to ask the right questions, and the resolve to begin the journey, one step at a time. The revolution in talent acquisition is here. Your leadership will determine if your organization is at its vanguard or in its wake.

Notes

1 Morrow, J. (2020) *Be Data Literate: The Data Literacy Skills Everyone Needs to Succeed*, New York, NY, Kogan Page

2 Ibid.

3 Ibid.

INDEX

NB: page numbers in *italic* indicate figures or tables

8-Step Process for Leading Change (Kotter) 105, 135–38, 181–83, 214
"90/10 rule" 118
"360° recruiter" approach 58

Agile 60
AIRS Certified Internet Recruiter 27
Amazon 75, 81, 84–89, 212
analytics 27, 120
  AI, role of 131, *131*
  predictive 62, 120, 204–05
  skills in 69
  see also data, use of
Applicant Tracking Systems (ATS) 8, 9, 27, 61, 88, 100, 120, 126
  AI, role of 131, 193
  function of 129
  "golden handshakes", data 132–33, 208
  outdated 193, 197
  see also Candidate Relationship Management (CRM)
Application Programming Interfaces (APIs) 133
artificial intelligence (AI) 7, 8, 10, 46, 120, 126–42, 203–20
  at Amazon 88
  for analytics 120, 131, *131*
  and the ATS 131, 193
  auditing and monitoring 213
  bias, combating 139, 194, 212–13, 217
  and candidate experience 161–63
  for change management 215
  for community management 209
  conversational AI 130, 162, 206–07
  as a co-pilot 210–12
  and the CRM 127, 128–29, 130, 131, 162
  for diversity sourcing 130, 131
  generative AI 120, 162, 193, 204, 205–06, 215
  "human-in-the-loop" 139, 213
  at IBM 35, 38–39, 40, 41
  impact on jobs 193
  and integration 24, 207–08
  large language models (LLMs) 205
  limitations of 216–17
  for nurture campaigns 128
  for outreach sequences 62
  for personalization 120, 193, 205, 211
  for pipeline rediscovery 128, 210
  for recommendations 27
  for scheduling 130
  for sentiment analysis 147–48
  transparency in 138–39, 212–13
  at Unilever 22, 23
  for workforce planning 209
Asana 8, 62
Atlassian 101–02
automation 8, 62, 196
  "golden handshakes", data 132–33, 208
  low-touch vs. high-touch roles *217*

bad hire, cost of a 111, 215
bias
  in AI 139, 194, 212–13, 217
  status quo bias 172
Bika, Nikoletta 54
brand, employer 12, 14, 43, 164–65, 202
Bratcher, Ronnie 53
Business Intelligence (BI) 9
buy-in, securing 75, 102

Calendly 8, 130, 207
candidate mindset, shifting 194–95
Candidate Net Promoter Score (cNPS) 147, 150
Candidate Relationship Management (CRM) 8, 27, 61, 88, 119–20, 127–29, 197
  AI, role of 127, 128–29, 130, 131, 162
  "golden handshakes", data 132–33, 208
  purpose of 127
  segmentation in 117–18
  see also Applicant Tracking Systems (ATS)
Cappelli, Peter 192, 194

Cathey, Glenn 70
certification 27
change management 105, 135–38, 171–87
  8-Step Process for Leading Change (Kotter) 105, 135–38, 181–83, 214
  AI, role of 215
  cognitive dissonance 172
  communication, strategic 183–84
  "learning anxiety" 172–73
  "messy middle", sharing the 177
  metrics, competing 178–80, 184, *185*, 186
  stakeholder fears 173–76
  status quo bias 172
  "why" vacuum, the 176–77
chatbots 8, 130, 162, 206–07
Cisco 23
cognitive dissonance 172
content planning 114, *114–15*
contractors, hiring 194
conversational AI 130, 162, 206–07
Craft.co 112

data, use of 46, 101
  at Amazon 86
  centralized repositories for 27
  data governance 140
  data hygiene 141
  data-driven decision making 9–11, 17–18, 63
  engagement tracking 128
  for future skills prediction 202
  "golden handshakes" 132–33, 208
  at Google 21
  at IBM 40
  segmentation in 117–18
  skills in 69
  see also metrics
Diversity, Equity, and Inclusion (DEI) *see* Equity, Diversity, and Inclusion (ED&I)

emotional intelligence 68
empathy, importance of 163–64, 216
Employer Value Proposition (EVP) 4, 14, 198
Entelo 8
Equity, Diversity, and Inclusion (ED&I) 18, 24, 111, 206
  AI, role of 130, 131, 206
  importance of to candidates 195
  at Johnson & Johnson 43
  metrics 28, 60, 88
  at Unilever 22–23
ERIN 116
Eventbrite 120
events 103–04, 115, 120
exercises
  current processes, mapping 24–25
  technology audit 25
experience, candidate 52, 55–56, 155–67, 214–15
  AI, role of 161–63
  empathy, importance of 163–64, 216
  friction points 165–66, 219
  improving 6–7, 8, 17, 98–99
  initial touchpoints 158–59, 202
  at interview stage 159–60
  measuring 145, 147–48, *152*
  post-interview 160
  reviews, checking 166
  "ripple effect" 159–60
  and technology 163–64

"firefighting" model 107, 203, 209, 218–19
flexibility, role 60, 68, 74, 89
  at Amazon 87
freelancers, hiring 194
friction points 165–66, 219
full-cycle talent partner approach 58

GE 44
Gehring, Sjoerd 42
Gem 116
generative AI 120, 162, 193, 204, 205–06, 215
Gen Z applicants 194–95
Gherson, Diane 35
gig workers, hiring 194
Glassdoor 14, 161, 166, 218
"golden handshakes", data 132–33, 208
"good-enough" hires 110–11, 144–45
GoodTime 130
Google 18–21, 29, 44
"Great Resignation," the 194
Greenhouse 62

high-potential candidates 12
high-touch vs. low-touch roles *217*
HireEZ 8, 129
"human-in-the-loop" 139, 213

IBM 21, 35–41, 46, 47
iCIMS 42
inclusion *see* Equity, Diversity, and Inclusion (ED&I)

inferred 130, 211
internal mobility 40
interpersonal skills 26–27, 54, 67–68, 70

Jibe 42
job descriptions, writing 206
Johnson & Johnson (J&J) 35, 41–45, 46, 47
joint projects 103
JPMorgan Chase 44

Kanban boards 62, 71
key performance indicators (KPIs) *see* metrics
Kotter, John 105, 135, 181, 214
Kumu 113

large language models (LLMs) 205
leaders
  buy-in, securing 75, 102
  input from 112
  resistance from 175–76
  role of 26, 71, 90
"learning anxiety" 172–73
LinkedIn 70
  Recruiter 129
  Talent Insights 112, 209
Looker Studio 120
low-touch vs. high-touch roles *217*
Luma 120

machine learning (ML) 10, 27
mentoring 76, 104
"messy middle", sharing the 177
metrics 104, 121, 143–54, 214
  candidate experience, measuring 145, 147–48, *152*
  competing 178–80, 184, *185*, 186
  Equity, Diversity, and Inclusion (ED&I) 28, 60, 88
  hire quality, measuring 146, 148–49, *152*
  hiring efficiency, measuring 145, 148, *152*
  leading vs. lagging 145
  outdated (legacy) 137, 178–80, 191
  pipeline health, measuring 145, 146–47, *152*
  setting 102–03
  shared 26, 60, 64, 78
  "watermelon scorecard" 144, 153, 214, 218
microlearning 27
Microsoft 44
  Microsoft Teams 27, 61
Millennial applicants 194–95
Morrow, Jordan 204

National Society of Black Engineers 111
native integrations 133
Natural Language Processing (NLP) 206, 208, 214
Natural Language Understanding (NLU) 206
Net Promoter Score (NPS) 14

pain points, identifying 74–75
Paradox 8
people skills *see* interpersonal skills
personas
  candidate 95–96, 211
  community 113, *113*
piloting changes 79, 104–05, 137
pipeline health, measuring 145, 146–47, *152*
"pod" system 58–59
Power BI 8
pre-screening 56, 72, 97–98
  bots for 62, 207
professional development 26–27, 41, 76, 81, 194
project management 70–71
psychological safety 97
purpose, desire for 195

quality, candidate 12, 55

RACI charts 183
recognition, employee 26
recruiter skills 69–72, 74
recruiters, traditional role of 53–54
"recruitment maturity" curve 35
rediscovery tools 62, 128
referral programs 116
"relay model" 55, 86
responsibilities, defining 28
reviews, checking 166
"ripple effect" 159–60

Salesforce 21
scheduling assistants 62, 130, 207
Schein, Edgar 172
Schneider Electric 23
SeekOut 129
segmentation 117–18
shadowing 103
SHRM Talent Acquisition Specialist 27
silos, risks of 11–12, 96–97, 126, 159

"silver medalists" 133, 160, 166, 210
Singel, Jon 81
skills
  in data use 69
  inferred 130, 211
  interpersonal skills 26–27, 54, 67–68, 70
  recruiter skills 69–72, 74
  "skills of tomorrow", the 194, 202
  skills shortages 34
  sourcer skills 67–69, 72, 74
  for strategic talent advisors 198
  training 26–27, 41, 76, 81, 194
Slack 27, 61
SmartRecruiters 62
SMS 8
"soft skills" *see* interpersonal skills
sourcer skills 67–69, 72, 74
sourcers, traditional role of 53
Spotify 59, 75, 81–84, 89
stakeholder fears 173–76
Sullivan, John 21

Tableau 120
Talent-as-a-Service (TaaS) *see* IBM
talent, losing 11, 51, 210
Tegze, Jan 69
Textio 43
training 26–27, 41, 76, 81, 194
Trello 8, 62

Unilever 21–23, 29

vacancy, cost of a 109–10, 126, 135
vanity metrics 131
vetting 56

Walmart 44
"watermelon scorecard" 144, 153, 214, 218
WhatsApp 8
"why" vacuum, the 176–77
wins, short-term 137, 182–83, 187
Women Who Code 111
workshops 103–04, 115

Zippia 112

Looking for another book?

Explore our award-winning books from global business experts in Human Resources, Learning and Development

Scan the code to browse

www.koganpage.com/hr-learning-development

More from Kogan Page

PEOPLE ANALYTICS

Using data-driven HR and Gen AI as a business asset

Cole Napper

ISBN: 9781398622166

ISBN: 9781398624801

From 4 December 2025 the EU Responsible Person (GPSR) is:
eucomply oÜ, Pärnu mnt. 139b – 14, 11317 Tallinn, Estonia
www.eucompliancepartner.com

www.ingramcontent.com/pod-product-compliance
Lightning Source LLC
Chambersburg PA
CBHW071554210326
41597CB00019B/3244

* 9 7 8 1 3 9 8 6 2 4 2 1 4 *